Broken Cities

Broken Cities

A Historical Sociology of Ruins

MARTIN DEVECKA

Johns Hopkins University Press

Baltimore

Johns Hopkins University Press
2715 North Charles Street
Baltimore, Maryland 21218-4363
www.press.jhu.edu

Library of Congress Cataloging-in-Publication Data
Names: Devecka, Martin, 1983– author.
Title: Broken cities : a historical sociology of ruins / Martin Devecka.
Description: Baltimore : Johns Hopkins University Press, 2020. | Includes
bibliographical references and index.
Identifiers: LCCN 2019056148 | ISBN 9781421438412 (hardcover) |
ISBN 9781421438429 (paperback) | ISBN 9781421438436 (ebook)
Subjects: LCSH: Social archaeology—Case studies. | Cities and towns—History—
To 1500. | Athens (Greece)—Antiquities. | Rome (Italy)—Antiquities. |
Baghdad (Iraq)—Antiquities. | Mexico City (Mexico)—Antiquities.
Classification: LCC CC72.4 .D39 2020 | DDC 938—dc23
LC record available at https://lccn.loc.gov/2019056148

A catalog record for this book is available from the British Library.

*Special discounts are available for bulk purchases of this book. For more information,
please contact Special Sales at specialsales@press.jhu.edu.*

Johns Hopkins University Press uses environmentally friendly book materials,
including recycled text paper that is composed of at least 30 percent post-consumer
waste, whenever possible.

CONTENTS

The book that follows is a tour of ruins across vast stretches of space and time; I could not have written it without the help of many friends and strangers. Credit for its virtues should therefore be widely distributed, though of course I bear all the blame for its vices. Emily Greenwood, David Quint, Katherine Harloe, and Julia Adams steered me away from many a cliff when I was starting out on this project; their insights and doubts led it to take on the shape it now has. Each of them set me an intellectual example that I have tried to follow after my fashion. I also thank my anonymous readers and my editors at Johns Hopkins University Press, Catherine Goldstead and Matt McAdam, for their valuable feedback.

Among faculty at the Yale Department of Classics, Christina Kraus, Egbert Bakker, John Fisher, Kirk Freudenberg, Joshua Billings, Victor Bers, and Noel Lenski deserve special credit for transforming my understanding of the ancient Greco-Roman material. I thank James Redfield, Chris Faraone, and Stephen Wheeler for inspiring me to study classics in the first place. When I was young and impressionable, Tahera Qutbuddin and John Parry introduced me to the worlds of Islamicate literature; later, Dimitri Gutas helped me see some of the connections between that literature and late antiquity that I explore in this book. Celia Schultz taught me how to study Roman history and culture; her encouragement and friendship have been more valuable than those lessons, by far.

Encounters with Amy Richlin, James Porter, Robert Hoyland, David Wright, Andrew Laird, and David Karmon transformed my thinking on several topics discussed in the following pages. I thank Frances Muecke, John Gagne, Francisco Marco Sillón, and Gregory Woolf for giving me opportunities to workshop parts of this project at conferences. I also thank Professor Woolf for early access to the proofs of a forthcoming publication.

Many are those whose conversation informed me of new evidence or led me to abandon old theories: from my graduate program, Thomas Biggs, Jessica Blum-Sorensen, David Danbeck, Patrick Duncombe, Meghan Freeman, Joshua Fincher, Benjamin Jerue, Nathaniel Jones, Bryant Kirkland, Sean Northrup, Jonathan Phillips, Claudia Portogallo, Christopher Simon, Francesca Spiegel, Caroline Stark, Jelle Stoop, Richard Teverson, and Katherine Wasdin; among my current colleagues at the University of California, Santa Cruz, Karen Bassi, Muriam Haleh Davis, Carla Freccero, Camilo Gomez-Rivas, Alma Heckman, Charles Hedrick, Grant McGuire, Guriqbal Sahota, Daniel Selden, Thomas Serres, Amanda Smith, and Zachary Zimmer.

Older friends, including Samuel Kurland, Joseph Scipione, Jacob Mikanowski, Julianne Werlin, and Carlos Grenier, have contributed to this book in ways both direct and indirect.

My parents have supported me through every stage of this project and through all the years of education that led up to it. This book is dedicated in part to them and in part to Maya, my perpetual editor and interlocutor, whose patience, wisdom, and affection kept me going.

Prologue

This book is a comparative study of four cities and their ruins. The main principle uniting the essays it contains is, in fact, that of diversity. One of my major aims in writing the book was to show that ruins mean different things at different places and times. Ruins were one thing for Athenians in the classical period, something else for imperial Romans, another thing for medieval Muslims, yet another thing for the Mexica and their Spanish conquerors at Tenochtitlan. It follows from this that we should see modern-day archaeological and antiquarian practices in a somewhat different light, not as science but as a contingent way human beings have of coping with the past.

Most scholars writing about ruins have depicted interest in them as a modern phenomenon. Christopher Woodward's *In Ruins*, one of the only book-length studies on the subject of historical attitudes toward ruins, asserts as much even as it acknowledges evidence to the contrary: for Woodward, despite the contributions of antecedents like Thucydides, ruins become an object of sustained reflection only with the Renaissance. In chapter 1, we'll see how far from the truth this is. Greek thought about ruins, however, is strange enough that a modern author might be forgiven for having mistaken it for something else.[1]

Woodward is far from alone in assimilating the genesis of a recognizably modern concept of the ruin to the emergence of antiquarianism (as a proto-archaeology) in the sixteenth and seventeenth centuries. Though there are reasons to qualify this equation and the search for antecedents (as conducted, for instance, by Alain Schnapp) has certainly been fruitful, (a new form of) ruin-gazing really does seem to have developed hand-in-hand with antiquarian thought in Europe. From Petrarch to the present, European scholars have seen ruins as an invitation to reconstruct the past from which those ruins emerge. Ruins were quarries; now they become a source of knowledge—for the expert, as disciplinary boundaries solidify over the nineteenth century, and through him for the layman also.[2]

Contemporary writing about ruins tends to make a Procrustean bed of this modern attitude. Non-European and non-modern representations of ruins, naturally, fail to fit. Bruce Trigger's encyclopedic and much-read *History of Archaeological Thought*, for instance, devotes a bare four of its almost six hundred pages to non-Western archaeologies. Song China gets a pat on the head for having developed forms of antiquarian inquiry that resemble those of Early Modern Europe. By contrast, Trigger writes of a "failure of antiquarianism to develop in the Islamic World" (2006, 75). In Greece and Rome, the study of material traces of the past was "at best vestigial and disorganized" (78). In chapters 3, 1, and 2, respectively, of the present volume, I show that Trigger's generalizations ignore the demonstrable, past-oriented interest in ruins shown by each of these societies.[3]

I do not cite these passages to criticize Trigger for pursuing a teleological history devoted to explaining the archaeological practices whose origins it traces. That's the right way to proceed if you think, as Trigger evidently does, that archaeology deserves to be ranked among the great scientific achievements of modernity. I only want to indicate that such an approach puts blinders on those who follow it. There are methods of looking at ruins (and the past) that have nothing to do with modern archaeology and that tend to relativize archaeology's claim to interpret the past. Each of the four parts of this book endeavors to illuminate one such method.

Someone might just object that the modern way of looking at ruins is "scientific"—empirical, controlled by data—whereas the four approaches I discuss in this volume are to a greater or lesser extent dependent on culturally specific mythologies about the past. Archaeology's contribution to nationalist narratives, exceptionalist and irredentist alike, belies this claim. Ask how to interpret the tomb of Philip II at Aigai: Greek and Macedonian nationalists will give you very different answers, each in the language of archaeology but inflected with patriotic longing. This is to say nothing of the urban legends and even religious ideologies, from the mummy's curse to Mormonism, that originate in archaeology and are inseparable from its modern history.

Leaving aside the question of whether modern archaeological practice has really managed to disentangle itself from myth, the objection is irrelevant in another, deeper sense. When we try to understand alien cultures, as Marshall Sahlins has argued, the "myth" is all that matters, since that's the version of the past that people use to structure their present. I see ruins as one such myth, diverse and ramified in a diversity of past societies.[4]

Another of my aims in writing this book is thus to show how ruins work as cultural objects. The observation that ruins (like everything else) are "socially constructed" is a trivial one; for any given society, the how and the why of that construction are both important research questions. Put simply, I am interested in knowing how different cultures make use of the material traces of the past—making history, but (to put a different spin on Marx's formulation) not just as they choose.[5]

Especially for those of us who deal primarily with written sources, "the past" is a matter of memory work—sometimes individual and idiosyncratic but usually collective. When we try to determine what "the past" looked like to peoples and cultures who themselves belong to our past, we look for forms of representation that seem to be doing this kind of memory work, controlling what's remembered (and how). In the field of classics, this line of investigation has already been taken rather far (by, for instance, the contributors to Karl Galinsky's *Memoria Romana*) in a direction that emphasizes individual agency and artistry. My own approach will be different. I'm interested in the structural constraints that some understandings of the past impose on the present: when you use the past, it also uses you.[6]

Thus understood, "the use of the past" headlines a broad inquiry of which ruins make up only a subsection. There are good reasons to see ruins as an important, not to say indispensable, part of that whole.

First—at least for the four societies that are the subject of this book—the typical ruin is of, or at least in, a city. That means these ruins are all political (in the Greek sense of the word, as relating to a *polis*). The way that the urban civilizations of Asia, Europe, and the Americas define their own past qua urban civilization entails political consequences for the present: as representations, ruins become tokens in political discourses by which these societies determine their own future. This happens in different ways at different times and places. Augustan poetry, for example, uses ruins to legitimate loyalty to Rome as the indispensable central point of an empire. For the early Islamicate polity, by contrast, ruins help explain why an empire founded on piety should have no fixed central point. The political valence of ruins is variable, but ruins always have a political valence.

Second, and consequently, representations of past ruins matter for the production of future ruins. Debates about urban abandonment, resettlement, and destruction often invoke ruins and run according to patterns set by culturally specific notions of what a ruin is. Tenochtitlan, for instance, would probably not have been destroyed if the conquistadors (and their Aztec victims, too) had not held the particular ideas about ruins that they did in fact hold, ideas that (on both sides) were the result of long cultural engagement with the ruins of past cities. Our ways of thinking about the past give us patterns for moving things into the past; ruination is one such pattern and has often been employed as such. All four chapters of this book will show how ruins are a representation with a peculiar potential for becoming real.

That approach means rejecting catastrophism, an old approach to ruins that one nevertheless encounters even in modern books. By catastrophism, I mean the idea that ruination happens overnight because of a natural disaster, a military defeat, or what have you. The idea is a useful one for people who want to make history into nothing more than a series of accidents in which divine or natural providence makes a mockery of human intentions. It exonerates us of our part in making ruins. If getting sacked by the Greeks is all it takes to ruin Troy, then Aeneas is innocent of betraying his *patria*; if getting sacked by the Goths is all it takes to ruin Rome, then Roman elites can seek their fortune elsewhere without guilt.

The truth that outs over and over again in these chapters is that catastrophe at most provides a pretext for ruination, not a cause. Citizens may respond to disaster by abandoning their city, but that's only one possibility among many. If they choose it, that's because they've prepared (or been prepared) to do so by long meditation in advance. You don't leave a city behind unless you're convinced (one way or another, by force or by fraud) that there's a better life elsewhere.

We'll see that elites have an outsized voice in deciding if or when to let a city fall to ruin. This should not distract us from what I take to be a central conclusion of this study: ruins are basically manmade objects. Disaster only provides an opportunity for the realization of a representation that predates it.

Taking all these points together, you could say that every culture's ruin constitutes a cycle, from representation (of past ruins) to political contestation (of or employing that representation) to reproduction (of new ruins, when the conjunctural moment is right). Each essay in this volume is an attempt to explain, for the culture that is its subject, these three elements of a basic plot that admits a lot of variation. In my epilogue, on the basis of the research findings of my first four chapters, I will address the same questions to modernity.

These questions, as I take them, are thus about much more than literary production and intellectual chatter. The ruin is a singular instance of what one might call an "effective representation," a figure that carries within itself a motivational and even a determining power over communal political responses and social organization. As my first chapter shows, this aspect of ruins emerges with special vividness in ancient Athens, a city where ruins made potent rhetoric long before they ever became a reality in lived experience. Representations of ruins in political oratory pointed up the vulnerability of Athens, with its massive reserve of public stone architecture. Thus, interested parties could use these representations to push the city toward a policy of caution and moderation in interstate affairs by revealing what it, especially, had to risk from defeat in war. Such representations did, and continue to do, an enormous amount of work in structuring an affective response to ruination that mediates the more visible effects of ruins in political discourse. Depictions of ruins teach us what we should desire or, more typically, fear.

This is a ticklish point. I am writing a history of representations that is not, for all that, *just* about representations—and yet the bulk of the material on which I rely is literary, with all that that suggests for its unreliability as historical documentation. In defense of this procedure, all I can say is that the subject of my historical narrative is a phantasm that has meaningful historical effects. Thus we might say of ruins especially what Maurice Godelier says of human ecologies in general, that they exist for their inhabitants in the form of perceptions made up "not only of more or less exact representations of the constraints upon the functioning of technical and economic systems, but also of value judgments and phantasmatic beliefs . . . an environment always has imaginary aspects, for it is the place where the dead exist, the house of supernatural powers (be they benevolent or malevolent) believed to control the conditions of reproduction of nature and society" (2011, 35). My book aims to show how Godelier's insight holds true of ruins: what are "the dead" here, what are the "supernatural powers?" These are questions that, for lack of a living object of anthropological studies, we can only answer by appealing to written representations. I think that literary texts approached in this way do give rise to a historical narrative about something else; I leave it to my readers to judge for themselves from the results of my investigation, whether they agree.

In a comparative project like this one, the selection of cases for detailed treatment is always going to be subject to doubt and second-guessing. Why write about Athens, Rome, Baghdad, and Tenochtitlan—as opposed, say, to Uruk, Memphis, Jerusalem, and Beijing? The reason for that choice of material is that, taken together, the four cases I've chosen amount to a historical narrative with a logic of its own, an account of the history of ruins from 500 BCE to the eighteenth century. The thread that leads from Athens to Mexico City has its loops and tangles, but I shall try to show that it remains unbroken.

I begin in chapter 1 with classical Athens, a city that turns out in practice to be unruinable. This is not to say that attempts weren't made, of which the one that lingered longest in Athenian memory was that by Mardonius and the Persian armies in 481–479 BCE. Athens' rapid recovery from that destruction is, as I'll show, emblematic of certain structural features of Greek city-state organization that led in almost all cases to the resettlement of ruined cities.

For all that, ruination grew to become emblematic of Athenian anxieties about the outcomes of wars, first the Peloponnesian and then the Macedonian. In the latter case particularly, we can read the rhetoric of speakers on both sides of the Macedonian Question to see how ruins worked as an "effective representation," by which a party that was at once antiwar, antidemocracy, and pro-Macedonian was able to coerce the population of Athens into surrendering its own political power. The threat of ruination was too great a risk to justify not only continued war with Macedon but even the political tradition of mass democracy.

On the other side, Alexander the Great used images of Athenian ruination for quite different purposes. By inserting himself into a cycle of ruination and revenge that stretched back to Xerxes, Alexander made himself out to be the avenger of Athens' destruction in 479 and asserted the legitimacy of his crusade against Persia in part on this basis. On this basis, too, he either chose or was compelled—depending on which source you trust—to burn down Persepolis, a city that stayed ruined. Since Herodotus, writers had recognized that permanent ruins were possible in the context of an extensive, imperial, state power—a political situation that Alexander's conquests were to induce elsewhere, and eventually also in Greece.

When their power began to extend across the Mediterranean, as I show in chapter 2, the Romans confronted this ruin-making tendency of empire—at Carthage and Corinth, not to mention closer to home, in neighboring cities that Rome's growth helped to drain of population. From the outset, as Polybius's narrative of Scipio weeping at the destruction of Carthage suggests, Rome's generals—or at least its historians—were thinking about this as something that could also happen to Rome itself.

One way of forestalling that possibility was to represent Rome as a necessary central point of the empire and as an object of migration from ruined cities elsewhere. Such a representation was already latent in the story of Rome's Trojan origins, which began to gain currency in the Middle Republic. Vergil, Horace, and other poets exploited these potentialities to show how Rome's legitimacy as a world power was grounded in the creation of ruins—elsewhere. Rome was the object of loyalty for refugees from a(ny) ruined city; as such, it could be wrecked but never ruined. We'll see that the discourse had two sides; Lucan, for instance, could turn it around to suggest that Troy still had a claim on Roman loyalties, especially as Rome was in the process of destroying itself.

These representational patterns gave writers faced with the apparent winding-down of the Roman Empire in the fifth and sixth centuries CE a way of imagining a world without Rome. Poets and prelates set forth their proposals for a post-Roman world in terms of a loyalty displaced from Rome by a ruination—Alaric's sack of Rome in 410—whose consequences they by turns exaggerated or obscured. Finally, part of the Ostrogoths' program of rule was to call for the repair of Rome's urban fabric, and thus to legitimate themselves as restorers of a city that was supposed to be eternal. What this meant in practice was that the city cannibalized itself, a process whose negative results were amplified by the Byzantine invasion of 535 CE—Rome's last civil war—and which would continue to unfold over the millennium to come.

In chapter 3, we'll see how the first Muslims radically reversed this Roman connection between ruins and allegiance. Informed by the Qur'an's persistent association of ruins with the pre-Islamic past and the rejection of prophecy, they regarded monumental building as risky, not to say diabolical, and eschewed the resettlement of ancient sites. The first Islamic cities were traditionally envisioned as waypoints on a migration, rather than the permanent dwelling places that they eventually became.

Medieval Islam was thus self-consciously postclassical, relating to the architectural traces of past societies with a degree of historical awareness unparalleled in contemporary Christian Europe. The forms of spoliation that Theoderic had legitimated as a last resort were reframed by Islamic historians as a means—sometimes successful, more often not—of confronting and overcoming the achievements of defunct civilizations. If the past was another country—one which, like the poet al-Buhturi, one could occasionally visit—then it was a country with which the present was often at war. Ruins were the terrain of this combat.

The forms of competition that developed—avoidance of ruined sites, foundation of new settlements, and spoliation—also came to articulate intercity relations within the Islamicate World itself. The outcome of a civil war, the foundation of a new dynasty, or even the ascension of a new caliph could bring new settlements into being. As the headquarters of a new (or renewed) polity, these cities thrived at the expense of their older neighbors, which began to fall into ruin. The same processes took place on a smaller scale between neighborhoods, within cities. By the time the Mongols besieged and destroyed it in 1256, much of Baghdad had already been ruined.

In chapter 4, I show how the early modern culture of ruin-gazing that informed Spanish procedures in Mexico emerges as an alternative to medieval Islamic practices: a different, but equally self-conscious, way of responding to the architectural legacy of the past. However—and especially in a Spanish context—the Renaissance relation to the past cannot be understood without taking into account the presence of an Islamic other. To cite an example that will play some part in my own analysis, Hernan Cortés calls the religious buildings of Tenochtitlan "*mezquitas*"—mosques—which is hardly an innocent lexical choice. He paints Mexico as another version of pre-Reconquista Spain, legitimating its conquest by highlighting the need for its Christianization.

Architectural descriptors also have a part to play in Cortés's eventual decision to make ruins out of the cities he had found. For centuries, but especially in the Early Modern phase of the Reconquista, Spain's rulers had preserved mosques and converted them to Christian use rather than destroying them. Across the Mediterranean, such a "conservationist" approach to architecture had become the norm by the end of the fifteenth century. Of Cortés it can also be said that his intention, at first, was probably to preserve Tenochtitlan for the greater glory of the Spanish Crown. He aimed to communicate the "reality" of conquest in other ways, for instance, by laying siege to the city—a gesture that signified defeat in the European idiom of war. Only once this attempt at communication had failed did Cortés begin to destroy Tenochtitlan, a move also envisioned by him—at first—as a communicative gesture designed to bring the war to an end.

The Mexica had their own tradition of thinking about ruins, however, in which only a particular and ritualized type of ruin-making could signal military victory. Cortés's attempted use of ruins was thus an *ineffective* representation, one that compelled him to ever-greater heights of destruction even as his enemies mocked him for doing "nothing but destroying buildings." From a Spanish perspective, this blunder was perhaps the worst of Cortés's career, and the victors worked constantly to cover it up—first by building a new city on the ashes of Tenochtitlan, then by writing Aztec monuments off as natural features of the landscape, and finally, hundreds of years down the line, by claiming that there had never been an urban civilization in Mexico at all. Still, a lesson had been learned. Ruin-making could also be a tool of policy—an argument made explicit by Machiavelli, which has echoed down to our own times.

This is, then, not only a collection of essays about ruins and their representations in four different societies. It is also a history in four parts of how urban civilization in Western Eurasia and the Americas has come to grips with the apparent fact that cities are ruinable. It is the history of therapies for an anxiety that modernity tends to forget unless it is explicitly coming to grips with the classical past. Such a history, as I'll show more fully in this book's epilogue, might come as a timely reminder to the present.

Athens

Democracy, Oligarchy, and Ruins in Classical Greece

At the center of Greek thinking and writing about ruins lies a paradox. Ruins of cities play an extraordinarily important role in Greek historiography and in other kinds of text through which the Greeks expressed their historical self-understanding. So true is this that the "classical" period of Greek history might as well be defined as what falls between two ruins: that of Sardis, made during the Ionian rebellion in 498 BCE, and that of Persepolis, made by Alexander in 330 BCE. Between those dates, however, the Greek mainland remained essentially free of ruins. Every city that was sacked in this period—and there were many of them—recovered within the space of a decade. So, if we define ruins as the physical trace of a depopulated city, then there were no ruins in classical Greece, even though ruins were a fundamental category of Greek historical thought.

That's the paradox: representations of ruins in Greek literature seem to have come apart from the presence (or rather absence) of ruins in lived Greek experience. In the pages that follow, I set forth the terms of this paradox in greater detail and offer some suggestions to resolve it. I show that ruins were "impossible" in classical Greece for structural reasons, particularly the polycephalous and rivalrous character of political power in Greece and the rarity of large territorial states on the Greek mainland. Despite that, the ruination that might follow on a military defeat was a terrible trauma in the life of a city's population; rhetorical representations of that trauma could have a powerful effect even on audiences who had never experienced it. Literary depictions of ruins were what I call an "effective representation," a linguistic object that could encode the threat of ruination and sway audiences accordingly. As such, they played a role in intracity political debates—a role that grew larger toward the end of the period under discussion. An important factor in Alexander the Great's eventual conquest of Greece—a conquest that, to follow my argument, necessarily undid the conditions that had prevented ruins from arising there—was precisely his use of ruins in a rhetorical way, as terrorism.

When the Ionian cities on the coast of Asia Minor revolted from Persian rule in 499 BCE, as Herodotus tells us, they enjoyed some early successes. With the support of their fellow Ionians at Athens, the rebels advanced into Lydia and captured Sardis, formerly the capital of an independent Lydian kingdom and then the seat of a Persian Satrapy. Their burning of the city would be the high-water mark of a rebellion that was, in Herodotus's view, doomed from the outset. For the Ionians, their defeat and resubjugation by Persia would be the end of their story. For Athens, on the other hand, this was only the beginning. It had attracted the anger of the Persian kings, whose mission of vengeance would only end with the city's utter destruction in 480 and 479.[1]

Herodotus sets this conflict within the frame of an older, tit-for-tat enmity in which the abduction of Europa and the Trojan War are only episodes. If hostility between Asia and Europe is not essential or eternal, it is at least, for Herodotus, a phenomenon of the *longue durée*. Nevertheless, the burning of Sardis seems to count for him as an escalation, one that initiates a decisive clash between Greece and Persia.[2]

In this sense, then, the ruination of Sardis is what sets the narrative of the second half of Herodotus's *Histories* in motion. It does so according to a logic of revenge that, as we shall see, dominates Greek thinking about ruins. But revenge for what? When Herodotus describes the Ionian sack of Sardis, he reports that the private houses (*oikiai*) were for the most part made of reeds and took fire easily. About these private houses he makes no further comment. With respect to the temples, however, he has more to say. After reporting that the Greeks burned many of these (in particular the temple of Cybebe, the local mother goddess), Herodotus remarks proleptically that the Persians, on this pretext, "later burnt the sacred precincts of the Greeks in revenge" (ὕστερον ἀντενεπίμπρασαν τὰ ἐν Ἕλλησι ἱρά) (*Hist.* 5.102.1).[3]

To draw a connection between the burning of the temples at Sardis and the Persians' later destruction of *hira* in Greece is already to assign the events at Sardis a pivotal role in the Herodotean narrative. *Antenepimprasan* is a nonce word, invented for the occasion in order to represent the Persians' burning of Greek *hira* as an exchange (and the Greeks always understood revenge as an exchange) for the damage inflicted by the Ionians on temples that, as Herodotus had pointed out earlier, belonged to the national wealth of the Persians.

The reason I have left *hira* untranslated in the preceding paragraphs is that the usual English rendering, "sacred buildings," is misleading in a Herodotean context where temples, *tel quel*, are certainly not the only buildings at issue. In Herodotus, *hira* signifies much more broadly. Ancient Greek lacks a single word to translate *public* as used, for instance, in the English phrase "public property." Later authors, with some inconsistency, use the adjective *koinon* or the genitive expression *tes poleos* to capture this concept. Herodotus (along with Plato and Xenophon) uses *hira* instead, frequently contrasting it with *idia*, or "private property."[4]

If this strikes us as strange at first, we understand his usage better once we realize that most "public" buildings in Greece were consecrated to a divinity. In classical Athens, for instance, Dionysus had the theater; the Areopagus, the court where intentional homicides were tried, belonged to Ares; altars to Athena and Zeus stood at the heart of the *bouleuterion*, or assembly hall. Divine ownership stood in for public ownership, so that few if any of the city's public landmarks were truly secular. There, and elsewhere in Greece, contrast between *idia* and *hira* is really an opposition between what humans own and what, being owned by no individual human, must instead be understood as belonging to the gods.[5]

When Darius asks a servant to repeat, each day after dinner, the phrase "master, remember the Athenians" (δέσποτα, μέμνεο τῶν Ἀθηναίων) (*Hist.* 5.105), what he wants to remember is the Greeks' destruction of "public property" at Sardis. The owners of the reed houses burnt by the Greeks are private individuals who can avenge their own losses if they want, but the public part of the city belongs to Darius and must be avenged by him. That obligation spurs Darius to launch an invasion of Greece, which fails at Marathon, not far from Athens. A generation later, Darius's son Xerxes will launch a second invasion that finds its mark.[6]

When, under Xerxes, Persian troops finally do reach Athens, their conduct there is axial for Herodotus's narrative in two ways. First, Mardonius, the leader of the Persian force in Greece, destroys the city and thus completes the narrative arc of revenge that began with the Ionian burning of Sardis. Second, and corollary to this destruction of its built infrastructure, Athens survives as a mobile, maritime city, which leads the Greeks in defeating the Persians at Salamis, a victory that Herodotus seems to treat as decisive for the war as a whole. When the victorious Athenians return to resettle Athens—because, in

Greece, nothing stays ruined for very long—they found a different city from the one they had left almost a year before.

The destruction of Athens takes place in a way that inverts the destruction of Sardis, which it avenges. The Persians begin by tearing down the sacred precinct of Athens: "After they had pillaged the temple (*hiron*), they burnt the whole Acropolis" (τὸ ἱρὸν συλήσαντες ἐνέπρησαν πᾶσαν τὴν ἀκρόπολιν) (*Hist.* 8.53.2). Herodotus's language here—his explicit mention of a *hiron* and his use of a verb, *enepresan*, that recalls the proleptic *antenepresan* of book 5—highlights the correspondence between this act of ruination and what the Athenians did to the *hira* of Sardis. The private houses of Athens don't get wrecked until appreciably later in the narrative, when Mardonius is already preparing to retreat from the city. He has kept them intact up to this point as leverage over their absent owners, with whom he hoped to make a separate peace (ἐλπίζων διὰ παντὸς τοῦ χρόνου ὁμολογήσειν σφέας) (*Hist.* 9.13.1).

That line deserves more attention because it reveals the strategic dimension of what otherwise looks like a pattern of wanton destruction. If the Persians have reasons for destroying the *hira* of the city, they do not therefore need or want to destroy the city as a whole. Mardonius' preference is to reach an agreement with the Athenians and make them into loyal, tribute-paying Persian subjects. He wants to capture the city, not obliterate it. His logic is not unlike that of Croesus at an earlier moment in the histories, when Cyrus has conquered Sardis and his soldiers are beginning to sack it. The troops, Cyrus says to his prisoner, "are pillaging your city and carrying off your possessions" (πόλιν τε τὴν σὴν διαρπάζει καὶ χρήματα τὰ σὰ διαφορέει); Croesus replies that Sardis no longer belongs to him, so the troops are actually carrying away Cyrus's newly acquired wealth: (φέρουσί τε καὶ ἄγουσι τὰ σά) (*Hist.* 1.88.3). Here, as elsewhere in the *Histories*, ruination works as a threat to bring unruly subjects to heel; the last thing a ruler wants is to have to carry it out.

Mardonius' aim is thus to *capture*, rather than destroy, the city and its subjects. The Athens he wants to capture, though, is not the Athens that existed before he arrived there. Since he has destroyed its public spaces and buildings, it will be no more than a collection of private dwellings—dwellings inhabited by subjects of the Great King, rather than citizens of an Athens that no longer exists.

Herodotus represents this Persian strategy as a program of selective ruination that aims to remake Athenian urban space. Alongside their Pisistratid allies, the Persians launch their assault on the Acropolis from the Areopagus, that bastion of oligarchic privilege, which has become the Persian base of operations in Athens. Far from aiming to destroy the city, Mardonius wants to transform it along oligarchic-aristocratic lines, to leave it governed by families who owe their power to Persia. That plan, and not piety, explains Xerxes' decision to invite a group of upper-class Athenian exiles to conduct a sacrifice on the Acropolis once the fires set by the Persians have gone out. That sacrificial procession adumbrates the new, more tractable version of Athens that Xerxes and Mardonius still hope to create.[7]

The inverse of Mardonius' failure at this task is the Athenians' success at remaining, in some meaningful sense, a city even without the built infrastructure and sense of place to which the Greeks usually attached that name. This is the right interpretation of the famous "wooden wall" prophecy, according to which, although the Persians will capture Athens,

> Great-eyed Zeus grants to Athena a wooden wall,
> Alone unconquered, that will profit you and your children.

> τεῖχος Τριτογενεῖ ξύλινον διδοῖ εὐρύοπα Ζεύς
> μοῦνον ἀπόρθητον τελέθειν, τὸ σὲ τέκνα τ' ὀνήσει.   *Hist.* 7.141.3

The Athenians who read these words literally will die staging a hopeless defense behind a wooden barricade on the Acropolis. Themistocles reads the prophecy figuratively as referring to the Athenian fleet, and those who follow him will live to resettle their homeland. In this state of emergency, Athens becomes a city at sea, unmoored from any particular place.[8]

Most commentators on Herodotus treat that episode as a sui generis narrative development. It can be better understood as a variation on the colonization myth, a narrative form that recurs throughout the early books of the *Histories*. The story of the foundation of Cyrene illustrates all the important features of the trope. Herodotus provides two accounts, which agree in some important details. In both, Battus leaves Thera with a troop of followers to found a city in Libya on the advice of an oracle; his departure is further encouraged by disasters that befall Thera—a drought in one account, a series of unspecified mischances in the other. Not knowing where to settle, Battus and his men first occupy an island near Cyrene, which Herodotus identifies, perhaps not without proleptic reference to later Athenian wanderings, as "Plataea." Finding this a poor site for a city, they move again to a place not far from modern Cyrene. The colony has to fight for its life against the Libyans and Egyptians, but eventually it comes to thrive.[9]

Formally, the narrative of Athens' removal to sea offers a close parallel to this and other Herodotean stories of colonization. Replace Thera with Athens, Plataea with Salamis (or even Plataea), Battus with Themistocles, the Libyans with the Persians: the rest falls into place, except that, on this account, Athens ends up colonizing itself.

What do we gain by treating the return of the Athenians to Athens as a case of colonization? In Herodotus's *Histories*, the travails that accompany the foundation of a new city are ethnogenic: they produce a cultural difference between colonists and metropolitans. The Cyreneans, for instance, are not the same as the Spartans from whom they descend. What makes the Cyreneans different is the shared experience of having had to travel to, and found, Cyrene. Likewise, the Athenians are not the same people when they return to their city as they were when they left it. Having been for some time literally a maritime city, they remain one in a metaphorical sense, even once they have returned to land. This means a new self-confidence based on sea power, but it also means a radical extension of citizen rights to the impoverished classes that provide oarsmen for the fleet. Herodotus would not be the only ancient author to have remarked on the causal nexus between thalassocracy and democracy.[10]

The episode of Athens' ruination in the Persian War thus concludes in a way that illuminates the political character of ruins in ancient Greek thought. For Herodotus (and not only for him, as we'll see) ruin-making is a tool of oligarchs and empire builders: the former have every interest in destroying the public spaces where democracy happens, while the latter see the destruction of public architecture as a way of transforming citizens into subjects. Sometimes—as in the alliance of Mardonius and the Pisistratids—these interests align. To resist ruination and to recover from it, as Athens does, is a sign of the strength or even the birth of democracy.

When he narrates Athens' ruin and recovery, Herodotus puts an idiosyncratic interpretation on a story that could have been told of many Greek *poleis*. Melos, for instance, was "sacked" by the Athenians themselves in 416 BCE, its adult male inhabitants put to death, and the rest of its population sold into slavery; despite this, the city was never uninhabited, since the Athenians sent their own colonists to the site and some of the original inhabitants, along with new Doric settlers, reoccupied the island at the end of the Peloponnesian War. Much the same could be said of Plataea, Thespiae, Thebes, and any number of other cities, large or small, that had been "ruined" over the course of the fifth and fourth centuries, in some cases more than once. Every one of these ended up getting resettled within a generation of its "ruination," often by the original inhabitants or their descendants. Like Athens, these cities underwent "ruination" without becoming ruins.[11]

Greek writers denote that state of affairs with an adjective, *anastatos*, which, when modifies a city, translators usually put into English as "ruined." That translation cannot be quite right. In this passage of Thucydides, for instance, the word appears twice with two distinct meanings:

> Since the Camarinans had been **displaced** through war by the Syracusans on account of their rebellion, Hippocrates, tyrant of Gela, at a later time became himself a founder and colonized Camarina. And, having been **ruined** again by Gelon, it was settled for a third time by the Gelans.

> **ἀναστάτων** δὲ Καμαριναίων γενομένων πολέμῳ ὑπὸ Συρακοσίων δι' ἀπόστα-
> σιν, χρόνῳ Ἱπποκράτης ὕστερον Γέλας τύραννος . . . αὐτὸς οἰκιστὴς γενόμενος
> κατῴκισε Καμάριναν. καὶ αὖθις ὑπὸ Γέλωνος **ἀνάστατος** γενομένη τὸ τρίτον
> κατῳκίσθη ὑπὸ Γελῴων. (Th. 6.5.3)

The word *anastatos* appears twice here. In its second occurrence, "ruined" works well enough as an English translation: "and once again, having been *ruined* by Gelon, it was founded a third time by the Gelans." In its first occurrence, however, *anastatos* is said not of the city Camarina but of its inhabitants, the Camarinans, and the only way to render it sensibly into English would be as something like "displaced" or "made into refugees." Etymologically, this must be the *primary* meaning of *anastatos*, since it is formed from the verb *anistamai*, "rise up and depart." Unless we are prepared to imagine buildings getting up and walking, *anastatos* can only apply to cities as a kind of transferred epithet.[12]

Nonetheless, this is the way that Greek prose authors usually use the word. What we (through our translators) read as ruination was for them just a depopulation—not the destruction of a city's urban fabric, but the displacement of its inhabitants. As such, it was easily remedied. The opposite of ruination— in the Thucydides passage just quoted, but also, surprisingly, in Herodotus's discussion of the sack of Athens, where the city's physical infrastructure really does get destroyed—is not rebuilding, but resettlement.[13]

What does it take to make a ruin? In the prologue to this book, I suggest that catastrophe is not enough. You need abandonment plus time, and I would even go so far as to say that you can't make a ruin without these two ingredients, no matter how much effort you put into wrecking things. Athens doesn't stay ruined because it doesn't stay depopulated: there's simply no time for ruins to emerge. What they couldn't burn in Athens, the Persians tore down; nonetheless, Athens was a living city again almost as soon as the Persians departed.

In classical Greece, the basic political situation—a polycephalous matrix of independent, competing city-states—always ensured that an abandoned city wouldn't remain abandoned for long. The effort required to keep a city depopulated was so much greater than the effort required to depopulate it in the first place that most *poleis*, most of the time, did not even try to do so. As scholars from Max Weber to Mogens Hansen have argued, the Greek political order emerged from the nucleation of a central place—the *polis*—within a space of agricultural hinterland, the *chora*. So long as a *chora* remained in use, whether to grow crops or to graze livestock, it would need a central place where its inhabitants could gather to trade and to make collective decisions. As such—and given what most scholars recognize as the secular population pressure characteristic of classical Greek demographics—a depopulated polis would always tend to be resettled, either from its own *chora* or by colonists from elsewhere. Only permanent military investment of the site of a depopulated polis—something that was beyond the will and the capacity of most Greek city-states—would have been enough to prevent this.[14]

The exceptions to this rule tend to prove it. In Sicily, we find cities like Megara Hyblaea, that do seem to have been kept empty long enough to turn into ruins. Sicily differed from mainland Greece, however, in that it was dominated by a series of tyrants who assembled stable multi-*polis* states that had a territory and were governed centrally. Mainland Greece, by contrast, remained polycephalous until the coming of the Macedonians, despite the attempts of various city-states to establish hegemony over it. Gelon and his successors had a level of extensive territorial control that the mainland *poleis* lacked. One of the things they could do with this novel form of power was to make ruins.[15]

The other exceptional ruin-making state—this time in mainland Greece— was Sparta. Like Syracuse, Sparta also exercised a territorially extensive control over the regions surrounding it—Thucydides claims plausibly that Sparta governed "a fifth of the Peloponnese"—and, like Syracuse, Sparta made ruins out of some of the *poleis* that fell within its sphere of domination. That was part of the process of capturing a class of helots who lacked citizen rights but did much of the hard work of agricultural production for those who enjoyed such privileges. Whenever the helots rebelled, they would try to establish a central place for refuge and collective decision-making. In the course of suppressing such rebellions, the Spartan *homoioi*, who did enjoy civic rights and who lived on Helot labor, would try to depopulate and destroy these central places.[16]

It took extraordinary exertions to keep the helots subjugated and disorganized. The extent to which Spartan culture was organized around violent suppression of these restive serfs is well-known, and at the same time suggestive of the lengths to which any other *polis* would have had to go if it wanted to keep its neighbors ruined. Even so, Sparta ended by having to relax this control. When the helots revolted after the Battle of Leuctra in 371 BCE (with the assistance of Thebes and other anti-Spartan *poleis*), they refounded Messene, a nearby city that had been ruined by the Lacedaemonians centuries earlier. Writing in the character of the king of Sparta, Isocrates gives voice to an astonishment that must have been widespread amongst the Lacedaemonians: "And they ruined (*anastatous pepoiekasi*) Thespiae and Plataea yesterday or the day before, but they are going to refound this [city, scil. Messene] after four hundred years?" (καὶ Θεσπιὰς μὲν καὶ Πλαταιὰς ἐχθὲς καὶ πρώην ἀναστάτους πεποιήκασι, ταύτην δὲ διὰ τετρακοσίων ἐτῶν μέλλουσι κατοικίζειν) (*Archidamus* 27). But what shocked Isocrates (and probably the real Spartans, too) was nothing more than the resubsumption of this city-state under a Greek historical norm. In a polycephalous territory like classical Greece, full of small, more-or-less independent states, cities only stayed ruined under exceptional conditions.[17]

Herodotus knows that norm and expects his audience to have a sense of it too: in the *Histories*, ruins belong elsewhere. Like later Greek writers—Xenophon, for instance, in the *Anabasis*—Herodotus is entirely capable of recognizing a phenomenon abroad that is effectively absent "at home." Overseas, even Greeks can make ruins. The Greek colonists in Egypt, forced to move out of their ancestral homes by Amasis, who wants to employ them as a bodyguard, leave traces behind: "In the lands out of which they were expelled still remain, up to my own day, the dry docks for their ships and the ruins of their houses" (ἐξ ὧν δὲ ἐξανέστησαν χώρων, ἐν τούτοισι δὲ οἵ τε ὁλκοὶ τῶν νεῶν καὶ τὰ ἐρείπια τῶν οἰκημάτων τὸ μέχρι ἐμεῦ ἦσαν) (*Hist.* 2.154.5). His lexicon for ruination here is familiar in part—*exanestesan* evidently bearing a relationship to *anastatos*, the word that Herodotus and other writers use to talk about depopulation—but there are differences, too. *Ereipion* is a noun of result from the verb *ereipo*, "to throw or dash down"; in classical Greek, it signifies the remains, no longer habitable, of a building that has collapsed or been destroyed. As such, it comes much closer than *anastatos* to what *we* mean by "ruin": a wreck that memorializes the presence of a building that is no longer there. This is the kind of ruin that, for Herodotus, belongs outside of Greece and helps mark the boundaries between civilizations.[18]

In the passage just cited, *ereipia* memorialize not only vanished buildings but also a not-quite-successful attempt to cross the border between cultures: the ruined houses of the Greeks in Egypt are autoptic proof of a Greek colonization attempt that failed. In a characteristic instance of the mirroring effect of Herodotean ethnography, similar ruins appear in the north as well, on the other side of the *oikoumene*. During his disastrous invasion of Scythia, Darius builds a series of fortifications along the Oarus River, which start to crumble after the withdrawal of what remains of his army. Herodotus claims that the ruins were preserved up to his own time (ἔτι ἐς ἐμὲ τὰ ἐρείπια σόα ἦν) (*Hist.* 4.124.1). Whether that's true or not, Herodotus writes them into the *Histories* as a commentary on the geographical structure underlying his narrative. Again, *ereipia* memorialize a cultural-geographical transgression, the failure of which seems to have been fated in advance.[19]

Readers of Herodotus's "Scythian logos" will have been primed to understand the folly of trying to build fortresses in Scythia. The Scythia of the *Histories*, as François Hartog has argued, is a radically open space where peoples move freely, unbound from central places. Darius treats this space as though it were Persia, a territory whose capture means the capture of its people, but the Scythians know how to take advantage of the porosity of the country in which they live. Herodotus describes these nomadic aptitudes in a tone of admiration that seems strange, coming from a *polis*-dwelling Greek:

> In that most important matter of human affairs, the Scythians have found the wisest tricks that we know. I do not praise their other customs; but in this greatest matter they have discovered how to escape without anyone's being able to attack them, and being proof against capture so long as they do not wish to be found. For they have neither settlements nor walls, but they bear their own houses with them and shoot arrows from horseback, living neither from the plow or from livestock, but carrying their homes on the backs of animals. How then should they not be impossible to fight and impossible to enter battle with?

> τῷ δὲ Σκυθικῷ γένεϊ ἓν μὲν τὸ μέγιστον τῶν ἀνθρωπηίων πρηγμάτων σοφώτατα πάντων ἐξεύρηται τῶν ἡμεῖς ἴδμεν, τὰ μέντοι ἄλλα οὐκ ἄγαμαι· τὸ δὲ μέγιστον οὕτω σφι ἀνεύρηται ὥστε ἀποφυγεῖν τε μηδένα ἐπελθόντα ἐπὶ σφέας, μὴ βουλομένους τε ἐξευρεθῆναι καταλαβεῖν μὴ οἷόν τε εἶναι. τοῖσι γὰρ μήτε

ἄστεα μήτε τείχεα ἢ ἐκτισμένα, ἀλλὰ φερέοικοι ἐόντες πάντες ἔωσι ἱπποτοξό-
ται, ζῶντες μὴ ἀπ᾽ ἀρότου ἀλλ᾽ ἀπὸ κτηνέων, οἰκήματά τε σφι ἢ ἐπὶ ζευγέων,
κῶς οὐκ ἂν εἴησαν οὗτοι ἄμαχοί τε καὶ ἄποροι προσμίσγειν; (*Hist.* 4.46.2–3)

How could Herodotus, writer of a history that chronicles the birth, growth,
and triumph of the city-states of Greece—a history that explicitly promises
to organize itself "going through both the small and the large cities of men"
(ὁμοίως σμικρὰ καὶ μεγάλα ἄστεα ἀνθρώπων ἐπεξιών) (*Hist.* 1.5.3)—praise
as the wisest custom of a "most ignorant" (*amathestata*) people precisely the
fact that they *do not have cities*? The deterritorialization of the Scythians
poses unique challenges to Herodotean historiography. For Herodotus, praising that deterritorialization is tantamount to praising the impossibility of
historical writing.[20]

   And yet, doesn't Athens—of all the Greek *poleis*, the one Herodotus seems
to admire most unreservedly—save itself from the Persian assault by adopting, if only for a moment, this *sophotaton heurema* of the Scyths? It is possible
to lay hold of (*katalabein*) the Athenians as long as they remain in their
homes; when they take to the sea, this is possible no longer.[21]

   This fantasy of the city's escape from its physical infrastructure remained
attractive for the Greeks long after Herodotus. Athens' flight to sea was, for
instance, a de rigueur component of the historical narratives that made up
much of the funeral orations delivered at Athens over the course of the fifth
and fourth centuries. In those speeches, it takes the place of and suppresses
Xerxes' simultaneous destruction of Athens. The important thing for the city's
identity was not that its buildings had once been destroyed, but that its people
had once been able to become mobile.

   Isocrates' *Archidamus*, a show-speech obsessed with ruins in a way that
was typical of mid-fourth-century productions, expands on and radicalizes
that idea. There, the speaker (imagined to be Archidamus, speaking before
a Spartan audience) advises his fellow citizens to leave their city behind rather
than give up control over Messene, as Thebes and its allies have demanded.
He then outlines a project for a Spartan version of Athens' flight to sea with its
"wooden walls." Sending their wives and children away to Cyrene or to Sicily,
the Spartans will abandon their homes, form a roving army, and pillage all the
cities of Greece. Sparta's enemies will quickly come to terms, especially when
they see their own cities besieged while Sparta itself has been "so ordered that
it can no longer suffer this misfortune" (οὕτω διεσκευασμένην ὥστε μηκέτι
τῇ συμφορᾷ ταύτῃ περιπεσεῖν).[22]

The attractiveness of these Scythian strategies highlights an essentially ambivalent feature of Greek thought about the *polis*. At once institution, location, and refuge, it provided security, freedom, a sense of identity and belonging; on the other hand, the *polis* was also a hostage to fortune, subject to siege and sack. Every city was a potential ruin, its citizens—just because they lived in a place—potentially subject to forced displacement (*anastatos*). It hardly mattered to the victims of such treatment that their city was going to be resettled by somebody else.

For the Greeks of the classical period, ruins were not so much part of everyday experience as a way of prognosticating about certain kinds of catastrophe that might befall the *polis*. The catastrophe that literary ruins evoke is a disaster of war: the prospective capture, pillage, and depopulation of a city by its enemies. Unlike their Hellenistic successors, fifth- and fourth-century writers paid little attention to earthquakes and volcanoes as causes of ruination. The reason why, I think, is that such natural disasters are not "up to us" and therefore not, by Greek standards, fit objects for deliberation—whereas whether or not to go to war (and, having begun a war, how to conduct it) were the objects of Greek public deliberation par excellence. I have been and will be arguing that Greek ruins have a rhetorical function; you can't argue against a volcanic eruption.[23]

In Greek literature, ruins almost always form part of a political project. We saw how this worked in Herodotus, where the ruination and resettlement of Athens map onto the triumph of a newer, democratic *polis* over the aristocratic forces that had been trying, with Persian assistance, to restore themselves to power. If ruination was an instrument of oligarchy, an egalitarian, public city could resist this by rebuilding itself on the ashes. Herodotus's framing of the issue is a perceptive one that reflects contemporary views, at least in Athens. As we'll see, antidemocratic partisans there used ruins as a monitory figure in a rhetoric designed to curb what they saw as the excesses of the popular will and even, near the end of the fourth century BCE, to restrict the scope of participation in civic life.

In the late fifth and early fourth centuries, Athens itself was changing in ways that encouraged these developments. More was getting built, and that meant more to ruin. The building program of Pericles during the fat years of the Athenian empire did more than just repair the damage the Persians had done; it reinvented the Acropolis as a new, monumental city, which immortalized in art and architecture the image of Athens as savior of Greece. This public complex continued to grow throughout the fourth century, especially under the stewardship of Lycurgus. Where most people saw visible signs of the wealth and confidence that had made Athens hegemon of Greece, some Athenian elites perceived and resented an enormous transfer of wealth from private households to the public treasury.[24]

It is in terms of these developments and the tensions to which they gave rise that we ought to interpret a passage from Thucydides' *Peloponnesian War* that proleptically turns Athens into a ruin. The book begins with a long, non-narrative essay, the so-called archaeology, which aims to validate its author's claim that the war he has chosen for his topic really is the greatest war of all time. In Thucydides' view, the other contenders for this title are the Persian War and the Trojan War—and behind both of these their historians, Herodotus and Homer, each in his own way rivals to Thucydides himself. Thucydides makes a show of scrupulous fairness. He would not want anyone to think that Homer is lying about the fleet that went to Troy just because the remains of Mycenae now visible are so paltry. Ruins, after all, can deceive, especially if we let our imaginations get the better of us:

> Now seeing that Mycenae was but a small city, or if any other of that age seem but of light regard, let not any man for that cause, on so weak an argument, think that fleet [described in the catalogue of *Iliad* 2] to have been less than the poets have said and fame reported it to be. For if the city of Lacedaemon were now desolate and nothing of it left but the temples and floors of its buildings, I think it would breed much unbelief in posterity long hence of their power in comparison of the fame. For although of five parts of Peloponnesus it possess two and hath the leading of the rest and also of many confederates without, yet the city being not close built and the temples and other edifices not costly, and because it is but scatteringly inhabited after the ancient manner of Greece, their power would seem inferior to their report. Again, the same thing happening to Athens, one would conjecture by the sight of their city that their power were double to what it is. (Hobbes trans.)

καὶ ὅτι μὲν Μυκῆναι μικρὸν ἦν, ἢ εἴ τι τῶν τότε πόλισμα νῦν μὴ ἀξιόχρεων δοκεῖ εἶναι, οὐκ ἀκριβεῖ ἄν τις σημείῳ χρώμενος ἀπιστοίη μὴ γενέσθαι τὸν στόλον τοσοῦτον ὅσον οἵ τε ποιηταὶ εἰρήκασι καὶ ὁ λόγος κατέχει. Λακεδαιμονίων γὰρ εἰ ἡ πόλις ἐρημωθείη, λειφθείη δὲ τά τε ἱερὰ καὶ τῆς κατασκευῆς τὰ ἐδάφη, πολλὴν ἂν οἶμαι ἀπιστίαν τῆς δυνάμεως προελθόντος πολλοῦ χρόνου τοῖς ἔπειτα πρὸς τὸ κλέος αὐτῶν εἶναι (καίτοι Πελοποννήσου τῶν πέντε τὰς δύο μοίρας νέμονται, τῆς τε ξυμπάσης ἡγοῦνται καὶ τῶν ἔξω ξυμμάχων πολ-

λῶν: ὅμως δὲ οὔτε ξυνοικισθείσης πόλεως οὔτε ἱεροῖς καὶ κατασκευαῖς πολυτε-
λέσι χρησαμένης, κατὰ κώμας δὲ τῷ παλαιῷ τῆς Ἑλλάδος τρόπῳ οἰκισθείσης,
φαίνοιτ' ἂν ὑποδεεστέρα), Ἀθηναίων δὲ τὸ αὐτὸ τοῦτο παθόντων διπλασίαν ἂν
τὴν δύναμιν εἰκάζεσθαι ἀπὸ τῆς φανερᾶς ὄψεως τῆς πόλεως ἢ ἔστιν. (Thuc.
Hist. 1.10.1–2)

Ruins, says Thucydides (and here we really are dealing with something close
to Herodotus's *ereipia*), bear no relation to power. That is, they are not a trace
of power. This raises two questions: *Why* don't they bear a relation to power,
and, if they're not a trace of power, of what exactly *are* they a trace?[25]

Thucydides answers both questions in a way that entails important consequences for his approach to historiography in general. The opposite of power,
he says, is not weakness but "sight" (*phanera opsis*). That's what ruins index:
if it does nothing else, a ruin can indeed give us a sense of what a city must
have looked like in the past. But just because they give us access to this, ruins
cannot tell us about the former power (*dunamis*) of a ruined city. For Thucydides, appearance and power are either detached or (at other times) in an inverse relationship; they never correlate. In the *Peloponnesian War*, those who
confuse the two always stumble into disaster.[26]

Here as elsewhere, this is an evidentiary principle that tends to work to
Athens' disadvantage. In his archaeology, Thucydides writes off as merely
phanera the *megale opsis* that Athens appears to be for the rest of Greece. The
city's magnificent public architecture, once we learn to see it as a vast and
imposing ruin, contributes nothing to what counts—which is, for Thucydides, power. He goes so far as to put a similar sentiment in the mouth of
Pericles, the leader most closely associated with Athens' impressive architectural façade. "Let us not lament," says Pericles, "over houses and land, but over
bodies: these [scil. houses and land] don't acquire men, but rather men acquire
them" (τήν τε ὀλόφυρσιν μὴ οἰκιῶν καὶ γῆς ποιεῖσθαι, ἀλλὰ τῶν σωμάτων: οὐ
γὰρ τάδε τοὺς ἄνδρας, ἀλλ'οἱ ἄνδρες ταῦτα κτῶνται) (Thuc. *Hist.* 1.143.1).
When it comes to war, bodies matter much more than land and buildings,
which are acquired by men but cannot themselves make men. Pericles makes
these remarks about the houses and farms of the Athenian *chora*, abandoned
at his insistence, but they apply in an ironic way to the Acropolis, which Pericles has dedicated his career to building up and which, near the end of his life,
he asserts will make a fitting monument to Athens even if she loses the war.
Thucydides regards this element of the "Periclean strategy"—which he more
than once compares with the Persian sack of Athens in 479—as one of the

great tragedies of the war, a sacrifice of private lands and homes to preserve the public architecture of central Athens, which is entirely unjustified by the value of the latter.[27]

By contrast, Sparta possesses a kind of latent power that is unevidenced by its public architecture and the ruins it might generate. Far more reliable as an index of this power, says Thucydides, is the city's *kleos*, a difficult word to translate in this context, but falling somewhere midway between "reputation" and "glory." Sparta's ruins would be deceptive, then, just insofar as they cause those who see them to have mistrust (*apistian*) for Sparta's *kleos*. In this respect, Sparta is much like Mycenae, whose ruins even now lead people to mistrust (*apistein*) its former reputation, wrongly:

> We ought not therefore to be incredulous nor have in regard so much the external show of a city as the power; but we are to think that the expedition [of the Greeks to Troy] was indeed greater than those that went before it but yet inferior to those of the present age, if in this also we may credit the poetry of Homer, who being a poet was likely to set it forth to the utmost. (Hobbes trans.)

> οὔκουν ἀπιστεῖν εἰκός, οὐδὲ τὰς ὄψεις τῶν πόλεων μᾶλλον σκοπεῖν ἢ τὰς δυνάμεις, νομίζειν δὲ τὴν στρατείαν ἐκείνην μεγίστην μὲν γενέσθαι τῶν πρὸ αὐτῆς, λειπομένην δὲ τῶν νῦν, τῇ Ὁμήρου αὖ ποιήσει εἴ τι χρὴ κἀνταῦθα πιστεύειν, ἣν εἰκὸς ἐπὶ τὸ μεῖζον μὲν ποιητὴν ὄντα κοσμῆσαι, ὅμως δὲ φαίνεται καὶ οὕτως ἐνδεεστέρα. (Thuc. *Hist.* 1.10.3)

In the end, Homer turns out to be a better guide to the erstwhile power of Mycenae than its ruins are, just as Sparta's *kleos*—a Homeric word, in this context undoubtedly employed for its Homeric resonances—will tell future generations more about its power than will its architectural remains. Thucydides is setting up a complicated series of parallels by which Sparta stands in for Mycenae, its *kleos* for the *Iliad,* and Thucydides himself (we might infer) for Homer—the second term in each pair being lesser (*endeestera*) than the first. An absent comparison, but one that is hard to avoid drawing, would be the one between Athens and Troy.

We might now ask why Thucydides opts to organize these analogies—and the evidentiary argument of *Hist.* 1.10 more generally—in terms of ruins at all. One way to answer this question would be to point out that a comparison drawn in other, more obvious terms—around the size of a city's fleet, for instance—would have given a different and, perhaps for Thucydides, less desirable result, associating Athens rather than Sparta with the victorious Greeks of Homer's *Iliad*. This points us toward a more general answer, namely, that ruins—unlike fleet size, army size, etc.—are for the Greeks almost definitionally proleptic. Jacqueline de Romilly incisively suggests that, in setting up this vista of future ruins, Thucydides intends to cast a forward glance, near the beginning of his narrative, toward what might happen at its end.[28]

Thucydides shows us Sparta and then Athens lying in ruins to show us what's at stake in the story he's about to tell: they are fighting not just for hegemony, but for survival. Leaving aside the vexed question of whether Thucydides lived to see the end of the war and thus knew that neither of the two lead combatants was going to be made *anastatos*, he surely did know about the ruinations suffered by a number of smaller *poleis* over the course of the conflict. One of the reasons he gives for treating the Peloponnesian War as the greatest of all wars is, after all, that it resulted in the depopulation of more cities than any previous war. This was a danger that also loomed—as Thucydides seems to think, ineluctably—over Athens. Or it might less speculatively be argued that Thucydides envisioned the war only ending with *both* its combatants ruined—in which case, our answer to the question mooted by Simon Hornblower, whether Thucydides could envision the end of his own civilization, would have to be yes.[29]

Thucydides exploits anxieties that were likely to have been broadly shared in Athens, if not at the beginning then at least toward the end of the Peloponnesian War. From the time of Aeschylus and even before, Athenian tragedy had been obsessed with the figure of the invaded city. The plots of the Theban and Trojan cycles from which so many surviving tragedies take their material orbit around ruination, and even "historical" tragedies like Phrynicus's ill-fated *Siege of Miletus* and Aeschylus's *Persians* derive their dramatic tension from the threat of a city's destruction. Euripides, however, raises the problem with an intensity unprecedented elsewhere. The *Trojan Women*, the *Hecuba*, and the *Andromache* all show us ruination from the victim's perspective. As with many Euripidean plays, critics have tended to read the contemporary Athenian political situation into these texts: for chronological reasons, the association between the *Trojan Women* and Athens' siege and sack of Melos is particularly compelling. It would nonetheless not have been hard for an Athenian watching any of these plays during the last decade of the Peloponnesian War to see past more immediate references and be reminded of his or her own potential fate should the war be lost.[30]

How did Euripides imagine ruination from the inside? In all three of his

Trojan plays, what drives the tragic plot is not the destruction of Troy's physical infrastructure but rather the displacement (through enslavement or kill-
ing) of its population. This is the trauma that Andromache suffers in the *Trojan
Women* and is compelled to repeat in the later play that bears her name. In her
monologue at the beginning of that play, she frames her life as consisting of
two movements—one, positive and identity-building, from her paternal home
to Hector's marriage bed, and another, altogether destructive, from the
wreckage of Troy to slavery in the house of Neoptolemus. Troy's fall has destroyed the household within which she once had a place; her displacement
has so overwritten her former identity that, subject to nightly rape by her
captor, she no longer even controls her own body. It is not difficult to imagine
the effects of such representations on a mixed Athenian audience of women
on the one hand and, on the other, men whose honor depended on their control of women.[31]

If the dramatic movement of Euripides' Trojan plays depends on displacement of populations, those same plays in performance make spectacle out of
the physical destruction of Troy's urban space. Here we run up against questions about the staging and viewing of Attic tragedy that are difficult if not
impossible to answer: Were the ruins of Troy visually depicted on the *skene*
and, if so, in what medium? Did audiences hear these plays with a visual image
of those ruins in mind? Poseidon's introductory speech for the *Trojan Women*
provides plenty of material for our imagination and the set designer:

> Since the day when Apollo and I put up stone walls, with straight measures,
> around this Trojan land, never has care for the city of my Phrygians been far
> from my mind—the city that smolders now, and, captured by the Greek gift,
> lies destroyed.

> ἐξ οὗ γὰρ ἀμφὶ τήνδε Τρωϊκὴν χθόνα
> Φοῖβός τε κἀγὼ λαΐνους πύργους πέριξ
> ὀρθοῖσιν ἔθεμεν κανόσιν, οὔποτ᾽ ἐκ φρενῶν
> εὔνοι᾽ ἀπέστη τῶν ἐμῶν Φρυγῶν πόλει·
> ἣ νῦν καπνοῦται καὶ πρὸς Ἀργείου δορὸς
> ὄλωλε πορθηθεῖσ᾽. (Eur. *Tro.* ll.4–9)

After its sack by the Greeks, Troy is "smoking" (*kapnoutai*); the sacred groves
are deserted, the gods' altars stained with blood. The city's spoils have been
loaded onto Argive ships. The evil of desolation (*eremia*) has fallen upon the
city; even the gods have deserted it.[32]

As the Peloponnesian War drew to a close, events would have brought such images constantly to mind. Athens' own behavior toward conquered cities, especially those that had rebelled from its alliance, grew increasingly savage in the final stages of the conflict. Thucydides and Xenophon narrate some half-dozen instances in which the Athenian people vote to demolish a city entirely, turning its citizens into permanent exiles or selling them into slavery—a practice that, if it was not entirely unknown in intrahellenic warfare, had at least been employed very rarely before. To the extent that we take Xenophon as a trustworthy source for public opinion in Athens just prior to its defeat and submission, he confirms that the Athenians feared their ruthlessness would come home to roost. They were sure they would suffer "what they had done to the Melians . . . taken by siege, and the Histiaeans, Scionians, Toronians, Aiginetans, and many others of the Greeks" (οἷα ἐποίησαν Μηλίους . . . κρατήσαντες πολιορκίᾳ, καὶ Ἱστιαιέας καὶ Σκιωναίους καὶ Τορωναίους καὶ Αἰγινήτας καὶ ἄλλους πολλοὺς τῶν Ἑλλήνων) (Xen. *Hell.* 2.2.3).[33]

With expectations thus raised, the Spartan defeat of Athens was a moment that would resonate in Greek political discourse for a long time to come. Plutarch, writing hundreds of years later and with a sense of what ruins were that owes everything to living under Roman rule, still found it puzzling. Why had the Spartans and their allies *not* destroyed Athens when they had the chance? In his biography of Lysander, the Spartan general, he says that some of Sparta's allies had wanted to do so: "Some among the allies proposed the punishment of enslavement, when Erianthus the Theban proposed to tear down the town, and to hand over its territory to stockherds" (ἔνιοι δὲ καὶ προτεθῆναί φασιν ὡς ἀληθῶς ὑπὲρ ἀνδραποδισμοῦ γνώμην ἐν τοῖς συμμάχοις, ὅτε καὶ τὸν Θηβαῖον Ἐρίανθον εἰσηγήσασθαι τὸ μὲν ἄστυ κατασκάψαι, τὴν δὲ χώραν ἀνεῖναι μηλόβοτον) (Plut. *Lys.* 15.2).[34]

It's hard to know whether Plutarch makes this claim on good information or, characteristically, to heighten the irony of the situation. He knew, as Erianthus could not have known, that Athens was going to play an essential role in Thebes' rise to hegemony some thirty years later, and that Thebes itself would be ruined at the hand of Alexander. Whatever the case, his Thebans have an immediate interest in "pastoralizing" Attica and thereby removing a city that has historically been their enemy and rival. Why should Sparta not also support this program? Plutarch's answer to this question is an ingenious fiction:

But when the generals had sat down to council in their cups, and a certain Phocian had sung the Parodos from Euripides' *Electra* that begins thus:

O daughter of Agamemnon,
I have come, Electra, to your rustic home,

everyone wept, and it seemed a dire deed to seize and destroy such a glorious
city, and one that had given birth to such men.

εἶτα μέντοι συνουσίας γενομένης τῶν ἡγεμόνων παρὰ πότον, καί τινος Φωκέως
ᾄσαντος ἐκ τῆς Εὐριπίδου Ἠλέκτρας τὴν πάροδον ἧς ἡ ἀρχή:

Ἀγαμέμνονος ὦ κόρα,
ἤλυθον, Ἠλέκτρα, ποτὶ σὰν ἀγρότειραν αὐλάν,

πάντας ἐπικλασθῆναι, καὶ φανῆναι σχέτλιον ἔργον τὴν οὕτως εὐκλεᾶ καὶ τοι-
ούτους ἄνδρας φέρουσαν ἀνελεῖν καὶ διεργάσασθαι πόλιν. (Plut. *Lys.* 15.3)

As though in answer to the Theban general's clumsy prose description of an
Athens given over to shepherds, along comes a Phocian singing some lines of
Euripides that describe such a pastoral space in much more arresting language. The beauty of the verse makes everyone present realize what a wretched
deed it would be to destroy the city that gave birth to (*pherousan*) "such men"
(as, apparently, Euripides). We as readers are meant to note that the lines
come from Euripides' *Electra*, a play that is of course about matricide.[35]

The obviously constructed character of Plutarch's historiographical fantasy should not make us lose sight of the broader narrative context in which
this passage appears. Athens' ruination is only at issue, as Plutarch tells us,
because Lysander accuses the city of having failed to live up to its obligations
under the terms of its surrender. In particular, the Athenians have not torn
down their own walls quickly enough. Lysander hurries them up by threatening to level the rest of the city as well. Rather than face ruination, the Athenians yield on all points; Lysander sends flute-girls to ensure that the walls are
torn down at a faster tempo. Ruination is a possibility so terrifying that it
leads the Athenians to ruin their city themselves.

This moment is prototypical for the Athenian political rhetoric of ruins over
the century to come. In an era when rivalries between Sparta, Thebes, Persia,
and finally Macedonia meant that the Athenian people were called upon to
choose sides more often than ever before, speakers of an oligarchic bent could
hold ruination over the heads of mass audiences in order to represent vividly
what they took to be the risks entailed by following the popular will. Though
these arguments were ostensibly about foreign policy, they tended to discour-

age and discredit Athens' unique form of radical democracy at home, as well. Ruins formed part of a broader rhetorical arsenal out of which Athenian elites constructed arguments (for their own and for mass consumption) against the extractive-redistributive policies of the democratic *polis* and in favor of the autarkic, aristocratic household.

In Athens itself, fourth-century politicians and writers showed little interest in Herodotus's glorification of the Persian sack as a triumphant moment of democratic self-re-creation. The epitaphic speeches (public orations that give narrations of the city's history in a patriotic tone) rarely mention Persia's destruction of Athens; the only exception is the *epitaphios* of Lysias, a learned and formally innovative instance of the genre that minutely follows the text of Herodotus.³⁶

Athens' defeat at the end of the Peloponnesian War had changed the political valence of ruins, which now brought to mind, not the city's resilience after the coming of the Mede, but the narrow margin by which Athens had escaped destruction at the hands of Sparta and its allies. The writings of Isocrates, for whom ruins are something of an obsession, are exemplary for this new tendency. In *On the Peace*, for instance, Isocrates uses ruins to argue that the Athenian *demos* must give up its imperial ambitions and instead pursue a "moderate," pacifist policy. To do otherwise would be to risk another Peloponnesian War, and everyone should remember how that nearly turned out: "We, hated by our allies and running the risk of enslavement, were saved by the Spartans" (ἡμεῖς τε γὰρ μισηθέντες ὑπὸ τῶν συμμάχων καὶ περὶ ἀνδραποδισμοῦ κινδυνεύσαντες ὑπὸ Λακεδαιμονίων ἐσώθημεν). Aside from the support they offer for the basic outlines of Plutarch's narrative, these lines illustrate Isocrates' own understanding of the events of 399 BCE: Athens came close to ruination, and the Athenians themselves were responsible for this. For Isocrates, it follows that the democracy ought to restrain its expansionist ambitions, lest it run again into the same set of dangers. The benefits such ambitions drive it to pursue are only apparent—"How should one praise that domination, which has such a wretched end?" (πῶς χρὴ τὴν ἀρχὴν ταύτην ἐπαινεῖν τὴν τὰς τελευτὰς οὕτω πονηρὰς ἔχουσαν); the *demos*, unlike Isocrates, does not know what's good for it.³⁷

Isocrates, who to a much greater extent than most Attic orators valued variety of expression and consciously avoided repetition within and between speeches, seems to have found the formula *peri andrapodismou kinduneusantes* so appropriate that he returns to it again and again when he wants to evoke Athens' defeat in the Peloponnesian War. The nominal term—*andrapodismou*—

varies from instance to instance, but the verbal term—*kinduneusantes*—always remains the same, so it is here that we should look for the formula's utility. Isocrates wants to represent ruination as a *kindunos*, a risk or a hazard that accompanies certain political actions. Because ruination is too great a catastrophe even to risk, the relevant kinds of political actions must be avoided at all costs. Each occurrence of this formula looks pacifist; taken together, however, the whole range of occurrences tend to indict not so much particular democratically chosen policies as democracy itself.[38]

Like many fourth-century elites, Isocrates looked back with nostalgia on an imagined, oligarchical "Solonian constitution" that differed in many respects—for instance, in the power it gave to the Areopagus and its use of election, rather than sortition, to fill public office—from the Athenian *politeia* of his own day. For him, one of the virtues of this ancient constitution was that it kept people at home, in the *chora*, rather than drawing them into the *polis* proper, where they were likely to engage in political mischief:

> And indeed for these reasons they lived with such security that their private houses and outbuildings out in the fields were better and more valuable than the ones within the city walls, and many of the citizens did not even come to town for festivals but preferred to remain among their own goods rather than enjoy the ones held in common.

> τοιγάρτοι διὰ ταῦτα μετὰ τοσαύτης ἀσφαλείας διῆγον, ὥστε καλλίους εἶναι καὶ πολυτελεστέρας τὰς οἰκήσεις καὶ τὰς κατασκευὰς τὰς ἐπὶ τῶν ἀγρῶν ἢ τὰς ἐντὸς τείχους, καὶ πολλοὺς τῶν πολιτῶν μηδ᾽ εἰς τὰς ἑορτὰς εἰς ἄστυ καταβαίνειν, ἀλλ᾽ αἱρεῖσθαι μένειν ἐπὶ τοῖς ἰδίοις ἀγαθοῖς μᾶλλον ἢ τῶν κοινῶν ἀπολαύειν. (Isoc. *Areo.* 52)

The "public city" itself, with its invitation to all to share in the practice of governing, was what Isocrates resented: better for people to build compounds in the hinterland and remain there, enjoying their private goods autarkically.

Isocrates is certainly an outlier, even among political theorists with oligarchic leanings, in speaking so openly against the city as a common good. Nonetheless, the thoughts he expresses here were not his alone. Xenophon often represents aristocratic characters in private conversation as lamenting the fiscal and personal demands made on them by the *polis*, demands that leave them unable to maintain their own *oikos* in a state of self-sufficiency. Given his interest in autarky as an aristocratic ideal, this is likely to have been Xenophon's own view as well. Melina Tamiolaki frames these and similar expressions in other authors as part of a trope of elite political discourse according to which the rich man, who would just as soon mind his own business, is made to become a "slave of the city." Isocrates and other authors stage this conflict architecturally, as a clash of values between the central, public, monumental city and the dispersed, private *oikoi* that house its population.[39]

The architectural culture of classical Athens prepared the grounds for this clash. As Matthew Christ has argued, Athenian elite complaints about fiscal exactions are bound up with efforts to evade these exactions, and the architecture of the private house plays a central role in such efforts. Whereas Athenian public architecture, as we saw, is paradigmatically open and available, private houses are a place for hiding. Christ gives ample evidence from Athenian courtroom rhetoric for the suspicion with which mass audiences viewed elite dwellings as potential hoarding places for secret wealth. I would add to his catalogue a statement made by Aristotle, in the *Physics*, so offhandedly that it must have seemed obvious to every Greek: walls are for "keeping and hiding something" (τοῦ κρύπτειν ἄττα καὶ σώζειν) (Arist. *Phys.* 200a6–8).[40]

The opposition between public and private architecture was a way for mass and elite to articulate conflicting views about what the city could expect of its citizens under democracy. It was also a way of framing the difference between democracy and other, less open forms of government. According to Aristotle (this time in the *Politics*), one of the traits that tyranny and oligarchy share is a tendency to "do the masses ill and drive them out of the city and scatter them" (τὸ κακοῦν τὸν ὄχλον καὶ τὸ ἐκ τοῦ ἄστεως ἀπελαύνειν καὶ διοικίζειν). In the *Athenaion Politeia*, Aristotle explicitly connects such behavior with Pisistratus's (in his view not-quite-) tyrannical government; we can see how these concerns lead us back again to Isocrates' idealized vision of an "old constitution," in which people stay on their farms instead of coming into town. In the *Ath. Pol.*, again, Aristotle is explicit about the oligarchico-tyrannical rationale behind these measures: to keep everyone busy with work and private affairs, "so that they should have neither the desire nor the leisure to concern themselves with common affairs" (ὅπως . . . μήτ᾽ ἐπιθυμῶσι μήτε σχολάζωσιν ἐπιμελεῖσθαι τῶν κοινῶν).[41]

By the middle of the fourth century, and thanks to the increasing politicization of an architectural contrast between public and private, the partisan valences of ruination that we recognized already in Herodotus had grown even more acute. This was the situation in which the Macedonians intervened, destroying first Olynthus and then Thebes in ways calculated to inspire terror in the rest of Greece and particularly in Athens.[42]

Here again, unfortunately, we have to rely on late evidence for Athenian reactions. In the *Life of Alexander*, Plutarch only reports that the Athenians "took Thebes' misfortune badly," but in his *Life of Phocion* he gives a more detailed narrative. There, Plutarch chronicles the rise and fall of the anti-democratic orator Phocion, whose fortune takes a turn for the better with Alexander the Great's military defeat of the allied Greek *poleis*. The politicians who had argued for Athens' participation in the anti-Macedon alliance having been discredited by events, Phocion takes a leading role in Athenian deliberations about how to make peace with Alexander. He advises full capitulation to Macedon's demands in a speech that ends as follows: "Men of Athens, and those who have fled here from Thebes, Thebes is sufficient matter for the Greeks to bewail. For which reason it is better . . . to take the advice of the powerful than to fight against them" (ἄνδρες Ἀθηναῖοι, καὶ τοὺς ἐκ Θηβῶν δεῦρο πεφευγότας, ἀρκεῖ δὲ τὰς Θήβας κλαίειν τοῖς Ἕλλησι. διὸ βέλτιόν ἐστιν . . . παραιτεῖσθαι τοὺς κρατοῦντας ἢ μάχεσθαι).[43]

Phocion leverages Thebes' ruination in the service of a Macedonian agenda. He reads—and expects his audience to read—that ruination as a threat against Athens. It is an "effective representation" on the Isocratean model, except that this time the ruins are not just rhetorical but also real. Rather than suffer what Thebes has suffered, Athens should "be convinced" (*peithein*) by Thebes' destruction to give up resisting the Macedonians. In practice, that means surrendering the leaders of Athens' democratic faction to Macedon and accepting a more oligarchic constitution, one that reduces the scope of popular participation in the government of the *polis*. The *ecclesia*, properly cowed, passes all these measures. With the power of Macedon behind it, elite Athenian discourse about ruination has finally become efficacious.[44]

That was the context for a curious incident in the political life of the city that came to pass a few years later. Lycurgus, a political moderate who found himself among the leadership of Athens' carefully managed "democracy" after its capitulation to Alexander, had been some years in preparing his prosecution of one Leocrates, for abandoning the city shortly before the disastrous battle of Chaeronea. Lycurgus's speech is a showpiece of patriotism that, accordingly, looks mostly toward Athens' past glory rather than its present abjection. Among the antiquarian documents presented by Lycurgus in the course of his argument, one that has attracted a great deal of modern attention is the so-called Oath of Plataea. This oath, purportedly taken by the united Greeks before that battle, commits them to mutual aid in the years to come. One clause in particular has occasioned a great deal of controversy in modern scholarship: "And I shall in no way rebuild the temples burnt or otherwise injured by the barbarians, but I shall let them remain as a reminder to coming generations of the impiousness of the barbarians" (καὶ τῶν ἱερῶν τῶν ἐμπρησθέντων καὶ καταβληθέντων ὑπὸ τῶν βαρβάρων οὐδὲν ἀνοικοδομήσω παντάπασιν, ἀλλ᾽ ὑπόμνημα τοῖς ἐπιγιγνομένοις ἐάσω καταλείπεσθαι τῆς τῶν βαρβάρων ἀσεβείας) (Lyc. *Leocr.* 81).[45]

If this clause were authentic, it would suggest the Greeks thought about ruins in a remarkably modern way, as indices and memorials of the past. However, it is almost certainly not authentic: this clause does not appear in an earlier, epigraphic version of the same oath discovered at Acharnae, and even that version of the oath, as Paul Cartledge has recently argued, may be a fourth-century confection. The question that lies before us is not so much how to interpret Athenian public architecture in light of this strange clause as why Lycurgus would have wanted to make it up.[46]

J. S. Boersma, who takes Lycurgus's version of the oath to be authentic, tries to square this position with the obvious fact that Athens *did* rebuild "the temples burned and damaged by the barbarians" by suggesting that they would have been able to set the oath aside in good conscience by the mid-fifth century, when they had avenged the Persian sack by launching a series of raids on Asia. That explanation is plausible, even if the *explanandum* turns out to have been a mirage. Revenge structures Greek thinking about ruination ever since Herodotus (and note the recurrence, in Lycurgus's oath, of the Herodotean verb *empimprenai*). Should we read the Lycurgan version of the Oath of Plataea as a reminder of ruinations past that is also a call for revenge?[47]

If this is right, then Lycurgus's patriotic set piece may also contain a piece of Macedonian propaganda. One of the ways in which Alexander the Great legitimated his invasion of Persia was as a Panhellenic crusade seeking payback for Persia's invasion of Greece, in general, and for its destruction of Greek sacred (read: public) buildings, in particular. To remind Athens of what it had suffered at Persian hands was to remind it that it, too, had a stake in Alexander's imperial venture, and to recruit this city, so afraid of being ruined, as a cog in someone else's ruination machine.

This line of propaganda contained an implicit promise of revenge that was, in some sense, kept. After the Persians had been broken militarily at Gaugamela, Alexander and his armies captured Persepolis, the Persian capital, without much resistance. They celebrated with a drinking bout at which various camp followers were also present:

The most famous among these women was Thaïs, an Athenian, the mistress of Ptolemy, who was afterwards king. She, partly in graceful praise of Alexander, and partly to make sport for him, as the drinking went on, was moved to utter a speech which befitted the character of her native country, but was too lofty for one of her kind. She said, namely, that for all her hardships in wandering over Asia she was being requited that day by thus reveling luxuriously in the splendid palace of the Persians; but it would be a still greater pleasure to go in revel rout and set fire to the house of the Xerxes who burned Athens, she herself kindling the fire under the eyes of Alexander, in order that a tradition might prevail among men that the women in the train of Alexander inflicted a greater punishment upon the Persians in behalf of Hellas than all her famous commanders by sea and land. As soon as she had thus spoken, tumultuous applause arose, and the companions of the king eagerly urged him on, so that he yielded to their desires, and leaping to his feet, with a garland on his head and a torch in his hand, led them the way. The company followed with shouts and revelry and surrounded the palace, while the rest of the Macedonians who learned about it ran thither with torches and were full of joy. For they hoped that the burning and destruction of the palace was the act of one who had fixed his thoughts on home, and did not intend to dwell among Barbarians. This is the way the deed was done, according to some writers; but others say it was premeditated. However, it is agreed that Alexander speedily repented and gave orders to put out the fire. (Perrin trans.)

ἐν δὲ τούτοις εὐδοκιμοῦσα μάλιστα Θαῒς ἡ Πτολεμαίου τοῦ βασιλεύσαντος ὕστερον ἑταίρα, γένος Ἀττική, τὰ μὲν ἐμμελῶς ἐπαινοῦσα, τὰ δὲ παίζουσα πρὸς τὸν Ἀλέξανδρον, ἅμα τῇ μέθῃ λόγον εἰπεῖν προήχθη τῷ μὲν τῆς πατρίδος ἤθει πρέποντα, μείζονα δὲ ἢ κατ᾽ αὐτήν, ἔφη γὰρ ὧν πεπόνηκε πεπλανημένη τὴν Ἀσίαν ἀπολαμβάνειν χάριν ἐκείνης τῆς ἡμέρας ἐντρυφῶσα τοῖς ὑπερηφά-νοις Περσῶν βασιλείοις ἔτι δ᾽ ἂν ἥδιον ὑποπρῆσαι κωμάσασα τὸν Ξέρξου τοῦ κατακαύσαντος τὰς Ἀθήνας οἶκον, αὐτὴ τὸ πῦρ ἄψασα τοῦ βασιλέως ὁρῶντος, ὡς ἂν λόγος ἔχῃ πρὸς ἀνθρώπους ὅτι τῶν ναυμάχων καὶ πεζομάχων ἐκείνων στρατηγῶν τὰ μετὰ Ἀλεξάνδρου γύναια μείζονα δίκην ἐπέθηκε Πέρσαις ὑπὲρ τῆς Ἑλλάδος. ἅμα δὲ τῷ λόγῳ τούτῳ κρότου καὶ θορύβου γενομένου καὶ πα-ρακελεύσεως τῶν ἑταίρων καὶ φιλοτιμίας, ἐπισπασθεὶς ὁ βασιλεὺς καὶ ἀναπη-δήσας ἔχων στέφανον καὶ λαμπάδα προῆγεν. οἱ δὲ ἑπόμενοι κώμῳ καὶ βοῇ περιίσταντο τὰ βασίλεια, καὶ τῶν ἄλλων Μακεδόνων οἱ πυνθανόμενοι συνέ-

τρεχον μετὰ λαμπάδων χαίροντες, ἤλπιζον γὰρ ὅτι τοῖς οἴκοι προσέχοντός
ἐστι τὸν νοῦν καὶ μὴ μέλλοντος ἐν βαρβάροις οἰκεῖν τὸ πιμπράναι τὰ βασίλεια
καὶ διαφθείρειν, οἱ μὲν οὕτω ταῦτα γενέσθαι φασίν, οἱ δὲ ἀπὸ γνώμης: ὅτι δ᾽
οὖν μετενόησε ταχὺ καὶ κατασβέσαι προσέταξεν ὁμολογεῖται. (Plut. *Alex.* 38)

Plutarch narrates the event at a level of complexity and detail that belies the historiographical difficulties it poses. Almost every ancient author who wrote on Alexander was at a loss to explain the destruction of Persepolis. Alexander could offer a kind of rhetorical-spectacular rationale for the ruinations of Thebes and Olynthus, but why would a world-ruler who promised to spread (Greek notions of) cosmopolitan justice destroy a city unnecessarily, when there was no one left to terrify and the city in question already belonged to him?[48]

Plutarch is not alone among ancient historiographers in shifting the blame to Thaïs, the famous Athenian courtesan, although he depicts her as a mouthpiece for the spirit of her fatherland (*patris*) in an original and highly suggestive way. Speaking through her, Athens explicitly demands that its burned-out temples be avenged on the private home (*oikos*) of the king who had burnt them down. Her role in the narrative is obviously to excuse Alexander for what appeared even to ancient observers as an absolutely irrational ruination. At the same time, however, she gives voice to a Greek logic of ruins and revenge that, even for Alexander (an outsider to Hellas, from a dynasty that, under his earlier namesake, conspicuously Medized during the Persian Wars), turns out to be ineluctable. If real ruins were impossible in Greece, destroyed buildings still did have a kind of permanence—not at objects but as grudges.[49]

The sight of a woman exacting a penalty from the Persians on behalf of Greece strikes the men of Alexander's army as a challenge, and they join the destruction while their king—initially, at least—does nothing to stop them. A riot ensues, rendered by Plutarch in Bacchic imagery that seeks to turn this madness into a daemonic expiation of Alexander's earlier destruction of Thebes. Plutarch, a Boeotian patriot, is still looking for revenge after all these years.

Speaking of Plutarch, what should we make of the remark on Alexander's remorse with which he concludes his account of the episode? He's certainly not the only ancient author to indicate that Alexander may have destroyed Persepolis on purpose and come to feel bad about it later, whether in order to give the full range of possible answers to an essentially unanswerable question or, in the end, to restore to Alexander some of the authority he had been made to surrender to the courtesan Thaïs. But what, exactly, is Alexander meant to feel remorseful *for*?[50]

Lasting ruins, I argue, were impossible in classical Greece. Instead, Athenian writers thought of ruination as a short-term phenomenon that nevertheless inflicted grievous hardship on the *anastatos* population of an *anastatos* city. Some writers held such ruins up as a threat to show what might happen if democratic enthusiasm went too far. These ruins were indeed effective representations, but for most of classical history they were just that—representations. Hence the paradox that I laid out at the beginning of this chapter: momentary ruinations on the ground, but permanent ruins in the antidemocratic imagination.

I have suggested a kind of rhetorical solution to this paradox, namely, that speakers and writers used ruins as tokens in a political conflict between mass and elite, public and private, *polis* and *oikos*. This solution, however, gives us no way of interpreting Alexander's remorse. Persepolis is already empty, so he hasn't committed ruination in the sense of making it *anastatos*; if he is going to extend the reach of Greece over the space of the old Persian Empire, then there is no reason to think that Persepolis is going to stay empty.

This might have been Alexander's view of things. With the benefit of hindsight, Plutarch knows better: The royal compound at Persepolis remained a ruin after Alexander's death and indeed long past Plutarch's own day. The truth was that, rather than expanding a "Greek" politico-cultural space where nothing stayed ruined for long, Alexander's adventure ended up destroying it. Plutarch knew how, in the sequel, the successor kings and then Rome had made ruins that lasted. Persepolis was the first ruin of a new age, an age that was not long in reaching Greece itself.[51]

Rome

Ruins and Empire in the Late Antique World

Isocrates says somewhere that cities are immortal. From all that we've seen so far, this is what we would expect a Greek to say. By contrast, a late Latin poet—Rutilius Namatianus, from whom we'll hear more later—remarks that we can hardly be angry about our own mortality when we see that cities can also die. The idea is an old one in Latin literature, going back at least to Lucretius. Seneca's spin on the trope in the *Consolatio ad Polybium* gives us a sense why such a thought might have preoccupied Roman writers in particular: Unlike Rutilius and Lucretius, who speak of *urbes* in general, Seneca names names: Carthage, Numantia, and Corinth, three infamous ruins made by Rome while it consolidated its grip on the Mediterranean basin in the second century BCE. The Romans knew that cities could die because they had killed a number of them.[1]

As a practice of empire, there was nothing new about this. The Persians made ruins to turn its empire into a governable space; Sparta did the same, and so did Alexander in his drive to build a world-kingdom. The interesting thing about Rome is the extent to which self-consciousness about its own ruin-making gets woven into the Latin literary tradition. In what follows, I investigate this by way of showing that Roman writers use ruined cities to think through two very nearly opposite projects, migration and staying in place, both tied up, in the Roman myth-historical tradition, with Rome's special status as the center of an empire. Ruins help Roman writers displace the contradiction between those projects, except in one worst-case scenario. If, for the displaced citizens of a ruined city, all roads lead to Rome, what happens when Rome itself gets turned into a ruin?

In the fifth and sixth centuries CE, when it seemed as if Rome really might be ruined, contemporaries discussed and understood that possibility by way of older themes and topoi derived from the Latin classics. If what Vergil or Lucan had treated as a limit case now seemed imminent, those earlier treatments set the terms of a Late Antique debate on ruinations that had very tangible results.

I say "debate" because people writing about ruins were really raising the question of whether Rome could or should be abandoned—and, if so, abandoned in favor of what? The answers that various parties offered to this question had, as I show, an effect on the way that Rome did, in the centuries that followed, start to crumble. They gave people ways of abandoning Rome, the physical city, without disloyalty to Rome, the imperial idea. That, more than any natural disaster or military defeat, was the main prerequisite for Rome's becoming a ruin.

Although most Roman writers probably would have disagreed or claimed to disagree with the Christian historian Orosius's claim that the expansion of the Roman Empire had brought more harm than good, they would have had a harder time countering some of his arguments in support of that claim:

> Then what value should be ascribed to this quantum of happiness, acquired with such great labor, to which is ascribed the blessedness of one city among such a great heap of unhappiness, by which the entire world has been ruined? But if those events are thought to be fortunate inasmuch as the wealth of one city has been increased, why should they not be judged rather misfortunes, through which a wretched devastation brought low the most powerful kingdoms of many civilized peoples?

> Quanti igitur pendenda est gutta haec laboriosae felicitatis, cui adscribitur unius urbis beatitudo in tanta mole infelicitatis, per quam agitur totius orbis eversio? aut si ideo felicia putantur, quia unius ciuitatis opes auctae sunt, cur non potius infelicissima iudicentur, quibus miserabili vastatione multarum ac bene institutarum gentium potentissima regna ceciderunt? (Oros. *Hist. adv. Pag.* 5.1.3–4)

Certainly the empire had brought happiness, but to whom? To Rome, a single city (*civitas*), and this at the cost of the overthrow of countless peoples and kingdoms—in short, the "ruin (*eversio*) of all the world." Orosius goes on to discuss, at more length and with greater vividness, the examples mentioned briefly by Seneca in the passage cited above. What kind of accounting could make the happiness of Rome outweigh the misery of ruined Carthage and Numantia?[2]

This was a question with which every Roman historian had to reckon. Rome used ruination as an element of policy, a means, as Machiavelli would interpret it many centuries later, of holding territories it could not colonize. If the Romans themselves took a less instrumental, more punitive view, the outcome was the same. Since Rome, unlike the Greek city-states, grew into a territorial empire of massive extent, it had the power to keep what it ruined uninhabited. Conversely, Rome also had the power to colonize those sites again, and it often did. The gap between ruined original and Roman imitation could occasion melancholy reflections. Orosius knew Carthage at firsthand: a thriving city in his day, it was nonetheless now "a small patch of ground, without walls, a part of the misery of which is to have heard what once it was" (situ paruae, moenibus destitutae; pars miseriarum est audire quid fuerit) (Oros. *Hist.* 5.1.5). The difference between that city's subject present and sovereign past was marked by ruins.[3]

One reason for this difference is the other, less dramatic, but in the long run probably more significant way that Rome made ruins. As the central place in an ever-larger imperial space, it drew toward itself the people and resources of a vast hinterland. At its height, Rome had a population in excess of one million people, astronomically high for a premodern city and requiring the resources of an empire to sustain: not only food and money, but also—since Rome, like every premodern metropolis, was a demographic sink—human beings. As Rome grew, (some) other cities had to shrink. Rival settlements in Rome's immediate neighborhood were the first to experience this effect. The importance of Gabii to Rome's early history is inscribed in the most archaic layers of Roman ritual, where certain rites had to be carried out *cinctu Gabino* or *in agro Gabino*. By Horace's time, though, Gabii was a byword for a one-horse town. In addition to siphoning off Gabii's most prominent citizens, Rome had literally stolen the ground out from underneath it: much of the city's original territory had been turned into a quarry for *lapis Gabinus*, a much-sought-after building stone.[4]

Livy writes a precedent for all that near the middle of book 1 of the *Ab urbe condita*, where Alba Longa—in a way Rome's mother city, but also its rival—has fallen forfeit to Rome because of the double-dealing of its chieftain, Mettius Fufettius. Roman legions arrive to lead its population off to Rome and level its buildings to the ground. But this isn't quite a military sack: "There was not, indeed, that clamor or terror typical of captured cities" (Non quidem fuit tumultus ille nec pavor qualis captarum esse urbium solet) (*AUC* 1.29), says Livy, only a sad silence and a universal grief among people now forced to leave their ancestral homes and familiar places behind. The distinction between war and peace grows blurry. It hardly matters, though, for the displaced Albans, driven to Rome by wings of cavalry—or for the Romans to whom this unlooked-for prize fell. Rome's population doubled all at once, a new hill and new senators were added; in short, says Livy, "Rome grew through Alba's ruin" (Roma crescit Albae ruinis) (*AUC* 1.30).[5]

It would grow from the ruins of many more cities in the centuries to come. There were local ruins, like Gabii, Alba, and Veii, that traced Rome's emergence as the premier central place of the Italian Peninsula; then more distant ruins, like Numantia, Carthage, and Corinth, towns destroyed punitively or preventatively in order to secure Rome's conquests beyond Italy. Recent research has shown that many *municipia* in Italy, far from being exhausted by their proximity to Rome, actually thrived on it, but these are precisely the images that Roman literature elides. Writers focus instead on disasters, which they characterize as unignorable: in the *Tusculan Disputations*, Cicero reports that refugees from these ruined cities have settled throughout the empire. He has met some of them himself, homeless (and enslaved?) Corinthians wandering the world. Strangely, Cicero says that the sight of the ruins of Corinth moved him more than it did the erstwhile Corinthians themselves. Why would that be?[6]

Experience taught Roman historiographers that Rome could make ruins anywhere, on purpose or not, whenever the occasion called for it. This line of thinking led more than one writer to ask whether Rome itself might ever be ruined. Via a quotation in Appian's *Romaika*, Polybius is the earliest writer we know of to face this possibility directly. There, the sight of Carthage in flames leads Scipio Aemelianus to consider how empires that are at the height of power (*arche megiste*) always fall into ruin. The destruction of Carthage, central place of a once-great kingdom, sends him into a downward and pastward spiral of imperial melancholy that ends with Troy and a line from the *Iliad*:

A day shall come when Holy Troy is wrecked
And Priam, too, and the people of spear-armed Priam."

ἔσσεται ἦμαρ ὅταν ποτ᾽ ὀλώλῃ Ἴλιος ἱρὴ
καὶ Πρίαμος καὶ λαὸς ἐϋμμελίω Πριάμοιο.   *Il.* 4.164–165

Polybius, Scipio's secretary and tutor, is standing by, puzzled as to the fit of that quotation with this context. Without hesitation, Scipio fills him in: "without dissimilation he named his fatherland clearly, on behalf of which, inspecting the course of human events, he was fearful" (οὐ φυλαξάμενον ὀνομάσαι τὴν πατρίδα σαφῶς, ὑπὲρ ἧς ἄρα, ἐς τἀνθρώπεια ἀφορῶν, ἐδεδίει) (App. *Pun.* 132). Polybius had supposed that Scipio was weeping over the fate of an enemy; as it turns out, he's mourning in advance for his home city. Someday, Rome is going to suffer the ruination that it has inflicted on Carthage.[7]

Polybius reads the object of Scipio's meditation here as a kind of supernatural force (*daimon*) that turns the wheel of fortune, for cities as for individual men. But if, as Arnaldo Momigliano argued, we are free to inquire as to the number of tears Scipio sheds during this episode, then I think we're also entitled to wonder whether Polybius has correctly grasped the intention behind Scipio's citation of Homer. The quoted lines come from book 4 of the *Iliad*, just after Menelaus has been treacherously felled by a Trojan arrow during a single combat between himself and Paris that was supposed to have decided the outcome of the war. Since both sides have sworn an oath not to interfere in the duel, and the Trojans have plainly violated that oath, Agamemnon remarks that Zeus will surely turn against them and allow the Greeks to raze their city. It would be hard not to read this as a pointed reference to the Romans' own abrogation of the terms under which Carthage had surrendered a short time before its capture and destruction. If we do read it that way, then Scipio would seem to be envisioning Rome's ruination, not by an indifferent turn of fortune, but as a result of the unjust means by which it has begun to pursue its imperial ends.[8]

In this series of analogies, Rome occupies the place of Troy—a substitution that can hardly be a coincidence, and one that shows us how deeply ruins were coming to shape Roman historical consciousness. Roman poets and historians were already drawing genealogical connections between Rome and Troy as early as the third century BCE, and the notion that Rome had been founded by Trojan refugees under the leadership of Aeneas was already current by Polybius's day. If, as many scholars have argued, this myth was a means of Roman self-insertion into a Hellenic cultural sphere, it was certainly an ambiguous one. Just when Rome was beginning to establish hegemony over the Greek-speaking world, it inscribed itself there as the Hellenes' great defeated rival—a city that, as we saw, was in Greek eyes the original ruin. Roman poets agreed: Troy's capture and ruination had been absolutely essential for its transformation into Rome.[9]

There were real historiographical stakes at play in the question of how to describe this ruination, because the Trojan refugees who were going to become Romans needed to be cleared in advance of the charge of having abandoned or betrayed their fatherland. Within the Greek and Roman mythographic tradition, Aeneas turns out to have been an ambiguous figure, more of an escape artist than anything else and possessed of a patriotism that was not beyond critique. Even Livy suggests that Aeneas only escapes Troy alive because the Greeks have made a separate peace with him and his family. Servius, the late antique commentator on Vergil, fills out this claim by recounting how Aeneas had been friendly to the Greeks throughout the Trojan War. He explains more than one line of the *Aeneid* with reference to Vergil's interest in dispelling the accusations of treachery that were still hanging over Aeneas's head in the fifth century CE.[10]

In book 2 of the *Aeneid*, Vergil confronts these allegations by writing his hero into a scene of ruination that both justifies his flight from Troy and shows how futile his staying behind and fighting would have been. The story of Troy's destruction begins with a dream in which Hector's ghost tells Aeneas to flee, because Troy is already becoming (or has become, since *ruit* is usefully ambiguous as to tense) a ruin:

> "Flee, child of the Goddess," he said, "and snatch yourself out of these flames.
> The enemy has the walls; Troy crumbles [*ruit*] from its great height.
> Enough has been given to Priam and the fatherland: if Troy
> Could have been defended by force of arms, it would still have been defended
>   by mine."

> "Heu fuge, nate dea, teque his" ait "eripe flammis.
> hostis habet muros; ruit alto a culmine Troia.
> sat patriae Priamoque datum: si Pergama dextra
> defendi possent, etiam hac defensa fuissent."   *Aen.* 2.289–292

There's nothing more to be done, Hector adds, as though anticipating Aeneas's protests and the reader's doubts. If Aeneas wants to interpret *ruit* as a present progressive verb describing an ongoing process that might still be reversed, Hector's ghost authoritatively interprets it as describing, in the perfect tense, something that's already come to pass. Troy's fall is a fait accompli; the sacrifices already made are "sufficient" (*sat*) to meet the requirements of patriotism. Aeneas can flee his fatherland in good conscience, knowing that Hector already has.[11]

Nonetheless, he strives to save it. This gives Vergil a chance to make a virtuosic display of *enargeia*, that sense of descriptive vividness so sought-after by ancient rhetoricians. Since the narrative here is strongly focalized through Aeneas, we witness the historians' *urbs capta* motif as it were from the inside out: the "*tumultus*" and "*pavor*," the "*clamor hostilis*" and the "*cursus per urbem armatorum*" (*AUC* 1.29.2), which Livy says tend to accompany the sack of a city—all get developed by Vergil at length. Out of these elements, Aeneas slowly assembles a picture of what's happening to Troy that matches what he has heard from Hector. Not until Venus gives him a peek behind the scenes and shows him how the gods are tearing down Troy's towers, however, does he finally realize that *ruit* means it's over and done with.[12]

A proper Roman—a Regulus or a Cato—might still have been expected to die for king and country. At the very moment he sees Priam struck down, though, Vergil reminds us that Aeneas is accountable for lives beyond his own:

I froze; the image of my dear father rose before my eyes,
Since I saw a king of equal age breathing out his life
Through a cruel wound, and the image of Creusa deserted
And my house torn down and the fall of little Iulus rose up too.

Obstipui; subiit cari genitoris imago,
ut regem aequaeuum crudeli vulnere vidi
vitam exhalantem, subiit deserta Creusa
et direpta domus et parvi casus Iuli.   *Aen.* 2.560–563

Aeneas's putative self-sacrifice for Troy would at the same time be a sacrifice of his entire *domus*, a collective that might yet survive the ruin of the *civitas* of which it had formed a part. His desire to save this *domus* excuses his failure to fight to the death for Troy: he's not running from battle, he's running home. There, his father, Anchises, still refuses to accept that his obligations to the city have ended: only divine intervention—the flames around Iulus's head and a thunderbolt from Jupiter—suffices to convince him that Aeneas's proposed flight is justified.[13]

If all this gives us the impression that Vergil (or Aeneas, since the whole of book 2 is in *oratio recta*, supported by Aeneas's authority rather than his author's) is protesting too much, this is probably because we no longer appreciate the extent to which fleeing one's fatherland at its time of greatest need could seem to ancient audiences like a betrayal and an utter moral failure. Aeneas needs to convince himself as well as us that Troy really has become a ruin, that the country to which he ultimately owes his loyalty no longer exists. At the beginning of *Aeneid*, book 2, Troy is a thriving city that acts as a collective entity, makes political decisions, and gives orders; at the beginning of book 3, when Aeneas sets sail, he is only leaving behind the "fields where Troy had been" (*campos ubi Troia fuit*) (*Aen.* 3.11).[14]

This is how Rome's history, as Romans understood it at the outset of the Principate, starts out of ruins: without the ruination of Troy, Aeneas would never have sailed to Italy, and Rome would never have come into being. Troy is the first of many ruins out of which Rome will grow.

The Roman Empire was thus in many senses built on ruins: emerging out of the ashes of Troy, it made ruins wherever its grasp extended as a condition of its own growth. A common thread in all this is what we might, for lack of a better expression, call loyalty to a place. The Roman Empire, if it is anything more than a historical abstraction, was made out of loyalty to Rome—a loyalty that, for each individual subject, was in the last instance supposed to trump more local commitments. In practice, attempts to defy or dissociate from Roman rule always organized themselves around another central place— Beneventum, Numantia, Carthage, or Jerusalem, for instance—which exercised a potentially profounder claim on the loyalties of erstwhile Roman subjects. These were the sites that Rome had to ruin in order to ensure that restive populations had no local alternative to Rome.

Generations of Roman subjects were thereby forced to experience the same transfer of loyalty that Aeneas had experienced in Vergil. The *Aeneid* writes this as a mytheme of migration, the hero as refugee (*profugus*) from a ruination that has left him nowhere to go but Latium. Later Roman writers problematized this mytheme in a variety of ways. Why, after all, had Aeneas not simply refounded Troy on the *campi* where it had once stood? And why did the Romans themselves never do so after they had come to control the ground it had occupied? It could seem surprising that a man and a people so notorious for their loyalty (translating, say, *pietas*) had shown so little of it toward their mother city. If the moment of ruination was surely a good time to get out of town, the ruins that resulted from ruination might serve as a powerful call to return.

In a poem that, given its historical emplotment and concern for merging history with theodicy, has to be read as a commentary on the *Aeneid*, Horace frames this problem in terms of historical repetition and the need to avoid it. *Odes* 3.3, like many of the so-called Roman odes, is in its way a poem about Augustus, the "*iustum et tenacem . . . virum*" of its opening line, a brooding figure, *impavidus* amid a world falling to ruin ("*fractus . . . orbis*"). The ode ends incongruously, with the apotheosis of Romulus and a commandment to the Romans from Juno never to rebuild Troy:

> But I give their destiny to the Romans,
> According to this rule: let them not, from an excess
> Of piety, and trusting in success, attempt
> To repair the houses of their ancestral Troy.
>
> For Troy, reborn, comes fate again
> Shaking its dark wings, to repeat old disasters,
> And I will lead the conquering hordes
> Myself, wife and sister of Jove.
>
> If a third time, on Apollo's say-so,
> The bronze walls rise, then a third time
> They will fall, cut down by my Greeks, a third time
> The captive wife will wail her husband and sons.

> Sed bellicosis fata Quiritibus
> hac lege dico, ne nimium pii
> rebusque fidentes avitae
> tecta velint reparare Troiae.
>
> Troiae renascens alite lugubri
> fortuna tristi clade iterabitur,
> ducente victrices catervas
> coniuge me Iovis et sorore.
>
> Ter si resurgat murus aeneus
> auctore Phoebo, ter pereat meis
> excisus Argivis, ter uxor
> capta virum puerosque ploret.   Hor. *Carm.* 3.3.57–68

In a trio of stanzas that enacts (*ter . . . ter. . . ter . . .*) the stuttering repetition from which it aims to discourage the *Quirites*, Juno cautions against an excess of *pietas* that would lead the Romans back into the historical dead end from which Vergil's *Aeneid* chronicles their escape. Troy is now what it was always fated to be, a ruin; if the Romans restore its buildings (*reparare tectas*), then the Greeks will come to knock them down again.[15]

The poem takes us backward in time from Augustus and a world in ruins to Romulus and a ruined Troy, thereby giving the lie to Juno's explicit claims about the irreversibility of time's arrow. It may be that Horace means to suggest that this kind of archaeology is permissible in fiction, but dangerous in practice. We could read *Odes* 3.3 as a gloss on one of the sharpest ideological tensions of the Augustan regime, which aimed—by antiquarian means that many modern scholars have come to recognize as fraudulent—to give the appearance of a return to the *mos maiorum* of the early Republic at the same time as, in fact, it constructed a radically new apparatus of power. The Augustan rhetoric of republican restoration, Horace suggests, is *just* rhetoric: a real return to the age of the Catos and Scipios would only re-expose Rome to the savage civil strife into which this era of elite competition had eventually debouched.[16]

For Horace (as well as for Vergil, who in the last three books of the *Aeneid* rewrites the Trojan war so that Aeneas and his allies can win it), the goal is to hold Rome and Troy at a distance from each other and, through ruination, banish Troy into the past. Rome is supposed to get nothing from Troy but an origin story. Its *pietas* toward this vanished metropolis has to take on an elegiac tone; Rome can mourn Troy, but not repair it. Troy is a source, not a goal.

In the *Bellum Civile*, in what is probably the most famous scene of ruinoscopy in Latin literature, Lucan subjects this line of argument to an acid bath. After slaughtering his countrymen at Pharsalus, Julius Caesar takes a victory lap around the Mediterranean. His first stop is at Troy:

> He circles the memorable name of burned-out Troy
> And looks for big traces of Apollo's wall.
> Already, though, the sterile woods and rotten oak trunks
> Have borne down on the house of Assaracus and the temples of the gods;
> Already these are bound with slack roots, and all Troy
> is wrapped in weeds: even the ruins have perished.

> Circumit exustae nomen memorabile Troiae
> magnaque Phoebei quaerit uestigia muri.
> iam siluae steriles et putres robore trunci
> Assaraci pressere domos et templa deorum
> iam lassa radice tenent, ac tota teguntur
> Pergama dumetis: etiam periere ruinae.   Luc. *BC* 9.964–969

Caesar really is behaving like a victor here: in the Trojan context, *circumit* suggests nothing so much as Achilles' hubristic defilement of Hector's corpse by dragging it around Troy's circuit walls. Since Caesar's family is supposed to have preserved a direct genealogical link with Troy through Aeneas's son Iulus, Lucan thus sets him uncomfortably in a double role. But there is no Troy left to conquer, since even the ruins have perished, and nothing remains but a memorable name. Trees have sunk deep roots into the wreckage and erased it. Around these rotten trunks cluster a range of associations—the "family tree," a metaphor as active for the Romans as for us; the *antiqua silva*, which for the Romans signifies the Latin poetic tradition; Lucan's own oft-employed figure of the great man as a tree—that point their accusatory fingers at Roman political and literary "overuse" of Troy. If the ruins of Troy are invisible, it's because they've been written over so many times already.[17]

At the same time, we have to read this image of an overgrown Troy as the endpoint of a trajectory of ruination along which Rome, according to Lucan, is already progressing:

> The fact that, now, walls hang from half-ruined roots
> and the stones lie, fallen from the great walls
> in Italy's cities, and the houses are guarded by no guard,
> and few are the inhabitants that wander in the old cities;
> the fact that Hesperia is hairy with weeds,
> neglected, unplowed for many years, and the begging fields lack labor:
> not you, fierce Pyrrhus, and not the Phoenician, source
> of so many calamities, will be to blame for this; no outside wound,
> but the blow of a civil hand, has sunk so deep.

> At nunc semirutis pendent quod moenia tectis
> urbibus Italiae lapsisque ingentia muris
> saxa iacent nulloque domus custode tenentur
> rarus et antiquis habitator in urbibus errat,
> horrida quod dumis multosque inarata per annos
> Hesperia est desuntque manus poscentibus aruis,
> non tu, Pyrrhe ferox, nec tantis cladibus auctor
> Poenus erit: nulli penitus descendere ferro
> contigit; alta sedent ciuilis uolnera dextrae. Luc. *BC* 1.24–32

The towns and cities of Italy are also, in their own way, going back to nature. The reason for this is that civil strife has depopulated them, leaving only the aged behind, their strength insufficient to keep the walls upright and plow the fields. Rome has managed to reverse its own upward trajectory; in an era of civil wars, Troy is at once Rome's future and Rome's past. Vergilian myth-history gives no insurance against a repetition of Trojan ruins at Rome.[18]

In the first century of the empire, historiographers and poets shared the project of imagining Rome as a ruin. In book 5 of *Ab Urbe Condita*, Livy goes so far as to rehearse it in a scenario that, as Christina Kraus has argued, is full of Trojan resonances. The Gauls have sacked Rome and pillaged everything but the *arx*. After their victory over the Gauls near Ardea, the Roman survivors face a city in ruins. At this point, somebody raises the question of whether it might not be better to abandon Rome altogether and migrate to Veii, a city captured and depopulated by Roman arms just before the coming of the Gauls. There, after all, the houses and walls are still standing, ready to shelter and protect a swarm of Roman refugees.

M. Furius Camillus, the dictator, gives a long speech opposing this plan, in which he details Rome's significance, not just as architecture, but as place. In particular, he says that Roman ritual practice is not simply transposable; Rome's gods and goddesses cannot be worshipped anywhere else than at Rome. Moreover, the task of rebuilding is radically easier than whatever might be meant by refoundation:

> If no better or more capacious house can be built in all the world than that hut of our founder, isn't it better to live among our sacred things and penates in huts, like shepherds or farmers, than to go as a people into exile? Our ancestors, shepherds and wanderers, when there was nothing here but woods and swamps, built a city in such a short time; are we too lazy to rebuild what has been burned, even though the Capitolium and the Arx and the temples of the gods stand unharmed?

> Si tota urbe nullum melius ampliusve tectum fieri possit quam casa illa conditoris est nostri, non in casis ritu pastorum agrestiumque habitare est satius inter sacra penatesque nostros quam exsulatum publice ire? Maiores nostri, convenae pastoresque, cum in his locis nihil praeter silvas paludesque esset, novam urbem tam brevi aedificarunt: nos Capitolio, arce incolumi, stantibus templis deorum, aedificare incensa piget? (Livy *AUC* 5.53)

The *maiores* created Rome from nothing, from swampland and forest. To restore, on a ground plan already given, is easier, especially if Romans are willing to forgo the luxury of a fully elaborated urban architecture and live, like their founder Romulus, in cabins (*casae*). Rome's ruination, unlike that of Troy, should not be the occasion for a general flight (*exsulatum*). The reason why Rome is no "second Troy" is because all lines of flight stop here.[19]

No less than Aeneas's flight from Troy, the Gallic sack of Rome is a foundation myth—one that might be understood, in fact, as the obverse side of the story that Virgil tells in the *Aeneid*. Here, by contrast with Aeneas at Troy, Rome's ancestors come out victorious: they have defeated the Gauls, and they have their choice of dwelling places. Where the Trojans are constrained to go to Rome, the Romans follow Camillus's advice and choose Rome freely. They adopt the Roman project not because it is all that they have, but because they prefer it over all other alternatives. The Rome that they rebuild will indeed represent a return to form, after a divagation into luxury and pride that resembles imperial historians' description of the last days of the Republic. If the rebuilding of Rome thus takes place in a much more conservative key than the resettlement of Athens, this probably shows the extent to which ruins, impossible in Greece, were baked into the historical experience of Roman empire.[20]

Livy's is a characteristically Augustan response to an ideological tension—always fruitful for Roman writers—between ruins that command loyalty and ruins that sever it. If ruination turns a population into refugees and potential Romans, it also leaves behind a trace—the ruin—that exerts a continuing pull on the *pietas* of its erstwhile inhabitants. This dialectic, paradigmatically staged between Rome and Troy, almost always resolves in a way that leaves Rome with an undisputed claim to the allegiance of its citizens. There were of course dissenting voices; Lucan is one example. Another, the pseudonymous author of the Book of Revelation, probably a near contemporary of Lucan, imagines the destruction of Rome in the guise of Babylon the Great. A holy remnant of its population flees in advance, but the rest are burned up. Not only will this Babylon-Rome never be refounded, there will never be a city like it again.

Roman writers observed and embroidered upon the role that ruins had played in Roman history. Between cultural background and historical experience, Romans learned to use ruins to think about the city's architectural future, particularly at moments of crisis or change. The Augustan moment brought ruins to the fore, and Diana Spencer has shown that Lucan wrote his ruins with a sidelong glance at Nero's radical building program. Interest in ruins waned over the more stable second century, while literary production itself waned over the more turbulent third and fourth centuries. In late antiquity, the literary record shows a renewed obsession with ruins that corresponds to an uncanny and unfamiliar sense of Rome's vulnerability. Unsurprisingly, then, ruins also have a privileged place in the range of Roman responses to Rome's capture and sack by the Visigoths, under Alaric, in 410 CE.[21]

This used to be one of the dates historians gave for the "fall of the Roman Empire," or at least its Western half. Modern scholarship, by contrast, has recognized how slight—in material terms, at least—the impact of this incursion really was. Some buildings were burnt, but not many, and the invaders preferred to milk Romans for their hidden wealth rather than slaughter them wholesale. Nor indeed can the Visigoths, settled by treaty within the empire and probably, by the time of Rome's sack, united more by opportunistic loyalty to Alaric than by ethnic identity, any more be thought of as a starkly barbarian other. The events of 410 CE are now seen, not as an unprecedented and unrecoverable disaster, but as one in a series of "falls" of Rome, beginning with Sulla's and proceeding with some regularity through Constantine's, which punctuate the city's long history of civil conflict.[22]

When earlier historians overstated the gravity of the "Gothic sack," however, they were repeating the (mis)representations of contemporary sources. Christians in particular tended to take an apocalyptic tone, but most everyone seems to have felt it as a trauma out of all proportion to the importance that modern historians assign it. Such exaggerations, far from being the product of panic, were part of an ongoing rhetorical-political debate about what should become of Rome (and other major cities) in an imperial space that, on many frontiers at once, was obviously collapsing. Within this debate, ruins were a figure that helped make the case for abandoning Rome. Alaric and his followers were not the only opportunists in 410 and the decades that followed; powerful groups and individuals who had long felt that they could "do without" Rome found in the Gothic Sack a chance that they had been looking for.[23]

Orosius's historiography—overtly anti-Roman, as we've seen—comes out of this cultural moment. So does Augustine's *City of God*, a long text that begins as apologetics but transforms, as it proceeds, into a call for Christians to transfer their loyalties from earthly cities (Rome included) to a heavenly city that exists on this earth only as metaphor. Augustine's immediate response to the sack, in a sermon only shortly postdating it, was to point out that it could have been much worse but for the fact that much of Rome's population had emigrated (*migraverat*) before the city's investment by Alaric's armies. As a piece of providence, the Goths had been sent by God to frighten, not destroy: not to wipe out Rome's citizens, but to set them in motion.[24]

Early on in *City of God*, Augustine—an astute but conflicted reader of Vergil—latches onto the tension between loyalty to Troy and loyalty to Rome, which that author had attempted to capture in the figure of the ruin. Citing extensively from book 2 of the *Aeneid*, he certifies Vergil's description of Troy's capture while pointing out the utter inconsistency—from a Christian perspective, naturally—of Vergil's and other writers' claims about the providential character of that sack. If the gods Aeneas had carried from Troy to Rome were worth saving, why hadn't they saved themselves or, for that matter, Troy? And didn't it follow from this that any city—say, Rome—that had committed itself to the protection of these gods was as likely as Troy to end up ruined? "What madness is it to suppose that Rome had been wisely committed to such protectors and, unless it had lost them, could not be sacked?" (Quae dementia est existimare his tutoribus Romam sapienter fuisse commissam et nisi eos amisisset non potuisse uastari?) (*CD* 1.3). The only really safe city was the City of God.[25]

Christians were the loudest but not the only party offering a project for a new *civitas* to be erected on the (real or figurative) ruins of the old; other writers articulated alternative programs in similar language but along more secular lines. Rutilius Namatianus, the Romano-Gallic poet who recorded his 417 journey by ship from Rome to Narbonne in a long elegiac poem now known by the title *De reditu suo*, has with some justice been read as one of the few really vehement anti-Christian writers we can identify in the fifth century CE. What motivates this hostility, I think, is not only religious animus: rather, Rutilius understood himself as engaged in a polemic against writers, like Augustine, who meant to turn Romanness into a religious identity. His own program was to re-create the city as a kind of distributed aristocracy, united by a shared sense of the past but not by place.[26]

Rutilius wrote *De reditu suo* in two books, of which only the first—a scant 644 lines of elegiac couplets—has survived intact. Brief verse portraits of the Roman aristocrats that Rutilius encounters on his travels or otherwise finds reason to mention occupy 111 of those lines, more than a sixth of the whole. He praises their genealogy, their estates, the high offices they have held; in particular, he praises their ability to create a kind of Roman space well beyond the city limits. So of Victorinus, who had once ruled as proconsul in Britain, he has this to say:

> He **took off** to the very ends of the earth,
> But governed as though he were in the middle of the City.

> Extremum pars ille quidem **discessit** in orbem,
>> sed tamquam media rector in urbe fuit   *DRS* 1.503–504

Rome is only secondarily a place. Primarily it is a past, a set of laws and customs that every true Roman carries with him everywhere. This is the sense in which Rutilius can claim that Rome, by giving laws, has made what used to be a world into a single city.[27]

This impulse to recreate the Roman senate as a distributed extraurban aristocracy is one that can be traced through a number of fourth-century writers, including Q. Aurelius Symmachus and Paulinus of Nola. These figures and their addressees shared a common wish to enjoy the privileges and prestige of a Roman senator without having to maintain an expensive and even dangerous presence in Rome, the empire's central place; their centrifugal project was in its way as anti-Roman as any Christianity. We should emphatically *not* understand it as a specific response to the Gothic Sack, any more than the Christian impulse to put the *ecclesia* in place of the *patria* can be grasped this way. What Alaric gave both these groups was an opportunity to intensify their rhetoric by connecting it to Roman ideas of antique provenance about ruins and the migrations these could entail.[28]

De reditu is a travel narrative that also involves, and therefore has to justify, a certain emigration from or displacement of Rome. In this sense, as apologetic travelogue, it forms part of a tradition that begins with the *Aeneid*, a text to which it is also united by important structural parallels. A product of Late-Roman baroque, it develops a learned pastiche out of that text and others (most importantly Ovid's *Tristia* and Homer's *Odyssey*) by way of demonstrating its author's ability to bring the Italian landscape within the scope of a literary tradition that was already classical. One way the *DRS* marks its belonging to this tradition is by using ruins to announce its apologetic aims.[29]

What Rutilius needs to do is justify his departure from—his abandonment of—Rome in terms that will still allow him to appear as a good Roman. He does this, first, by evoking the ruins of his ancestral estates near Toulouse, estates that call him back from Rome's "beloved shore:"

> Indeed they are too ugly with the scars of long wars,
>> But all the more to be pitied, as they are less pleasant.

> Illa quidem longis nimium deformia bellis,
>> Sed quam grata minus, tam miseranda magis.   *DRS* 1.21–22

The latent affective ties that bind Rutilius to these estates, the origin point of his family's earlier Rome-ward migration, have been, as it were, reactivated by the damage they suffered during or because of the recent invasions. *Pietas* compels Rutilius to repair a property to which, as long as it remained intact, he was able to pay no mind:

> It is not licit to ignore any further their prolonged ruination.

> Nec fas ulterius longas nescire ruinas. *DRS* 1.27

Now that they have fallen into ruin, his refusal to know or acknowledge these ancestral lands is a failure to meet a most sacred obligation.

We see in this compulsion to return to a ruined homeland something that earlier Roman authors, with respect to Troy, had tried to resist. For Vergil, Horace, and Livy, Rome was to be the endpoint of all lines of flight rather than the starting point of new migrations. Rutilius sees the dilemma and navigates it as deftly as he can. Sometimes, as in the lines that follow, allusive language blurs Rutilius's departure point and destination:

> Now is the time to build even shepherds' cottages
>> On farms torn by fierce fires.

> Iam tempus laceris post saeva incendia fundis
>> vel pastorales aedificare casas. *DRS* 29–30

In the rare word *casas*, here again collocated with *pastorales*, we should see an allusion to the passage of Livy's *AUC* book 5 in which Camillus exhorts the Romans not to abandon the site of their ruined city. In that passage, which I discussed earlier, Camillus highlights Rome's pastoral origins to argue that its modern citizens should be happy to live there even in cottages, like shepherds— a rhetorical move, I think, that lies behind Rutilius's otherwise hard-to-explain "*vel*" in the lines just quoted. What it amounts to is an identification of Rutilius's Toulouse with Camillus's Rome as the truest locus of the poet's loyalty and obligation. This is, of course, all in keeping with Rutilius's project of re-presenting Rome, not as a place, but as a distributed feeling-world united by history, law, and culture.[30]

But what about Rome itself, the physical city from which Rutilius sets out? Here, he surprises us: Rutilius's Rome, despite its recent sacking, appears totally intact. He even goes so far as to point out that the city is *not* smoldering but rather seems to fill the sky above it with a purer air. To this claim, one might reply that poetry, like the unconscious, knows no negation. However that may be, Rutilius gives us no mise-en-scène of ruination to match the one that justifies Aeneas's flight from Troy. His depiction of a Rome unharmed or restored forms part of a paean to the city and a prediction of the empire's recovery that has been read by modern critics, with the advantage of hindsight, as unaccountable optimism or even as propaganda.[31]

To take it this way would be to ignore Rutilius's careful depiction of Roman Italy as a landscape in ruins. Half the cities his ship sails past are uninhabited, and most of these are falling apart:

> We sighted the old ruins that had no watchman
>> And the crumbling walls of deserted Cosa.

> Cernimus antiquas nullo custode ruinas
>> et desolatae moenia foeda Cosae.   DRS 1.285–286

In this context, the collocation "*nullo custode*" has to remind us of Lucan, a poet on whom Rutilius leans elsewhere, too. The point of the allusion would be to make us think of the abandoned Italy, already almost reclaimed by nature, which Lucan depicts in book 1 of the *Bellum Civile*. The Italy of *De reditu* is also showing signs of escaping human control. The very reason that Rutilius has chosen to travel by boat is that, after the depredations of the Goths, Roman bridges and roads no longer bind Italy together. Even along the coast, as Jacqueline Clarke has shown, the borders between land and sea in *De reditu* are beginning to blur.[32]

The slow dissolving of Italy depicted in the *DRS* forces us to reconsider that text's representation of Rome as eternal city. We could resolve the contradiction by reading Rutilius's Rome as a symbol, his Italy as the Real, which that symbol obscures: in that case, the city of Rome would figure as the abstract object of Rutilius's loyalties, while a ravaged Italy would play an apologetic role by justifying Rutilius's flight from the center of the empire. In any case, it is clear that *De reditu* reverses the polarity of the Vergilian migration scheme: from rather than to Rome, toward rather than out of ruins.

The aim of the poem is to present, and justify, a new way of thinking a post-410 Roman world. In this respect, it has much in common with works by Augustine, Jerome, and other Christian writers who saw in Rome's ruin a chance to shake Christianity free of the dominance of secular powers. All of these projects involved, to a greater or lesser extent, the abandonment of Rome, and as such all of them sketched out a future "imagined community" that their authors wanted to make real. For Rome to be ruined, only one of these projects had to succeed. By talking about ruins as they did, these writers also helped bring ruins into being.[33]

If we can say with certainty that Rome did end up ruined, the date at which it actually became a ruin is harder to pin down. That's in the nature of the question: ruination can always be followed (as was usually the case in Greece, for instance) by rebuilding, so that catastrophic events matter less than long-term trends. The closest thing to a date of birth that we can give for ruins, then, might just be the moment when people give up on rebuilding. Rodolfo Amadeo Lanciani, the great nineteenth-century Italian archaeologist, makes a strong case for identifying the Byzantine-Gothic Wars of the mid-sixth-century CE as an episode of depopulation and ruination after which there was to be no restoration for a very long time. On the whole I endorse this view, but it poses a further puzzle: Why did people choose to stop rebuilding Rome at just this point?[34]

To answer this question means taking into account not just the centrifugal narratives I've just been discussing, but also their knock-on effects in the late fifth and early sixth centuries. In these years—from a Constantinopolitan perspective, at least, which many modern historians have also adopted—the West could seem "post-Roman" because it no longer had an emperor who bore the title Caesar or Augustus. The *reges* who ruled Italy from 476 CE onward did not see things this way. Though they claimed (and worked hard to construct) an Ostrogothic identity for themselves and their soldiers, they sought to maintain Roman institutions and loyalties among their subjects. The success or failure of this program would depend on how those subjects received it.[35]

We are fortunate to have an extraordinarily thick documentation of this period from multiple perspectives. Procopius, the chronicler of Justinian and Belisarius, gives us a circumstantial narrative of Ostrogothic rule in Italy at the beginning of book 5 of his *Wars*. He is evidently interested in justifying Justinian's invasion of Italy, and his narrative should therefore be read with a healthy skepticism. Cassiodorus' *Variae*, a portfolio of letters written by the state secretary to a series of Ostrogothic kings, gives us the materials to compose a more detailed and less tendentious account—although, as M. Shane Bjornlie has pointed out, this portfolio was assembled in by its author in Byzantium after the fall of Ostrogothic Italy and thus cannot be taken to give an unfiltered image of events.[36]

Like some among the last Roman emperors, the Ostrogothic kings governed Italy from Ravenna rather than Rome. Nevertheless, they took an extraordinarily close interest in the management of Rome's urban fabric. Theoderic in particular—the first and by all accounts the best of the *reges*—worked to represent himself as the restorer of Rome and thereby to legitimate his rule on the time-honored Roman pattern of inscribing himself on the city's built infrastructure.[37]

Cassiodorus, who knew the rules of the game, gave a rhetorical framing to Theoderic's program that made it appear of a piece with the Ostrogoths' general interest in maintaining the old order of things:

> And so greater care is to be had in preserving a thing than in founding it, because while the praise for beginnings is owed to the thing founded, perfection acquires its praise through preservation . . . so former princes justly owe us their praises, to whose buildings we gave an extended youth, so that they shine with the newness of their antiquity, which were formerly dimmed by aged maturity.

> Atque ideo maior in conservandis rebus quam in inveniendis adhibenda cautela est, quia de initiis praedicatio debetur invento, de custoditis adquiritur lauda perfectio . . . ut antiqui principes nobis merito debeant laudes suas, quorum fabricas dedimus longissimam iuventutem, ut pristine novitate transluceant, quae iam fuerant veternosa senectute fuscata. (Cass. *Var.* 1.25)

Cassiodorus gives the rationale for Theoderic's program in terms of a series of paired oppositions: preserving-discovering, beginning and caring for, ancient and new, youth and old age. At issue in all these antitheses is the passage of time, and their tendency in combination is to give the present, despite its "late" status, a privileged position with respect to the past. Rome's past rulers owe Theoderic a debt of gratitude for the measures he's taken to preserve their buildings: restoration is perfection.

Indeed, the king's legitimacy seems bound up with his power to maintain the city of Rome, as though the extinguished *principes* who sit in judgment over their Gothic successor can be induced to approve him by his approach to building and repair. We would probably not be wrong, either, to see in this passage a latent condemnation of the *imperatores* who had immediately preceded Theoderic on the throne, and through whose mismanagement the city's *senectus* had become apparent.[38]

In his study of the end of civic euergetism in Roman Italy, Bryan Ward-Perkins argues that the flow of private and imperial wealth into urban infrastructure continued in Rome for centuries after it had ceased in smaller cities. By the end of the fifth century CE, however, both these sources of funding had fallen off dramatically, especially when it came to repairing older structures. This was in part for what we might anachronously call religious reasons: with the conversion of the emperor to Christianity, the dissolution of temple endowments, and eventually the banning of pagan ritual practices, the many temples of Rome lost their attraction as objects of patronage. The imperial gaze was attracted elsewhere, as Hendrik Dey has shown: to the walls and porticoed central streets that came to characterize even small cities in late antiquity and after. The urban gestalt had changed: cities served ever more as stages on which magnates could demonstrate their magnitude, ever less as sites for shared rituals that predated, or claimed to predate, the empire itself.[39]

It is interesting to note, in this connection, that Cassiodorus shows Theoderic undertaking the repair of at least one temple—that of Hercules, in Ravenna—and a synagogue at Rome, but not repairing or building any churches. This is to some extent an artifact of Cassiodorus's editorial policies: we know from other sources that Theoderic did finance the construction of at least one basilica at Ravenna. The most likely reason that Cassiodorus culled any documents connected to this church from the *Variae* was that it served Arians, the Christian sect to which Theoderic (and most Ostrogoths) belonged. Since most of Theoderic's Roman subjects, as Nicene Catholics, were violently opposed to Arianism, Cassiodorus generally avoids any mention of his sponsor's heterodox religious beliefs. There was little demand for an Arian church in Rome, so Theoderic didn't patronize Christian architecture there.[40]

Not that Christian architecture in Rome needed much help from the *rex* by then. Since the early fourth century, the popes had overseen the building of dozens of basilicas in and around the city, most of which had been given substantial endowments for their own upkeep through private or imperial largesse. The built infrastructure of the Christian world was now growing of its own accord, and with it an administrative structure that would lend cohesion to much of what had been Roman space during and after the breakup of the empire.[41]

At the same time, and in adumbration of the *incastellamento* that would spread across Italy later on, elites who might in earlier centuries have devoted their wealth to euergetism were now spending instead on the extension and fortification of their private estates. In some parts of Italy, this involved the removal of whole populations to walled-up hilltop positions, a trend that Theoderic worked hard to stop. In Rome, too, Cassiodorus represents him as calling senatorial elites to meet what he considered their obligations to the city that was at least nominally their home. In a letter calling on Symmachus, father-in-law of the philosopher Boethius, to repair the Theater of Pompey, he makes the point clearly:

> Since you show such zeal for private buildings that you are seen to have built walls on your own property, it's fitting that you, that great institutor and outstanding decorator of structures, be counted as one of the miracles of Rome, which you adorned with your houses, since both these things stem from prudence— namely, to plan rightly and to decorate existing buildings well.

> Cum privatis fabricis ita studueris, ut in laribus propriis quaedam moenia fecisse videaris, dignum est, ut Romam, quam domuum pulchritudine decorasti, in suis miraculis continere noscaris, fundator egregius fabricarum earumque comptor eximius, quia utrumque de prudentia venit, et apte disponere et extantia competenter ornare. (*Var.* 4.51.1)

The expense to which Symmachus has gone in fortifying his own villa gives evidence of his capacity also to participate in Theoderic's project of Roman restoration. Private building and public works, Cassiodorus writes, stem from the same *prudentia*. A magnate like Symmachus should be eager to help preserve Rome's architectural past. It is revealing, then, that Theoderic needs to send him a letter reminding him to do so, and to offer, later on in the same letter, a subvention for the project out of the royal treasury.[42]

That letter is only one of many in the *Variae* that give the impression that Theoderic is beating against the current. This is true: the Rome he wants to restore is one that already belongs to a distant past. What I have elsewhere called Ostrogothic "classicism" was a program that sought to recreate Rome as a governable entity by referring to models from the third century CE and even earlier. These models, which left important administrative roles open to Italian elites, were supposed to secure Roman loyalty and gratitude. That they failed to do so is at least in part testament to the extent to which Roman citizens had shifted their affective attachments away from Rome as a central place, a process in which, as we saw, the rhetoric of an Augustine or a Rutilius had its part to play.[43]

The reality was that Romans were now working actively to destroy their city, not to restore it. The form of architectural recycling known as spoliation had been a problem in Rome since at least the time of Majorian, the first emperor whom we know to have legislated on the subject. Since building materials of the highest quality, such as Carrera marble and *lapis Gabinus*, were no longer being imported to Rome, the easiest and in some cases the only way to acquire them for new construction was to reuse what was already there. People quarried from buildings that had collapsed and in some cases from buildings that were still standing. Given his program of restoration, this was a particularly acute problem for Theoderic: to restore one building might mean to destroy another, or, more significantly, to acknowledge that it had already fallen into ruin and was beyond saving.[44]

A number of letters in Cassiodorus's *Variae* show that Theoderic understood spoliation as a matter of necessity. It was Cassiodorus's job to clothe this necessity in a rhetoric that made it appear compatible with the ideal of a Rome restored. In one letter authorizing a *comes* with the Gothic name Suna to manage spoliation of marble blocks for public purposes, he makes it seem like part and parcel of that ideal:

> It is not fitting for that which could increase the elegance of the city to lie without use, since paying no attention to what might bring profit is no counsel of wisdom. And therefore let your high sublimity take measures that those marble blocks, which having fallen down lie everywhere neglected, be put back into walls wherever this may seem necessary, so that old construction may once again redound to the public elegance and stones lying after their fall may provide some adornment.

> Sine usu iacere non decet, quod potest ad decorem crescere civitatis, quia non est sapientiae profutura contemnere. Et ideo illustris sublimitas tua marmorum quadratos, qui passim diruti negleguntur, quibus hoc opus videtur iniunctum in fabricam murorum faciat deputari, ut redeat in decorem publicum prisca constructio et ornent aliquid saxa iacentia post ruinas. (Cass. *Var.* 2.7)

Decus, as Valerie Fauvinet-Ranson has recognized, is a keyword in Cassiodorus's architectural language. Midway between the ethical and the aesthetic, it motivates the reconstruction of Rome as a project not only of beautification but also of moral regeneration. Here, characteristically, Cassiodorus structures it in opposition to the *iacentia*, whatever is uselessly lying around. The scattered stones are made to seem not only ugly, but lazy—both vices that Suna can fix by making them stand upright again.[45]

By designating and identifying such stones, though, Cassiodorus is effectively recognizing and legitimating the category that we would call a ruin. Some buildings are so decayed that they are no longer deserve to be called buildings: they are only stones, *sine usu* after a decisive and irreversible *ruina*. This was the only dimension of the Ostrogothic building program that was to have a lasting impact on Roman building practices and landscapes. Cassiodorus's rhetoric turns ruins into a natural resource—one that was irresistible even to Theoderic himself, whose palace at Ravenna was decorated with columns that had been despoiled from Rome.[46]

Read closely, the letters of the *Variae* that deal with Rome's urban fabric reveal that any program to restore or preserve that fabric in the sixth century CE was going to have to be imposed from the top and would face resistance from many parties who viewed the collapse into ruin of Rome's ancient buildings with eagerness or indifference. This was why the multiple sieges and sacks that Rome suffered during the Byzantine-Gothic Wars led to ruin rather than rebuilding. That war marks the transformation of Rome into a ruin, not because it was particularly damaging to the city's urban fabric, but because nobody cared anymore to clean up the mess that it left behind. Survival meant a retreat from the glorious but risky and high-maintenance monumentalism that had been the legacy of the Caesars.[47]

In a letter that comes toward the end of the *Variae*—in fact, it is the last letter in the collection that can securely be dated to before the landing of Byzantine troops on the coast of Italy in 534—Cassiodorus describes the desperate measures that need to be taken to prop up an elephant. The elephant in question is a statue that has long stood on Rome's Via Sacra but now trembles on the brink of ruin. Scholars agree that Cassiodorus has selected and placed this letter so as to make a point, allegorically, about the state of Italy on the eve of the Byzantine invasion. Under Theodahad's bloody and incompetent rule, Cassiodorus hints, not only the elephant but Rome itself is ready to fall.[48]

Is Cassiodorus evoking Rome's ruin in advance to justify, Aeneas-like, his own opportunistic transfer of loyalties from the Goths to the Byzantines early in the war? If so, he is inaugurating a rhetorical move that the Byzantine historian Procopius will employ in his own later account of the conflict, a narrative that, whatever else it does, at least seconds Justinian's interest in obliterating Rome as a center of specifically imperial loyalties. When he describes the state of Rome after its final capture from the Goths in 552, Procopius comments extensively both on the feebleness of the modern population of Italy and on the crumbling state of Rome's monuments, which that population is no longer competent to repair.[49]

In a passage that has intrigued critics and, like Cassiodorus's elephant, given rise to a diversity of interpretations, Procopius then gives a detailed description of Aeneas's ship, which he claims to have seen in a specially built shed on the banks of the Tiber. The vessel, he says, is marvelously well-preserved—an understatement, given that it would then have been more than 1500 years old by the normal Roman chronology.[50]

Probably this is all a Procopian fiction. But to what end? Is it that, having shown a Rome in ruins, he wants to summon up the means by which Romans or would-be Romans have been fleeing forward out of ruination since the fall of Troy? In that case, Rome will pass its empire on to Constantinople, there to continue making ruins for centuries to come.

CHAPTER THREE

Baghdad

Postclassical Ruins and the Islamic Cityscape

In the *Muqaddimah*, his guidebook to the study of history, the fifteenth-century Maghribi scholar Ibn Khaldun reports on a belief, widely held among his contemporaries, that the ancient monuments were built by giants, men twice or more the size of modern men, strong enough to heft stone blocks and tall enough to roast fish by proximity to the sun. He himself knows better. The great buildings of the past were built by collective effort and with tricks of engineering still well-understood in his own day. If the Arabs have failed to build anything that compares with these ancient ruins, this is only because the royal dynasties of the past were longer-lived and ruled larger territories. For Ibn Khaldun, ruins are historical evidence that condemns the frailty—political, not biological—of the present.[1]

The *Muqaddimah* devotes a full seven chapters to the right way of reading monuments as documents. On this topic at least, Ibn Khaldun writes with a methodological rigor and complexity that goes far beyond anything in Greco-Roman literature. Ibn Khaldun's engagement has deep historical roots: Islamicate civilization was born in ruins,[2] a nativity that shaped its awareness of its present as much as of its past.

For many Muslim thinkers, before and including Ibn Khaldun, ruins framed the relationship between that present and that past as a rivalry. There was a sense in which, as the Qur'an made clear, the present was always going to come out on top: After all, Muslims survived and thrived thanks to their piety and their obedience to God's commands, while the erstwhile inhabitants of ruins had been exterminated for their rebelliousness and ingratitude. Ruins were thus a warning about the dangers of disobedience. But they were also a challenge, one that—as historians represented it, at least—Muslim rulers were often unable to meet. Islamicate urban planning tried to duck this challenge, with important consequences for the layout and self-consciousness of early Muslim cities. If the architectural remains of the *jahiliyya* articulated an emphasis on monumentality and permanence, early Islamic cities eschewed both of these. In their planning and construction, they favored adaption and mobility instead. To the extent that these new cities were "arguments in stone" (or wood, in the earliest cases), they were arguments against the ruins of the classical past. Such arguments in stone gave rise to arguments in words, an Islamicate discourse on ruins that united literary cultures high and low, pious and secular, around a shared anxious relation to the past.[3]

The Qur'an, which initiates this discourse as it initiates Islam writ large, is a difficult document to localize—in time as much as in space. To a great extent, the *sira* (historiographical) and *tafsir* (interpretive) traditions surrounding it aim exactly to establish that placement of scripture within a particular spatial/ historical context that the Qur'an itself withholds. The Qur'an's interests are different, after all, and not exactly or at least straightforwardly historiographical. It constructs itself as the unadulterated self-presentation of a revelation. Consequently, and unlike other scriptures in the Mosaic tradition, it foregoes a narrative-historical framing that might have been taken to distort its inspired content.[4]

These evidentiary constraints leave the ruined cities of Islamic revelation with a lot of work to do. By placing the Qur'an within a geography of dead civilizations, they lend the document a sense of space; by locating Muhammad within a local history of Arabian prophecy, they help create a sense of historical time. Within this Qur'anic framework, ruins are evidence of a very special sort.

You don't have to look too far for evidentiary claims in the Qur'an. They're everywhere: *ayat* (signs), *burhan* (proofs), and *bayyinat* (clear evidence) establishing the truth of Qur'anic revelation in ways that Muhammad's bare assertion could not have done. This is part of the document's peculiar rhetoric. Usually what counts as evidence is nature: the rain and the order of day and night and the way the earth, more or less reliably, comes back to life after a dry dead season. As manmade objects, ruins are anomalous among the categories of Qur'anic evidence.[5]

On the other hand, ruins in the Qur'an don't become meaningful because of the human work that has gone into building them. What turns them into signs worth attending is rather what God has done to them by taking the people out of them. A ruin is a ruin because God made it so. In this sense, a ruin is as natural as a plant growing out of the earth. One hadith on the creation of the world shows God making the urban landscape on the fourth day:

> God created the Earth on Sunday and Monday, and the mountains on Tuesday along with the useful things that are in them, and, on Wednesday, trees and water and cities and inhabited places and the wastelands (*kharab*). (al-Tabari, *Ann.* 1966, 22)

خلق الله الأرض يوم الأحد والاثنين, وخلق الجبال يوم الثلاثاء وما فيهن من منافع, وخلق يوم الأربعاء الشجر والماء والمدائن والعمران والخراب.

The hadith just quoted thus makes cities and wastelands anterior to people, who are created on the sixth day. This will seem perverse to anyone who takes for granted that cities are only an index of human history, but it reflects an originary Islamic theology of ruins. In the Qur'an, ruins are not just archaeological traces of past societies but also part of a system of signs made by God to help us know him better.[6]

The Qur'an expects that its audience will know about ruins by firsthand experience. Again and again, it asks: "أَوَلَمْ يَسِيرُوا فِي الْأَرْضِ" (have they not traveled in the land? Q30.9, inter alia). Have they not seen the houses or monuments that stand there empty of people and considered the fate of their occupants? Those structures, the Qur'an insists, are all that remain of ancient tribes who were "أَشَدَّ مِنْهُمْ قُوَّةً . . . وَعَمَرُوهَا أَكْثَرَ مِمَّا عَمَرُوهَا" (greater than them [i.e., Muhammad's contemporary audience] in strength . . . and inhabited more than they inhabit). Having played their part in prophetic history, they vanish from a land of which God has made the Arabs inheritors. Their disappearance, in turn, contains a moral for audiences in Muhammad's own time and after.[7]

In the Qur'an there are many of these vanished peoples—'Ad, Thamud, and Midyan make up the canonical list—but they more or less share a common story. With local variations, the story runs something like this. God "sends" to each people a messenger from among that people—literally, a "brother" (أَخَاهُمْ) (Q7.65). The message is that everyone should worship God alone, and no one else beside him (اعْبُدُوا اللَّهَ مَا لَكُم مِّنْ إِلَهٍ غَيْرُه). His people call this message a lie or a fiction—the messenger, after all, is just a man like them—and refuse to leave the traditions of their forefathers (مَا كَانَ يَعْبُدُ ءَابَاؤُنَا). God saves the messenger and his few followers, but annihilates the rest of his people.[8]

In context, the most obvious function of these narratives is to establish historical precedent for Muhammad's mission. The 'Adites and Thamudites reject God's messengers in the same terms that, elsewhere, the Arabs of his own time are shown as using to reject Muhammad. Like him, these earlier prophets are mortal men and bring no, or insufficient, miraculous support for their revolutionary message. Like him, they bring is a call to strict theolatry, a simplification of worship against the background of some kind of polytheism. Like him, they are accused of retailing their own free invention as divine revelation. The Qur'an represents Muhammad as a figure in the same kind of narrative structure, for which it proposes—if the Meccans continue to reject his message—the same apocalyptic ending.[9]

The shared plot structure and rhetorical function of these ruin-histories were recognized by Islamic readers from an early date. More recently, scholars approaching the Qur'an as a "stratigraphic" document, containing layers of material that preserve not one, but many versions of Muhammad's self-representation, have noticed something else: extensive narrative treatments of 'Ad, Thamud, and Midyan are restricted to suras that, as far as the evidence allows us to reconstruct, were delivered at a point in Muhammad's mission before his and his followers' flight from Mecca to Medina. As such, they may preserve a significant but temporary and later abandoned turn in Muhammad's prophetic project.[10]

The pioneering Qur'anic philologist W. Montgomery Bell has plausibly argued that we should see in these stories a trace of an early moment in the development of Islam, a moment at which this religion—like those propounded to 'Ad, Thamud, and Midyan by their respective messengers—was still essentially local in scope. At this moment, Muhammad's message would not only not have been universal; it would not even have been, as on Patricia Crone's revisionist interpretation, intended for all Arabs. Muhammad's call would have gone out only to the inhabitants of Mecca: a local call to right worship, to be followed, if rejected, by a strictly local apocalypse.[11]

Extending Bell's argument, I would suggest that this phase in the history of Muhammad's prophetic mission should also be understood as anti-urban in a way that would have lasting consequences for the development of the Islamic city. In the Qur'an, ruins record a history of "local apocalypses" in which a city and its citizens are held hostage to the proper reception of a prophet's monotheistic kerygma. The repeated failure of cities to accept this kerygma is no coincidence: something in their political organization, where a few proud chief citizens (الملأ, a word the Qur'an uses to identify political authorities in an urban context) control the opinions of all the rest, makes it difficult if not impossible for cities to abandon the customs of their forefathers. The city, an infertile ground for the spread of Islam, is transformed through the "local apocalypse" into a monument to the consequences of unbelief.[12]

I would not be the first to see in this narrative a reflection of Muhammad's own situation at Mecca as the *sira* tradition has represented it. That city's leading families—including, eventually, Muhammad's own—are supposed to have rejected the Qur'anic revelation for the threat it posed to their profitable position as stewards of one of the central places of Arab polytheism. These magnates are reported to have hounded Muhammad and his followers out of the city, driving some of them to Ethiopia and others to Yathrib (the future Medina). Muhammad's apparent interest in placing himself within a sequence of Arabian prophets emerging from, and working in opposition to, an urban context at least tends to corroborate this account. The Arabic word for this migration itself embodies the double-sidedness of Muhammad's relationship to Mecca: *Hejira* is usually glossed in English as "flight" or "emigration," but comparison with cognates in related languages strongly suggests it must have meant something like "retreat from the countryside to the city."[13]

In combination, all these narratives tend to devalue the built, monumental city as irrelevant or perhaps even detrimental to faith in the Islamic revelation and its earlier adumbrations. The architectural marvels left behind by vanished tribes tend to aggravate rather than counterbalance the weight of their unbelief. As Salih, the prophet sent by Allah to Thamud, tells his people:

> Now remember how he made you [the Thamudites] successors after 'Ad and placed you in the land. You took its plains as sites for fortresses and burrowed into the mountains for your homes. So remember the blessings of God and do not go about the land spreading corruption. (Q7.74)

وَٱذۡكُرُوٓاْ إِذۡ جَعَلَكُمۡ خُلَفَآءَ مِنۢ بَعۡدِ عَادٍ وَبَوَّأَكُمۡ فِى ٱلۡأَرۡضِ تَتَّخِذُونَ مِن سُهُولِهَا قُصُورًا وَتَنۡحِتُونَ ٱلۡجِبَالَ بُيُوتًا فَٱذۡكُرُوٓاْ ءَالَآءَ ٱللَّهِ وَلَا تَعۡثَوۡاْ فِى ٱلۡأَرۡضِ مُفۡسِدِينَ

If the Thamudites have been able to build on a grander scale than their predecessors, this is only because God has cleared them the space to do so. Their monuments demonstrate God's favor, not the skill, power, or wealth of the Thamudites themselves. In this light, the corruption they spread on the earth seems all the more grievous. When they reject the prophetic call, their *qusur* and *buyut* will stand as monuments of their impiety for whatever people replaces them.[14]

Ruined buildings in the Qur'an thus survive to condemn their vanished builders. In the first age of Muslim expansion, the founders of new cities might understandably have wished not to repeat the mistakes of the past. As we shall see, the Islamic historiographical tradition does indeed represent the Muslims of that generation as resistant to the monumental impulse, and even to the idea of building permanent cities at all. But even as the Qur'an spoke against the hubris and impiety that ruins represented, it turned the attention of its earliest readers toward these ruins in an altogether original way. Ibn Khaldun's disquisition on ruins in the *Muqaddimah*, which I discuss at the opening of this chapter, comes at the end of a tradition that, beginning from this scriptural impulse, was always prepared to see ruins as evidence.[15]

The evidentiary significance of ruins in the Qur'an stems from something that both the text itself and the interpretive tradition surrounding it represent as a central dilemma for Muhammad. His prophetic mission involved, at least in part, the confirmation of earlier divine revelation—the Torah and the Gospels—which in his view had been distorted and misunderstood by earlier generations of notional monotheists. To Jewish or Christian audiences, these recognizable parts of the Islamic revelation could seem cribbed. At an early date, polemicists from both these faiths invented intermediary figures—a disgraced rabbi, a defrocked monk—from whom Muhammad was supposed to have received whatever narrative elements of the Qur'an happened to resemble earlier scriptures. The Qur'an itself records his contemporaries' dismissal of such stories as *asatir al-awalin* (tales inherited from the ancients).[16]

As part of a prophetic tradition that recognizes the Torah and the Gospels, the Qur'an necessarily shares some content with its antecedents, a content that thus can always be represented by hostile parties as having its source in earthly documents rather than divine revelation. This is the double bind of Qur'anic originality from which ruins represented an escape. They were assuredly monuments of *something*, but as monuments rather than written documents they were not straightforwardly legible by everyone or even by a class of specially trained scribes. The Qur'an could thus adopt them as narrative "sources" without thereby being accused of copying. If ruins were illegible, then whatever Muhammad could "read" out of them had to come by way of God's assistance. The accounts of the past to which ruins gave rise were thus also evidence of the Qur'an's revelatory originality.[17]

The precise meaning of the first word in the phrase *asatir al-awalin*—that slander against it which the Qur'an itself records—is obscure. Elsewhere in the Qur'an, and in other Semitic languages, the root *sTr* refers to writing or monumental inscriptions, but commentators have often taken the derived noun form to refer to oral folktales. An older hypothesis (which is at least phonologically plausible) saw the Arabic word as a borrowing from the Greek ἱστωρία. With closer attention to Semitic cognates, some very old, this hypothesis has fallen by the wayside, but it nonetheless highlights something essential about *asatir* and its substitutes in the Qur'an. There, ruins duplicate the function of those deprecated *asatir* by grounding the construction of an original Qur'anic historiography. Where its self-presentation forces the Qur'an to discard the usual supports of a historiographical tradition—textual accounts, oral reports—ruins take the place of these in providing an authoritative connection between Qur'anic narrative and the truth about the past. This is something that scholars who censure the Qur'an as an "ahistorical" document have largely ignored. The Qur'an does have a historical dimension, one centered on ruins; Islamic historians inherited this approach to monuments as documents, which opened for them a window onto the past that would remain closed to European writers until the Renaissance.[18]

The ruins of the Qur'an belong to pre-Islamic Arabia, long a terra incognita for modern historians. Thanks to inventive use and reinterpretation of sources by scholars like Irfan Shahid, Robert Hoyland, Glenn Bowersock, and Aziz al-Azmeh, our ability to reconstruct the *histoire eventuelle* of the *jahiliyya* has grown tremendously in recent decades. Nonetheless—both because sources are lacking and because the sources we do have are colored by hagiographic and Qur'an-hermeneutic impulses—we have a great deal of trouble reconstructing the cultural milieu and everyday experience of life in Arabia before Muhammad. The opacity of this material poses a problem for anyone who wants to write about the origins and development of Islamic urbanism, let alone its imbrication with pre-Islamic ruins.[19]

Reconstruction of pre-Islamic social history must begin at the broadest level. The consensus view holds that Central Arabia, in Muhammad's time and for a long time before, was a tribal rather than a state society. As the historian Patricia Crone has argued (echoing in the Arabian context Pierre Clastres's general suggestion about anti-state organization in surviving non-state societies), a tribal society is by no means necessarily an undeveloped mass of people loosely organized and awaiting the coming of the state to set them in order. Tribal organization is better understood as an *alternative* to the state, one that serves many of the state's functions but also works to prevent a state-style social organization from coming into being.[20]

The balance of evidence suggests that the tribal society of pre-Islamic Arabia had developed along these lines, elaborating mechanisms for the regulation of economic exchange, the enforcement of legal norms, and the defense of local populations against outside threats. When outside state actors—Rome or Persia—wanted to make confederates in central Arabia, they did so by dealing with tribes and tribal confederations. It's worth noting, incidentally, that these tribal structures were more effective than state formation in preserving the independence of the Arabs: Northern Arabia and the Yemen, which were closer to the great empires of late antiquity and where secondary state formation had reached an advanced stage, ended up directly subjugated to the Byzantines, Persians, and Ethiopian Axumites.[21]

The enduring tribal structures that resisted imperial encroachment in Arabia were based, at bottom, on an almost contractual exchange of loyalty for protection: since tribes enforced economic and moral norms, a person could only enjoy the protection of these norms as a member or client of a tribe. Member or client: a dramatic hierarchy of status existed within the tribe itself, embracing not only these terms but also age, gender, and genealogy. One's experience of tribal life thus varied substantially depending on one's place within it. At the bottom and the margins, it was probably quite oppressive, a situation that the tenets of Islam tended to remedy in theory, if not in practice. For the freeborn male, the threat of marginalization produced a drive to ascend through the ranks of the tribe by exercising violence against its enemies. For the *jar* or *mawla*, the client or slave, oppression was a structural factor of an existence that was still better than that of an exile or refugee, who lived unprotected by any tribe and thus at the mercy of all.[22]

Pre-Islamic Arabia has also been described as a city-state society. If that's right, then this city-state society was dramatically different from the one that existed in classical Greece. There, as we saw, political and ethnic identities were largely bound up with urban habitation or belonging, such that the capture or destruction of a city-state was the worst disaster imaginable for its inhabitants. In Central Arabia, cities were by contrast secondary and subject to tribal structures: they were part of a tribal patrimony rather than independent political entities. Living in a city conferred no special rights or protections, and an urban dwelling or occupation could even count as an obstacle to advancement within tribal structures that privileged, both ideologically and practically, the life of the desert stock herder or warrior.[23]

The anti-urban prejudices of the Qur'an, such as they are, should be understood as reflexes of this structured interplay of town and hinterland. For Muhammad's audience, the destruction of a city was not a world-ending disaster but indeed, as has been said, just a local apocalypse. Cities and city life could be represented as deviations from the norms of a tribal social structure that could do without cities and tended to despise their inhabitants. Although Muhammad's mission began in an urban setting, with an urban audience, the Qur'an condemns cities in terms that would have resonated with the extra-urban groups that held the balance of power in Central Arabia.[24]

This tendency to privilege the tribe over the city continues in the first centuries of Islamic expansion, during which time it has a clear impact even on the reading of the Qur'an itself. The majority of the early Qur'an interpreters whose views are summed and evaluated in the polymath al-Tabari's magisterial ninth-century collection of *tafsir* (gloss and explication), replace cities with tribes wherever possible. Relying on their testimonies, al-Tabari generally takes the Qur'anic word *qarya*—which means "town," both in Modern Standard Arabic and in the other ancient languages of the Arabian Peninsula—to mean "people" or "inhabited district." Al-Tabari is prepared to accept the text's specific references to built settlements at face value in most but not all cases. In Sura 89, for instance, the Qur'an describes Iram dhat al-'Imad, a particular settlement of the Thamudites usually rendered into English as "'Iram of the Pillars." Many later interpreters, especially those in the *qass*, or folkloric tradition, tend to take the toponym literally, representing 'Iram as a vast and colonnaded city. Al-Tabari rejects this architectural reading, instead following the alternate tradition that makes "Imad" refer to tent poles or to the extraordinary height of the Iramites. He claims that this represents the opinion of most scholars up to his time, an opinion that treats 'Iram not as a city, but as a tribe.[25]

Despite the anti-urban biases outlined above, the expansion of Islam in the seventh and eighth centuries gave rise to a period of city-foundation whose intensity is perhaps only rivaled in world history by Rome's conquest of Gaul and Germany or the European invasion of North America. The dilemma faced by that first generation of Islamic city-builders is palpable in our sources. The available precedents for urban settlement had been judged inadequate in advance, by the Qur'an and also by the social formation in which they lived: as Paul Wheatley has pointed out, no Islamic settlement ever followed the model of Mecca, Medina, or any other Arabian city. Still, the soldiers who spearheaded Islam's conquest of the Near East needed a place to live. In 'Iraq especially, the cities that already stood were inadequate to this purpose. The first Islamic city-builders resolved this dilemma in a revolutionary way, one that tried to foreclose the possibility of repeating the Qur'anic ruinations.[26]

Kufa was among the first of these new foundations. It would eventually become one of the great metropoleis of Islamic 'Iraq, a city whose dynamic culture would make it a major source both of scholars and of scholarly traditions. It began, however, as a kind of armed camp, laid out by the general Sa'd ibn Abi Waqqas as an alternative to nearby Ctesiphon (former capital of the by-then-defunct Sassanian Persian Empire). In his *Futuh al-Buldan*, the ninth-century historian al-Baladhuri reports that the Muslim soldiers refused to settle in Ctesiphon, both because of its insalubrious atmosphere and because its urban plan would have left them dispersed, unable to come together for aggression or defense. The first ground plan of Kufa was laid out in a way that mirrored the military organization of its settlers: ibn Abi Waqqas divided it into *aktat*, or neighborhoods, such that each tribe could settle together and muster quickly in the event of an emergency. In its first incarnation, then, Kufa represented a continuation of tribal forms of social organization in an urban framework. It was, says al-Baladhuri, quoting the Caliph 'Umar, a *Dar hijra* rather than a *madina*: an abode of migration, a point on an outward trajectory, rather than a terminus in itself.[27]

The provisional character of this settlement entailed rejecting monumentality. Al-Baladhuri records that Sad ibn Abi Waqqas built a mosque at the moment of Kufa's foundation and a *Dar al-Imarah*, or house of government, shortly thereafter. Both buildings were simple structures, made of wood and reeds. The early traditions record many attempts to adorn them or remake them out of some more permanent material, attempts strenuously resisted by 'Umar or some other paragon of traditional piety. The first such attempt, reports al-Baladhuri, was made by ibn Abi Waqqas himself:

> Sa'd ibn Abi Waqqas got himself a paneled door made out of wood and set aside for his headquarters a hut made out of reeds. Then 'Umar ibn al-Khattab, may God be pleased with him, sent Muhammad ibn Maslama al-Ansari to burn the door and the hut. (al-Baladhuri, *Futuh*, 1916, 167)

اتخذ سعد بن أبي وقاص بابًا مبوبًا من خشبٍ وخص على قصره خصًا من قصبٍ. فبعث عمر بن الخطاب رضي الله عنه محمد بن مسلمة لانصار حتى أحرق الباب والخص.

In part, the persistence of such traditions doubtless belongs to the hagiography of the first generation of Muhammad's companions, a group the Islamic tradition represents as at once exemplary and, by contrast with all that came later in Islamicate civilization, exceptional. The topos itself still highlights the extent to which Kufa's earliest organization, in spite of its apparently provi-

sional character, fully represented an ideological and religious orientation
that stood in conflict with older, monumentalizing patterns of city-building.
The provisional character of early Kufan architecture made this a city that
could never become a ruin.[28]

Is it possible to conceive of an "anti-urban" city? If this is what we want to
call Kufa, then we do so from a teleological perspective that looks forward to
a trajectory of development that is by no means implicit in the first ground
plan of this or the other early Islamic settlements outside Arabia. The founders of these settlements, at least as our sources represent them, were animated
by social models distinct from those of the Greeks and the Romans, which
have been the subject of this book so far: they were trying to set up "civilization" without the *civitas*. From this standpoint, monumental cities could only
stand as obstacles to outward flight (*hijra*) or as ruined graves for peoples
whose faith God had found wanting.[29]

The first Islamic historians were themselves writing under teleological
constraints, since Kufa and the other *Amsar* had by the ninth century ossified
into cities that, if they followed a ground plan quite distinct from that of older
Roman and Persian settlements in the region, at least spoke a language of
monumentality that had historical connections with that of classical antiquity. The Kufa of al-Baladhuri's day was, like most ancient cities, an argument
in stone; the plan of its earliest wooden buildings only survived in the oral
traditions on which al-Baladhuri relied to write his history. The story of this
transition from wood to stone is also the story of Islam's second reckoning
with the architecture of the pre-Islamic past.

A few decades after Kufa's founding, the chief men of the city decided to rebuild its mosque in stone. In this rock-poor part of 'Iraq, it was easier to spo-
liate nearby, older cities than to quarry fresh materials. Al-Baladhuri reports
that the ruins near Hira, built in the fifth century CE by kings of the Lakhmids,
an earlier Arab kingdom, were the first to go:

> In Qaratis were located the ruins (*hadam*) of the palaces of Hira, which be-
> longed to the tribe of Mundhir. The Friday Mosque in Kufa was built with some
> pieces of these palaces, and the people of Hira accounted this value against
> their poll tax. (al-Baladhuri, *Futuh*, 1916, 167)

وجد في قراطيس هدم قصور الحيرة التي كانت لآل المنذر . إن المسجد الجامع بالكوفة بني ببعض نقض
تلك القصور وحسبت لأهل الحيرة قيمة ذلك من جزيتهم.

That these stones could be reckoned as part of the *jizya*, the poll tax paid to their overlords by non-Muslim subjects of the caliphate, remind us that the inhabitants of Hira were separated from the Kufans not only by distance but by religion. Hira's Christianity was a trace of earlier Byzantine and Persian interventions in Arabia; from the Islamic perspective, it had been superseded both politically and soteriologically by Muhammad's revelation. The stones that the Kufans strip from the ruins (*hadam*) of Hira thus represent a tax levied on the past by the present. In this episode, spoliation becomes an apt metaphor for the political and ideological triumph of Islam.[30]

Such stories of spoliation gone right are relatively rare, and should be read against the narratives of failed spoliation that are far more prominent in the Islamic historiographical tradition. Often, the ruined monuments of the past turn out to be surprisingly resistant to physical (and even ideological) appropriation by the present. They constitute a legacy from the pre-Islamic past that Islamic rulers, as much as they might deprecate it, are unable to overcome. Even ruined, such monuments cannot be destroyed.

From the outset, the great buildings of Islam invited comparison with those of Rome and Persia. The early Islamic caliphs understood this and meant to win the monumental contest if they were going to participate at all. In 'Iraq, as we have seen, the first Islamic settlers rejected the grounds of the comparison, building on purpose in non-monumental materials. In the Levant, already crowded with settlements, the caliphs built in the heart of the ancient cities new monuments that argued for the superiority of their new religion. The tenth-century historian and geographer al-Muqaddasi records a conversation that lays out the stakes of the contest. His uncle explains the expenditures undertaken by the Caliph al-Walid to build Damascus' Friday Mosque in the following terms:

[al-Walid] saw the Levant was a land of Christians, and he saw that they had churches in it that were ornately decorated and widely renowned ... So he undertook to build a mosque for the Muslims by which they should be more engaged than by these [churches] ... Don't you see that 'Abd al-Malik, when he saw the magnitude of the dome of the Church of the Nativity ... feared it would loom large in the hearts of Muslims, so he erected the Dome of the Rock which you now see? (al-Muqaddasi, *Ahsan at-Taqasim*, 1906)

رأى الشام بلد النصارى ورأى لهم فيها بيعة حسنة قد افتن زخارفها وانتشر ... فاتخذ للمسلمين مسجدا اشغلهم به عنهن ... الا ترى ان عبد الملك لما رأى عظم قبة القمامة...خشى ان تعظم في قلوب المسلمين فنصب على صخرة قبة على ما ترى؟

Monumental urban architecture lacks the utility of fortresses and roads, but what it lacks in power it makes up for in glory. The visual and spatial appeal of the great Christian churches is a temptation to Muslims, a testimony to the enduring power of Christianity despite its supersession; the Great Mosque at Damascus shows that Islam can outdo Christianity in architecture, too. In this way, al-Muqaddasi suggests, it has done more to advance the cause of Islam that any number of roads or fortresses.[31]

The earliest monumental architecture of Islam should thus be read—and, as other scholars have observed, it invites itself to be read—as part of a polemic against rival monotheist traditions, in particular Orthodox Christianity. But the Islamic historiographical tradition also records a parallel polemic, harder to understand in the pragmatic/propagandistic terms invoked by al-Muqaddasi, between the architecture of an Islamic present and the ruins of a more distant, pagan past.

The story of the 'Abbasid Caliph al-Mansur's attempt to tear down the great palace ('Iwan) of the Sassanids at Ctesiphon gives us a sense of what was at stake in this contest of strength and will against a long-dead foe. Al-Tabari records the earliest version of a narrative that will be recycled by later historians up to and including Ibn Khaldun. Tradition remembers al-Mansur, among other things, for building Madinat at-Salam, the new 'Abbasid capital, which would grow into Baghdad. He chose to situate this city not far from Kufa, and (like the early improvers of Kufa) al-Mansur faced a shortage of rock. Al-Tabari represents him as trying to address this crisis by spoliating the 'Iwan of Khusraw, the famous White Palace of Ctesiphon, capital of the now-vanished Sassanid Persian Empire. His vizier, Khalid ibn Barmak—a Persian by ethnicity and founder of a great dynasty of viziers—advises him at the outset against the attempt. The 'Iwan, Khalid claims, whatever its provenance, is now an Islamic monument:

> It is a monument among the monuments of Islam, a glance at which indicates that a people like its builders (aṣhabihi) was not going to be swept away by worldly affairs but only by religion; and along with that, oh Commander of the Faithful, there is a prayer place of 'Ali Abi Talib inside. (al-Tabari, *Ann.* 1990b, 10, 336, modified Kennedy trans.)

لأنه علم من اعلام الاسلام يستدلّ به الناظر اليه على انه لم يكن ليزال مثل اصحابه عنه بأمر الدنيا, وانما هو على امر الدين ومع هذا يا أمير المؤمنين فإن فيه مصلّى علىّ بن ابي طالب صلوات عليه

The story of Ali ibn Abi Talib's having prayed there repeats in a pious register the main thrust of Khalid's argument, which is that, since the conquest of

Persia by Muslim armies, the monuments built by the Persians now function as signs, landmarks, and monuments (*'alam*) in an Islamic landscape.[32]

What they signify turns on an ambiguity in Khalid's language, one over which the caliph is going to stumble. When Khalid says of the 'Iwan that its masters (*ashabihi*) will never withdraw in worldly affairs, the semantics of Arabic *ashab* allow it to designate one of two groups: either the Persians who built the palace, or else the Muslims who now control it. The first of these readings agrees with the Qur'an in making the vanished builders of ruined cities out to be stronger and richer than the men of the present, and this is what al-Mansur takes his vizier to be saying. However, al-Mansur further interprets this claim in terms of an ethnic rivalry, still very much open, between Arabs and Persians within Islam. He dismisses Khalid's advice as stemming from "الميل الى اصحبك العجم" ("your inclination toward your friends, the Persians") and proceeds to order the palace's destruction, which will once again demonstrate Islam's superiority over everything that has gone before it.[33]

This ideologically attractive program, however, turns out to be impossible to execute in practice. A first assay reveals that the cost of tearing stones down from the 'Iwan and transporting them to Baghdad will amount to much more than that of working fresh stones elsewhere, and al-Mansur is prepared to abandon the project. Khalid ibn Barmak, consulted once more, now reveals the pragmatic concerns that had motivated his earlier, pietistically and politically framed advice:

> I gave my opinion before that you shouldn't do it, but, now that you've done it, I'm of the view that you should wreck it (*tahdama*) until you reach its foundations, so that it is not said that you were impotent to ruin it (*hadmihi*). (al-Tabari, *Ann.* 1990b, 10, 336)

قد كنت ارى قبل ان لا تفعل فلمّا اذ فعلت فانّى ارى ان تهدم الآن حتى تلحق بقواعده لئلّا يقال انك قد عجزت عن هدمه

Khalid had counseled his caliph against trying to tear down the 'Iwan, not just because its monumental status could now redound to the advantage of Islam, but because the risk of failure in this destructive project was too great. At all costs, he had wanted to avoid setting up a contest between past and present that would end by showing the present up as weaker than the past. Now that al-Mansur has entered on this project of ruination (*hadm*), though, he must see it through; otherwise people will infer (correctly, in Khalid's view?) that Iran's new Muslim rulers are feebler than the Persian shahs of old.

For reasons that al-Tabari's narrative does not make clear, al-Mansur rejects this advice and calls the ruination to a halt.

Al-Tabari's circumstantial narrative of an act of spoliation that is recounted in more general terms elsewhere is especially interesting to the extent that it lays out, through the two speeches of Khalid ibn Barmak, a "double logic" of architectural conservation. On the one hand—and this is a politic argument, intended, if not to flatter the caliph, then at least not to demean him—Khalid suggests that the 'Iwan of Krusraw should remain untouched because it is a mighty monument to its *ashab*, ambiguously either its "builders" or its "current masters." One should therefore avoid spoliation, because to command the monuments of empires is to command their imperial legacy. But the truth of the matter, as Khalid reveals once al-Mansur has already gotten himself inextricably involved in this doomed project, is that the monuments of the past still pose a challenge to the present. It is better not to take up this challenge than to take it up and be found wanting.[34]

The art historian Oleg Grabar has suggested that something like that attitude may lie behind the bold innovations of Islamicate decoration and architecture in the first few centuries AH. Apart from a few early experiments, Islamic architecture did not imitate older—Greco-Roman or Persian—building types. The 'Iwan, as the basic form of the Sassanian royal palace, marks a limited exception to the rule. In explanation of this phenomenon, Lionel Bier has argued that the caliphs' reliance on Persian-inspired court ceremonial—visible in early Arabic political manuals from the anonymous treatise *'Ahd Ardashir* to the *Kitab al-Taj* of al-Jahiz and beyond—necessitated the borrowing of the palace architecture that supported this ceremonial. In this instance, then, to borrow the function was also to borrow the form.[35]

According to this schema, spoliation is the most important field of interaction between Early Islamic and pre-Islamic architecture: on this point, at least, what gets torn down is more significant than what gets built. In Rome, as we saw, emperor and law regarded all ruins indifferently, as belonging to a "classical" past in which the meanings of individual structures were usually lost. Islamic interest in reading the functional "meaning" of despoiled buildings is an innovation against classical practice: here, for the first time, we find architecture intersecting with a form of historiography.[36]

The frequency of such encounters between Islamic rulers and the monuments of the past—not just in 'Iraq, but also in Egypt and, to an extent that deserves a book of its own, in formerly Roman North Africa—is an index of the extent to which, in the period of its expansion, just as during the early years of Muhammad's prophetic mission, Islam developed across a landscape of ruins. As we have seen, one way that Muslims understood these ruins was as part of a rivalrous monumental competition, one that they could not be assured of winning. If the Qur'anic revelation sealed the superiority of Islamicate society over all previous forms of social organization, there remained, embodied in the 'Iwan and the Pyramids and the Aqueducts of Malga, the disturbing specter of ancient powers that were in excess of anything that the Muslims of the early centuries could conjure up.[37]

The first generation of Muslims avoided living in the old cities of the Middle East, preferring to build cities of its own that could reflect its own needs and ideals. These cities still turned out to be "dependent" on their ancient rivals—not for their form, which was new, but for their material. The practices of spoliation that emerged out of these early encounters were to shape the Islamic imaginary for centuries to come by creating an axis of rivalry with the past that was difficult to escape and along which—unlike in other arenas—the pre-Islamic *jahiliyyah* could turn out to be superior. This was how Islam confronted the ruins of "past" civilizations. But the mode of this rivalry could easily be turned inward to produce a self-confrontation, a kind of architectural civil war. In that case, the Islamicate world began to produce ruins of its own.

In a discussion of Kufa which begins with its construction on the wreckage (*kharab*) of Hira, the tenth-century geographer al-Muqaddasi observes that the city of Kufa itself, in some neighborhoods, has started to fall into ruin (*kharaba*). Al-Muqaddasi was a well-traveled man, not an armchair scholar, and observations like this one are common enough in his chorographic text *Ahsan al-Taqasim* to give us the impression of an Islamicate world that, even at the height of its pre-Crusades prosperity, was also decaying. That impression is not, I think, an incorrect one, but it would be easy to misinterpret. The ruination of certain neighborhoods and cities in the medieval Near East goes alongside the explosive growth of others, while the ideological fractures of Islam's first centuries continue to replace old cities with new ones.[38]

The story of Kufa is emblematic of a process that was taking place—making allowances for various historical conjunctures—all over the Islamic world in the eighth and ninth centuries. Kufa began life as a sort of temporary city or enormous armed camp, but it soon grew by parasitizing the remains—both material and human—of nearby Hira. By the early eighth century, Kufa and Basra were known as al-'Iraqan, the two poles of Islamic 'Iraq. Even at this early date, though, shifts and transformations in the structure of 'Iraq and the

Islamicate world as a whole were under way that would end by depopulating Kufa (and, to a lesser extent, Basra).[39]

In the seventh century, Islam had been divided by a pair of *fitnas* (civil wars), both notionally set off by debates as to the claim of 'Ali ibn Abi Talib and his descendants to rule all Muslims. First, 'Ali himself fought unsuccessfully to defend his caliphate against the allies of his recently assassinated predecessor, 'Uthman; then, a generation later, the Bani 'Umayy were split between supporters of the dynastic claimant 'Abd al-Malik and a collateral relative, Ibn al-Zubayr, who put himself forth as avenging the murders of 'Ali and his sons. In both these conflicts, Kufa supported the losing side. Accordingly, the triumphant 'Umayyads came to regard it as suspect and as a hotbed of Shi'ite sympathies—a view somewhat confirmed by Kufa's importance as a transmission center for both Sunni and Shi'i hadith.[40]

In 702 CE, not long after the end of the second of these *fitnas*, al-Hajjaj— the general who had finally quashed Ibn az-Zubayr's rebellion—came to 'Iraq to confirm 'Umayyad rule there. Rather than setting his seat of power in Kufa or Basra, as might have been expected, he instead built a new settlement that would come to be known as al-Wasit—literally, "the middle." He thereby evaded political constraints that would have been imposed by the mixed sympathies of Kufa or its resentment of the new regime. Al-Hajjaj was remembered as a strict, almost tyrannical governor; not coincidentally, he also left Kufa in a dramatically weakened position within 'Iraq's urban hierarchy. Al-Wasit drew away people, material, and wealth from its northern neighbor. Basra, to the south, was able to weather these trends because of its indispensable role as port city for the entire region, but the intrusion of al-Wasit had almost deprived Kufa of its raison d'être.[41]

Strategic and ideological reconfigurations within the Islamicate world as a whole had thus already worked to Kufa's detriment even before the Third Fitna, which was to entail the further depopulation of the city as one of its long-term results. This conflict pitted the 'Alids and other restive descendants of Muhammad's clan against an 'Umayyad dynasty whose chauvinism and self-interest had earned it many enemies among those who did not directly benefit from its dominance. At stake now was not only leadership of the Islamic community but also the Arabs' so-far unchallenged primacy within it: an ever-increasing number of converts from other ethnicities, Persians most of all, chafed at rules and conventions that made them second-class citizens in this community of faith.[42]

With the victory of the rebellion and its co-option by the house of 'Abbas came a major shift in the center of gravity of the caliphate. The 'Umayyads had ruled from Damascus, a city close to the Arab heartland that also provided a window onto the world of the Mediterranean. The 'Abbasids, by contrast, turned toward Persia, both as a base of support and, as Patricia Crone has skillfully documented, because it had already become a source of new rebellions. They founded a new capital not far from al-Wasit, the Madinat al-Salam that would come, in the span of a few generations, to be called by the Persian name Baghdad.[43]

As we have already seen, this was a city that would mine the great monuments of Ctesiphon, but it would also siphon material, human and otherwise, from nearby Muslim settlements. Al-Wasit and Kufa, being nearest, lost the most; the former dwindled to a mere town, while the latter, a greater city to begin with, was half-ruined when al-Muqaddasi visited in the late tenth century.[44]

A widely circulated hadith that has been shown by G. H. A. Juynboll to be of Kufan origin gives us a sense of how this progression might have been viewed by those on the losing side of it. Probably an eighth-century forgery, it had, by the tenth century acquired an *isnad*, or chain of transmission, that took it all the way back to the companions of the prophet and a place in historiographical texts that, themselves showed no anti-Baghdadi or anti-'Abbasid bias. Here is one of the several versions recorded by al-Khatib in his eleventh-century *History of Baghdad*:

A city will be built between the Tigris and the Euphrates, the fields of Qatrabbul and the river Sara, and the treasures of the *Amsar* and their oppressors (*jababira*), and it shall be swallowed up in the earth faster than an iron tent peg sinks in wet ground. (al-Khatib, Tarikh, 1931, 28)

تبنى مدينة بين دجلة ودجيل وقطر بل والصراة، تجبى اليه خزائن الامصار وجبابرتها، يخسف بها وبمن فيها لهي اسرع ذهبا في الارض من الوتد الحديد في لارض الرخوة.

The first part of text evidently functions as a *prophetia ex eventu*, ascribing to Muhammad foreknowledge of Baghdad's founding and the social consequences of that founding for nearby cities. This formulation is of special interest because it describes Baghdad—evidently the city "built between the Tigris and the Euphrates"—as attracting to itself "the riches of the *amsar*." In this context, *amsar* can only mean Mosul, Basra, and Kufa, the three original Islamic foundations in 'Iraq. Other versions of the hadith extend Baghdad's gravitational field to the entire world, but this one is more straightforwardly local and, not coincidentally, may also be the oldest.[45]

The second part of the text we might still call *prophetia ex eventu*, although in a slightly different sense. There, in all its versions, the hadith predicts that Baghdad is going to suffer the same ruination it has already begun to inflict on its neighbors, sinking into the earth "faster than an iron tent peg." The image evoked here is Qur'anic, though it comes from a context that has nothing to do with ruins: *yakhsafa*, the verb here translated as "will swallow up," occurs in a passage that shows God destroying a particularly proud and wealthy member of Moses' people by opening a sinkhole beneath him.[46]

In this respect and in others (*jabbar*, for instance, is a term almost as freighted with political significance in classical Arabic as *tyrannos* is in classical Greek), the language of the hadith links Baghdad's predicted dominance over the urban hierarchy of its region to illegitimate forms of political domination. The hadith thus reframes a phenomenon I have already highlighted— the tendency of structural transformations in the Islamicate world as a whole to redound on the urban organization of its regions—in pietistic terms. From either point of view, it was a process that worked to resolve social and political tensions by ruining older cities even as it built up new ones.[47]

This was perhaps the most innovative element of the Islamicate urban pattern. The contrast with classical antiquity is not complete: archaic Greek colonization and the establishment of Constantinople as a "Christian Rome" might both be seen as adumbrations of the Islamic practices that I have been discussing. Greco-Roman historians often represented such fissional events as stemming from or as attempts to relieve social tensions that might otherwise have led to open conflict. What was rare in classical antiquity, however, seems to have been the norm in the early centuries of Islam. Until the time of the Mongol invasions, a spate of new city foundations follows every major conflict within the Islamic community: rather than fight to win over the populations of older cities, the winners prefer to build new cities of their own. Accordingly, the domination of metropolis over colony that characterized Greco-Roman ideology now reverses itself: the junior city is in a dominant rather than a subservient position, and it grows directly at the expense of the senior one.[48]

In short, early Islamic patterns of city-building look wildly dynamic against the background of classical models governed in great measure by stasis and hysteresis. While ruins indicated a breakdown in the Roman system, they were a normal part of Early Islamic urbanism. Ruins are what gets left behind when the mobile parts of the city leave an old site for a newer, more promising one.

These transfers of wealth and population operate between neighborhoods in much the same way as between cities. The complete abandonment of old neighborhoods in favor of new, commercially vibrant ones is so common in early Islamic cities—whether conquered or newly built—that, as the comparative urbanist Paul Wheatley has suggested, ruined neighborhoods are a diagnostic feature of early Islamic urbanism. The progress of ruination was especially noticeable in Baghdad, where more than one caliph chose to build a new royal neighborhood rather than live in the palace of his predecessors. Even great monumental structures like the Green Dome, the centerpiece of al-Mansur's original Madinat al-Salam, were abandoned and allowed to crumble within a generation of their construction. In a passage recording the date of the Dome's collapse, al-Khatib remarks that it had been a marvel to see and an *'alam* of the region, a "monument." *'Alam* is also, we should remember, what al-Tabari has Khalid ibn Barmak call the 'Iwan of the Sassanids. Now that the caliphate is building monuments of its own, it can ruin them, too.[49]

Did the sense of rivalry that governed Islamic spoliation of pre-Islamic monuments have a parallel in the way that newer Islamic cities related to older ones? Al-Muqaddasi reports an encounter on the docks in Cairo that seems to speak to that question:

> One day, I was walking along the quay and marveling at the multitude of boats at anchor and sail. A man out of the crowd said to me, "Where are you from?" I said, "from Jerusalem." He said, "A great country. But know, sir—and may God bless you—that the boats on this quay, along with others that have gone a-sailing to towns and countries, if they went to your country, could carry away its people and furniture and stones and wood—so that it would be said, 'there once was a city here.'" (al-Muqaddasi, *Ahsan al-Taqasim*, 1906, 198)

وكنت يوما امشى على الساحل و تعجب من كثرة المراكب الراسية والسائرة فقال لي رجل منهم من اين انت قلت من بيت المقدس قال بلد كبير يعلمك يا سيدي اعزك الله ان على هذا الساحل وما قد اقلع منه الى بلدان والقرى من المراكب ما لو ذهبت الى بلدك لحملت اهلها وآلاتهم وحجارتها وخشبها حتى يقال كان ههنا مدينة.

Jerusalem was a great city but also an old one, and by the tenth century, Cairo had undeniably grown bigger than it and more prosperous. Al-Muqaddasi's interlocutor makes the point by way of a counterfactual: if the Cairene merchants were given permission to do so, they could bring all the people and treasures of Jerusalem home with them. Cairo is at least potentially to Jerusalem what Baghdad was to Kufa and what, before that, Kufa had been to Hira.

With this anecdote, al-Muqaddasi captures the spirit of a rivalry between new cities and old that closely parallels the rivalry between Islamic cities and pre-Islamic monuments. If cities were arguments in stone, one way in which such an argument could be successful was by ruining cities that argued against it. In al-Muqaddasi's day, Cairo and Jerusalem were indeed separated by more than distance. Cairo was the capital of the Fatimids, a Shi'i dynasty that had begun as a heterodox movement within the 'Abbasid Caliphate, while Jerusalem remained within the sphere of proto-Sunni piety. The growth of one city at the expense of the other would have been, in some sense, an argument in support of the politico-religious program for which it stood. In this connection it is worth mentioning that one of al-Muqaddasi's biographers believes him to have converted to Shi'ism while in Cairo.[50]

Medieval Muslims had not only inherited ruins as part of a theological heritage that, beginning with the Qur'an, made them out to be monuments both of vanished civilizations and of God's wrath. Those Muslims that lived in cities, at least—which is most, if not all, of the ones that wrote anything down—also lived among ruins and could even, over a lifetime, see ruins being made. This left considerable traces in the culture at large. Ruins gave Muslim writers across a range of genres a way of thinking the past in the present, of articulating a relationship between these poles that cut across the radical break of Islam.[51]

Ruins thus acquired an allegorical value that transcended historiography and made a serviceable figure in every genre of Islamicate literature. In an early-eleventh-century collection of pious discourses and wisdom sayings assembled by al-Qadi al-Quda'i and attributed to 'Ali ibn Abi Talib—the fourth of the Rashidun caliphs and the first Imam of the Shi'ites—we find the following exhortation against the pleasures and temptations of this world:

> O worshippers of God, know that, as long as you are in this world, you are following the path of those who have passed away, who were greater than us as to buildings and stronger than you as to force and built greater houses than yours, and more long-lasting monuments. Their voices have been extinguished after a long run of power, their bodies rotten, their houses collapsed and their monuments obliterated. They have traded their mighty palaces and thrones and cushioned seats for the stone cairn of the grave, a crushing shelter, which

has revealed the depopulation of their palaces and the crumbling of their buildings to dust. Their dwelling places are near to hand, but the inhabitants are estranged, like people who share a house but are lonely and too busy to show concern for one another. They do not enjoy prosperity nor do they communicate in a neighborly way, even though there is a brotherhood between them on account of the closeness of their neighborhood and the nearness of their dwellings.

اعلموا اعباد الله أنكم وما أنتم من هذه الدنيا على سبيل من قد مضى ممن كان أطول منكم عمارا وأشد منكم بطشا وأعمر ديارا وأبعد آثارا. فأصبحت أصواتهم هامدة خامدة من بعد طول تقلبهم وأجسادهم بالية وديارهم خالية وآثارهم عافية. قد استبدلوا بالقصور المشيدة والسرر والمنارق الممهدة والصخور والأحجار المسندة في القبور اللاطية الملحدة التي قد بين الخراب فناءها والتراب بناءها فمحلها مقترب وساكنها مغترب بين أهل عمارة موحشين وأهل محلة متشاغلين لا يستأنسون بالعمران ولا يتواصلون كتواصل الجيران والإخوان على ما بينهم من قرب الجوار ودنو الدار.

(al-Qadi al-Quda'i, *Dastur*, 66–68)

Like most works attributed to 'Ali in the Islamic Middle Ages, this one is almost certainly pseudepigraphic. We should instead see this homily as roughly contemporary with the anthology in which it appears, and as reflecting a form of piety that could find an audience in that Fatimid Cairo which al-Muqaddasi so admired.[52]

The text brings into play a whole range of themes that we have already encountered in the preceding pages. The notion of Muslims as successors to a long sequence of now-vanished societies is Qur'anic, as is the semiotics of ruin-gazing that follows from it. There is, again, a topos of rivalry between the present and the past—one that, as in al-Tabari's account of the attempted spoliation of the Sassanid 'Iwan, seems to resolve in favor of antiquity. This passage could count as a general theological commentary on ruins in Islam, beginning with an invocation of eons-old dead civilizations and ending, on a more human time scale, in terms (*mahalla, sakin, jiran*) that invoke the urban sociability of a medieval Islamic city. Ruins are diachronic metaphors for the synchronic, everyday experience of urban life.

We know that Cairo, like the other cities I have discussed and by similar means, produced its own ruins. Thanks to the trove of everyday documents contained in the Cairo Genizah, in fact, we have more exact information on this point for Cairo than for elsewhere. In one of his early publications on the documents recovered from the Cairo Genizah, the historian S. D. Goitein expressed amazement at the frequency with which those documents discussed abandoned and ruined buildings—residential structures, in this case, rather than grand public monuments. The archive thus confirms something that al-Quda'i's language would already have led us to expect: for al-Quda'i, as for his contemporary readership, ruins are not only a term of relationship to the distant past but also an element of contemporary experience.[53]

This double approach to ruins is characteristic of medieval Islamic piety, where ruins often appear as figures for the transience of a worldly life that, if from a pietistic point of view it needs to be rejected, still has its attractions. Muslim writers of this period are still following through on the Qur'an's command to travel the earth and see the ruins there. This vision reminds them, and their readers, that a monumentality beyond their power to achieve was also useless to those who, in the past, did achieve it. Not only ascetics found this point of view congenial.[54]

Al-Buhturi's late ninth-century *Siniyya* is the best known of many poems in the *qasida* tradition that are organized around the topos of ruins. Since the poetic conventions of the *qasida* are pre-Islamic in origin and meant to represent (or simulate) the life of tribal herders living in the back country of Arabia, it is at least superficially surprising that this genre should turn out to be so open to urban ruins. On the other hand, one traditional element of the *qasida* form is the poet's evocation of an abandoned campsite and elegiac or apostrophic treatment of the people who had lived there only a short time before. The campsite, like the ruin, is a trace.[55]

Al-Buhturi replaces the formulaic campsite with ruins of Ctesiphon in a way that was to be imitated by later writers. Fleeing from a dangerous situation at the court of the 'Abbasid Caliph al-Muntasir, he arrives at the *abyad al-Mada'in*, the Sassanid 'Iwan that al-Mansur had tried to destroy almost a century earlier. Although the building and its surrounding structures are *dars*—"effaced, obliterated," a word used by earlier *qasida*-writers to describe the abandoned campsite of their beloved—al-Buhturi conjures up a vivid hallucination of Sassanid court life in which he and his son, envisioned as the Sassanid kings Anushirvan and Khusraw Parwiz, also participate.[56]

At this ruined palace, the past comes so close to the present that

It is as though the meeting was two days ago, and the haste of parting was yesterday, and the one who wishes to follow will be eager to encounter them on the fifth day [hence].   (al-Buhturi, *Sin*, 48–49, in Arberry 1965, 72–79)

كأنّ اللقاء اوّل من امس وواشك الفراق اوّل امس

وكأنّ الذي يريد اتّباعاً طامع في لحوقهم صبح خمس

The measurement of space in terms of days of riding time is a convention of early Arabic poetry and of the *qasida* form in particular. Following an old formula, poets introduce that measurement to show how quickly their pursuit—of a beloved, of an enemy—may be brought to a close, provided their patron is willing to help. In al-Buhturi's case, naturally, the project of a pursuit is always going to remain incomplete; for him, days of riding serve to measure not a crossable zone of space but an impassible chasm of time.

The poem's concluding appeal for a patron's generosity is likewise, and self-consciously, destined to fail. While other poets address living patrons either by their own names or under pseudonyms, al-Buhturi devotes this section of his *Siniyya* to the vanished Sassanids themselves. If the kings of Persia have, as al-Buhturi points out, done the Arabs favors in the past, they are certainly no longer in any position to do so; their sponsorship of al-Buhturi's project can only be metaphorical, by way of a cultural heritage that continues to inspire. Al-Buhturi's poetic archaeology is by nature a thankless work.

Most *qasida*s are aspirational poems that aim, both inside and outside the poetic fiction, to improve their authors' lot in life. Al-Buhturi's *Siniyya* departs from this norm, as we have seen: a truly backward-looking poem, it uses ruins to recreate past glories that are beyond recovery in the present. By proceeding this way, al-Buhturi writes the Islamic theology of ruins into his own poetic biography. The dominant tone of the poem, despite its rich evocation of wine-soaked banquets in the palace of Shah Khusraw, is one of hopelessness: al-Buhturi no more hopes to recover his position in the Abbasid court than he really expects to catch the Sassanids after five days' riding.[57]

In its comfort with the pagan past and with pleasures notionally forbidden under Islam, al-Buhturi's *Siniyya* follows an orientation by all appearances utterly distinct from the intensely ascetic pietism of al-Quda'i's homily. Despite the ideological chasm that separates them, they use ruins in remarkably similar ways. Both writers treat them as emblems of the (worldly) superiority of ancient men, a superiority that the moderns can never hope to match or overcome; both also use ruins as an index of the inevitable shipwreck confronting our (worldly) hopes in the present. To be sure, al-Quda'i takes ruins to teach a lesson about the human condition, while al-Buhturi's *qasida* reads ruins with respect to its author (or his poetic persona) alone; but these differences are diacritics in what the late Shahab Ahmed might have termed a shared Islamic discourse. What allows us to identify both al-Buhturi and al-Quda'i as Islamicate authors is not that they say the same things about ruins—for indeed they do not—but that, when they talk about ruins, they talk about the same thing.[58]

This notion of the ruin circulates in other, more vernacular genres, too. Readers of the *Arabian Nights* will recall the City of Brass, an ancient, abandoned place that challenges those who visit it to resist the temptation of returning to the past. It is a monument to the kind of worldly power that brings destruction in its train; as the story illustrates, Muslims do better to develop their own piety than to borrow the wealth and monuments of the past, however seductive these might be. Through the inscriptions that they have left behind, the builders of the City of Brass address its Islamic explorers in terms that recall what both the Qur'an and later *zuhd* literature have to say about ruins. If the material wealth the explorers recover has a certain taint of *jahiliyyah*, the knowledge they harvest only confirms the truth of Islamic revelation.

The trope is a common one in the medieval Islamic storytelling tradition. Less well-known may be the narrative dependence of Islamic esoteric philosophy on the ruin as source, a dependence that accents the threat posed by ruins rather than taking them as occasions for pious reflection. The Pseudo-Aristotelian *Sir al-Asrar*, a hodgepodge of political advice and magic recipes, is only the most famous of many theurgical or astrological manuscripts that begin with an editor's note claiming to have found the original document in a crumbling Greek or Roman temple or church. The tendency of these prefatory notes is to authenticate the texts they accompany as likewise fragments of an insurmountable past—dangerous and seductive, like ruins themselves.[59]

In this literature, the ruin has a tendency to take the form of a no-place: the prototype ruin for Arabic-language narrative fiction from the ninth to the twelfth century is not Ctesiphon, a well-known landmark that anyone can visit, but (once again) Iram dhat al-'Imad, an ancient city of unknown location that was even, as we saw, thought by some philologists not to have been a city at all. Writers in the *qass* tradition of theologically inflected fictional narratives embroidered on a Qur'anic pattern seem to compete to give the most fantastical elaboration on the Qur'an's laconic description of 'Iram. Lost in the sea of sands, accessible only to those chosen by God, by the thirteenth century this city had acquired a crown of mile-high colossi (which were, the storyteller al-Tha'labi suggests, no more than scale representations of its gigantic inhabitants) and a treasury to dwarf that of a Sultan.[60]

These imaginary ruins are of a piece with a generally speculative trend in medieval Islamic popular narratives. What allowed them to join the ranks of the treasure caves, enchanted animals, and magical islands which give so much of that proto-science fiction its subject matter, was that ruins, for an

Islamic audience raised on the Qur'an and living among crumbling buildings both ancient and modern, were part of a familiar space in which to confront the past. The sense of rivalry between past and present that almost always subtends early Islamic discourse on ruins gave this trope both its narrative tension—would living people be able to outwit or triumph over the built legacy of their dead ancestors?—and, since ruins were physical artifacts demanding particularly sublime forms of verbal description, a special aesthetic appeal as well.

Ibn Khaldun understood these speculative ruins as inimical to a historiography that wanted to use ruins as evidence. Near the beginning of his *Muqaddimah*, in a chapter dedicated to showing the virtues of good historical method as well as some of the elementary errors it could help students avoid, Ibn Khaldun takes the *qass* tradition to task for having invented a version of Iram al-ʿImad that defied the conditions of historical possibility—a city-state in the desert that was greater, as to manpower and as to monuments, than the empires of Rome or Persia. Such a great power should surely have left some ruins behind, but nobody can—or has ever been able to—point out where these ruins are. For that reason, Ibn Khaldun ends up agreeing with those of al-Tabari's sources who take Iram dhat al-Imad to have been nothing more than a tribe of tent-dwelling Bedouin.[61]

In the wake of five centuries of antiquarian inquiry, it seems obvious that ruins should matter for how we imagine the past. Ibn Khaldun's Western European contemporaries, however, would likely no more have understood his interest in Iram dhat al-Imad than they would have appreciated Schliemann's reason for trying to dig up Troy. Khaldun and most of the other Islamicate authors whom I have discussed in this chapter seem to me to have in common with modernity a sense of having come late, of arriving after great empires, whose ruins we can still see and touch. For the first Muslims to leave Arabia this was, of course, literally true: they themselves had put to bed the two great powers of their day, Persia and Rome.

I have been arguing that Islam had emerged as a ruin-gazing culture even before this point. The Qur'an, from almost the very beginning, had located itself within a history of ruinations whose traces Muhammad's audience could see themselves if they wanted. This audience may have been predisposed to hostility toward cities; a preference for nomadic lifestyle over traditional urbanism certainly shows through in the cities they built. Given time, though, these cities entered into a rivalry with the past, and then with each other. In

CHAPTER FOUR

Tenochtitlan

Preservationism and Its Failures
in Early Modern Mexico

Renaissance ruins seem like familiar ground: here, at last, casual students and experts alike find a literature that conceptualizes the decayed buildings of the past in a way that looks similar to the knowledge-producing, reconstructive practices of modern scholarship. The writers of this period treat ruin-gazing as archaeology and, not coincidentally, as a historicizing mode of thinking our own relations with the past. They turn ruins into monuments in their own right, deserving conservation and even pilgrimage. This is the moment when antiquarianism takes root in Europe and turns material remnants into a rival of written history. We have inherited from the fourteenth, fifteenth, and sixteenth centuries CE a certain way of behaving around ruins. In this respect, the Renaissance anticipates what comes later and would seem to deserve to be called "Early Modern."[1]

I end my book with a chapter on the Renaissance for two reasons. First, because going further forward would bring us to epochs that think about ruins in ways that, even under the estranging gaze of scholars, turn out to be all too familiar. Second, because I think that Renaissance ruins don't yet seem to us as strange as they should. By way of demonstrating this second point, I focus my attention on the Spanish destruction of Tenochtitlan, an episode of ruin-making that stands at a certain distance from what people usually think of as the cultural centers of that era. If Renaissance Europe learned how to understand ruins at home, in the heartland of Italy, it learned how to make them abroad, in the New World.[2]

Hernán Cortés's destruction of Tenochtitlan—on the wreckage of which Mexico City would be built—was not the first in a series of Spanish encounters with indigenous urban spaces, but it was probably the most significant for the trajectory of Spanish colonialism in the Americas. What I argue is that the outcome of this encounter was the unintended—at least on Cortés's part— result of a certain rigidity in Renaissance patterns of thinking about ruins and conquest. Cortés had imagined these patterns as reflecting a universal lan- guage of architectural destruction and preservation, but in the end they proved to be only particular, unable to accommodate or translate the slight differ- ences that distinguished an indigenous Nahuatl discourse on ruins that was in many respects surprisingly similar to European models.

The aftereffects of the encounter appear to have stimulated a darker, more occlusive Early Modern discourse on ruins, one that aimed to undo, efface, or disavow Cortés's handiwork rather than monumentalizing what traces were left of Mexica urbanism. This firsthand experience of ruination resonated quite differently in Early Modern Europe than did the historically distant de- struction that the monuments of Rome or Greece had undergone. European writers drew freely on the latter as a source of intellectual and political legit- imacy; what happened in Mexico, by contrast, became a challenge to Europe's self-understanding as a "civilization" built on ruins and committed to rescuing ruins from "barbarism."

In 1444, the merchant, traveler, and—as we would now say—amateur archae- ologist Cyriac of Ancona revisited the site of the ancient Greek settlement of Cyzicus. The temple there, as he knew from reading Pliny, had been one of the architectural marvels of the Hellespont, its masonry inlaid at the joints with bits of golden thread. He had also, on an earlier visit, seen the temple in a good state of preservation—minus the gold, of course, but with most of its colonnade still intact. "But how much more wrecked now," he writes: less than a decade later, almost half the surviving colonnade has come down. Cyriac says that the Turks (*barbari* in Cyriac's Latin) are to blame, their spo- liation of the site to provide materials for nearby cities having destroyed much of what time's passage had left standing. If some of the statuary has been pre- served, he thanks Olympian Jove and not the Turks.[3]

This image of the Turks as destroyers of the classical heritage is one that will prove popular in Europe, especially after the Ottoman capture of Con- stantinople in 1453, which European commentators represented as the sack and utter destruction of that second Rome. Writers after Cyriac, from Ogier de Busbecq in the sixteenth century to Volney at the turning of the nineteenth, reproduce Cyriac's image of Turkish spoliation and neglect. This image is at least an exaggeration: the Ottoman sultans had antiquarian interests of their own and were as interested as any European ruler in laying claim to the Greek legacy. Certainly the Ottomans, like the Romans, quarried old structures in order to build new ones. In Istanbul and elsewhere, though, the Ottomans worked to protect and conserve the greatest ancient monuments—the Hagia Sophia, for instance, or the Serpent Column, both still intact today. A glance at the documentation surrounding Cyriac's first visit to Cyzicus reveals, in fact, that the statuary at the site survived for him to see again because the Turkish governor, Canuza Bey, had agreed to preserve it at Cyriac's request.[4]

By the fifteenth century, Italians and Ottomans alike had come to value the architectural legacies of the past, both classical and, in the Ottoman case, Early Islamic. The wanton destruction of these legacies became an accusation that served the rhetorical needs of an intercultural polemic that was to last through Volney's lifetime and beyond. We know this maneuver best from European writers, but the Turks employed it too: one of the *casus belli* they alleged in favor of their invasion of Cyprus was the presence there of ruined mosques from the last time Muslims had ruled the island, many centuries earlier.[5]

The sources of this value, as scholars like Leonard Barkan and Andrew Hui have argued, were multiple. Ruined or partly ruined buildings could provide artistic models for Renaissance craftsmen, who saw themselves as returning to a kind of architecture untainted by the Gothic. As in the landscape backgrounds favored by Raphael, ruins could generate an aesthetic all their own. Renaissance thinkers and artists were also moved by a simple awe at the very old, which, if medieval guidebooks are any indication, they shared with generations of pilgrims to Rome.[6]

Many Renaissance observers, however, also saw ruins as stores of antiquarian knowledge and as means of access to a past that humanists were coming to know better, but still primarily through literature. Livy, Cicero, and others ancient writers were revealing, under humanist interrogation, an image of past Rome's greatness that seemed to dwarf the present. In a letter to Pope Leo X, Baldassare Castiglione and Raphael Santi allege that some of their contemporaries take such written accounts for fables rather than truths. In a complete inversion of the logic of Thucydides' archaeology, ruins now turn out to be the cure for this skepticism:

> Estimating the divinity of those ancient souls on the basis of the remains of the ruins of Rome which can still be seen, I do not think it unreasonable to believe that many things seem impossible to us which were very easy for them.

Considerando delle reliquie che ancor si veggono delle ruine di Roma la divi-
nità di quegli animi antichi, non istimo fuor di ragione il credere che molte cose
a noi paiano impossibili che ad essi erano facilissime. (Cast./Sanz., *Lettera*, sec.2)

In their size and their sheer physicality, ruins stand surety for any story about
ancient Rome, no matter how incredible. As such, they reveal dimensions
to human capacity that have been forgotten in the intervening centuries. By
confirming the truth of certain narrative and descriptive accounts about the
past, ruins open up new possibilities for the present.

That attitude is in stark contrast to a medieval ethical reading of ruins that
saw the decay of magnificent structures as setting limits on what humans
could achieve and—in a topos as widespread in Europe as in the Islamic
World—showing the ephemerality of all worldly things. This critique, popular in Christian and Islamic homiletic traditions alike, persisted into early
modernity as well. Collucio Salutati, for instance—in *De seculo et religione*, a
text that scholars have characterized as atavistic in many respects—asks his
viewers to sit with him on one of the hills outside Florence and examine that
city's rapidly changing skyline. The Palazzo Vecchio (not yet *vecchio*) "already
collapses under its own weight and, worn down by cracks both internal and
external, already seems to tell its own slow distant ruination" (*De sec.* 27.8);
the Duomo (still under construction) "seems likely to end up, at last, in the
ugliness of ruin, so that in not long it will be no less in need of repair than
of being finished" (27.9) Everywhere he looks, Salutati sees virtual ruins as
a futurity threatening to undo the monumental works of this (temporarily)
thriving city-state. If even collectives work under those constraints, what of
any worth can we hope to accomplish as short-lived individuals except the
work of our own salvation?[7]

In my view, the most compelling interpretation of *De seculo* is that it is
essentially a rhetorical exercise, written as a favor for and in encouragement
of a friend of Salutati's who had recently taken monastic vows. *De seculo*
would then be a kind of hybrid document, making old medieval arguments
using the innovative intellectual toolkit of early humanism. Scholars have
already recognized this with regards to the text's Ciceronian rhetoric and,
respecting the passage under discussion, Salutati's apparent re-creation of a
painted landscape in prose. Salutati's visual evocation of ruins is modern; his
application of that technique for destructive rather than reconstructive purposes is a throwback.[8]

The contrast becomes especially clear by comparison with the walking tour of Rome in Petrarch's famous letter to Giovanni Colonna (*Epistolae Famili-ares* 6.2), which belongs to the same discursive universe as Castilglione's much later epistle, even though it predates Salutati's *De saeculo* by several decades. Here Petrarch sees not ruins but restored, completed buildings; what he de-scribes in most detail are narratives, drawn from Roman history and epic, which take place among that scenery. His vision is an inverse of Salutati's: restorative, not destructive. And Petrarch's project, by his own estimation, is not just antiquarian:

> These days, who is more ignorant of Roman affairs than Roman citizens? I say it against my will: nowhere is Rome less known than at Rome. With respect to which fact, I bewail not only ignorance—although what is worse than igno-rance?—but the flight and exile of many virtues. Who can doubt that Rome would straightaway raise itself up from this position if it began to know itself?

> Qui enim hodie magis ignari rerum romanarum sunt, quam romani cives? invitus dico: nusquam minus Roma cognoscitur quam Romae. Qua in re non ignorantiam solam fleo—quanquam quid ignorantia peius est?—sed virtutum fugam exiliumque multarum. Quis enim dubitare potest quin illico surrectura sit, si ceperit se Roma cognoscere? (*Ep.* 6.2.14)

For Petrarch and his interlocutor, archaeology is a means of knowing, not only about the past, but about the self—of reestablishing a broken continuity between the imperial Rome of the historians and Rome as it now exists. Pe-trarch draws attention to this discontinuity by his constant equivocation be-tween two meanings of "Roma"—one pointing toward the present, the other toward the past—even as he works to close the gap between them. His phras-ing in this passage is purposely (and wisely) vague, but what else can be the end of a Roman "uprising" (*surrectura*) on the basis of ancient virtues than some form of imperial restoration?[9]

When Italians write to Italians, as both Petrarch's and Castiglione's exam-ples suggest, ruins take on a certain nationalist dimension. Petrarch imagines ruin-gazing as a restorative for Rome's *virtus*, and all that that entails; for Castiglione and Raphael, Rome is a "nobil patria" (sec. 3): of all Christians, of course, but of Italians in particular. The history of Rome's decay is also the history of that fatherland's subjugation, pillage, and partition by various waves of barbarians. Castiglione portrays Father Time as lacking confidence in his own "devouring file and poisoned bite" and as calling in "profane and crimi-nal barbarians" to help him complete the task of ruining Rome. Driven by an "impious madness," the barbarian invaders are supposed to have destroyed Rome's buildings with fire and sword.[10]

We saw in chapter 2 how misleading this image is, and my argument there was based in documentation that, for the most part, would also have been available to Castiglione. His lack of interest in this material is something he shares with other humanist writers, especially historiographers, who were invested to a surprising extent in building a nativist myth according to which the Roman Empire's fall and Italy's subsequent troubles were, by and large, the result of outside interference. In this narrative, ruins functioned as a double trace—first of the epoch of Rome's former greatness and then, by their very ruination, of what Rome had suffered since then and who was to blame.[11]

Renaissance writers, then, read ruins also as a sign of conquest. As I argue in chapter 2, this is a logic that Roman historiography anticipates with respect to the victims of Rome's imperial expansion. Leonardo Bruni, for instance, seems to be following Orosius when he writes that the cities of Italy were *inanatae*, "emptied out," by the establishment of the Roman Empire. With the collapse of that empire (he goes on to say with a sense of historical irony not yet available to Orosius), some of these cities came back to life. Others, however, were crushed and destroyed by subsequent waves of barbarian invasions in which, again, the Ostrogoths figure prominently. The topography of Italy in his own time encodes all this history: "Finally, whatever Italian cities survived the barbarian flood began to grow, flourish, and raise themselves day by day back to their old status."[12]

Bruni observes that Italy's topology has changed since antiquity, new cities replacing old to create a palimpsest that indexes the passage of centuries. The enumeration of ruined cities alongside their present-day names becomes a commonplace device in Renaissance historiography and chorography for demonstrating how far the present falls short of the past and identifying a scapegoat (usually the Goths or the Turks) for this decay. Cristoforo Buondelmonti and Cyriac of Ancona use it to file briefs against the Ottomans; in addition to Bruni, Flavio Biondo and many others employ it to condemn ultramontane intervention in Italy. By the early sixteenth century, such treatments are enough of a commonplace that Machiavelli can broadly parody them in a comparison of past and present toponyms that blames Christians rather than barbarians for Italy's decline. Not only the cities have changed names, but the people too: instead of Caesar and Pompey (great generals), we now have Peter, John, and Matthew (apostles of a religion of passivity).[13]

Italian humanists use ruins to trace imperial myths that, in turn, help produce national identities. Sometimes, as with Bruni, the identities in question belong to city-states, but ruins—especially the ruins of the Roman Empire— also lend themselves to larger imperial projects. Castiglione and Raphael, as we saw, revive the figure of Rome as *caput mundi*, a note also struck by Biondo in his *Roma Illustrata*. Ruins are monuments that mark out territories as the object of irredentist ambitions—those of an existing empire, as for the Ottomans, or, as for the Italians, an empire yet to be. Even Bruni, the city-state historian par excellence, wrote about ruins in a way that tended to justify the territorial ambitions of Florence with its tiny empire.[14]

These ambitions reflect a political trend in the Early Modern period toward the growth of states, the fusion of territories that had previously only been united by tenuous cultural and linguistic ties into larger blocs that adumbrated the map of modern Europe. Scotland and England came under the control of one king; France swallowed up Burgundy and Brittany; the Ottomans consumed the remains of Byzantium and the Mamluks. The archetypal case of state formation, however—for contemporaries as well as for many modern historians—was Spain's emergence out of a merger of Castile, Aragon, Navarre, and recently reconquered Andalusia. A crown whose power on the European stage had been negligible a generation earlier now threatened to achieve the dream of medieval theorists: universal empire.[15]

From the eleventh until the late fifteenth century, during its conquest of Islamic southern Spain, Castile established traditions of architectural preservation that in some ways anticipated humanist interest in ruins. Many of Spain's medieval monuments are the work of one of the Islamic dynasties that ruled there before 1492, though most bear the traces of later modifications by Christian rulers. The cathedral mosque of Seville, its counterpart in Cordoba, and the Alcázar in Zaragoza are only three of the many Islamic monuments that survived under Spanish stewardship. Ferdinand and Isabella, the first rulers of a united Spain, continued this tradition after their conquest of Granada. If Renaissance thought had mapped the choice between ruining and preserving onto a dialectic between barbarism and civilization, the Spanish were making it clear which side they wanted to be seen to be on.[16]

This was the Europe from which Hernán Cortés departed when, in 1504, he set sail for the New World. The New World was then just Cuba, Hispañola, and other, smaller islands. On Cuba, Cortés enjoyed a rich and easy life as secretary to the governor, his necessities more than provided for by the labor of indigenous slaves. Cortés's ambition ran further than this: when rumors began to circulate, following Grijalva's disastrous expedition, of vast lands to the west, Cortés assembled men and ships and departed with the governor's blessing. This the governor soon revoked, sending a second expedition to bring Cortés to heel. Given Cortés's ruthlessness in fighting off this challenge to his authority, it was easy for the governor of Cuba to depict Cortés as a rebel against the Spanish Crown. The *Cartas de Relación*, letters accounting for his conduct in Mexico, which Cortés dispatched to King Charles I, work hard to counter such depictions, representing their author as a scrupulous and law-abiding agent of Spain.[17]

Cortés needs to justify his every decision, great or small, from the smallest expenditure to the overthrow of kings, as being either in Spain's best interest and according to its laws, or else beyond his control. Cortés thus represents his conquest of Mexico as what we could call a value-maximizing proposition, so long as we understand that the values cherished by Cortés and his readership back home are not our own. Alongside gold and silver, the monetary commodities par excellence, we have to account for the Spanish (and, more broadly, Early Modern European) interest in what theorists from Montesquieu to Agamben, while characterizing it in different ways, agree in calling "glory." Cortés's conquests are supposed to increase not only Spain's wealth, but the power and prestige of its ruler, Charles I, then also Holy Roman Emperor, whose claims to universal monarchy the addition of Mexico did much to make good.[18]

One element of Cortés's depiction of Mexico that, however true it may also be, needs to be understood in this context is his depiction of the Aztecs as a civilized nation (almost) on par with those of Europe. Where earlier writings about the New World (again, Cuba and Hispañola, but also the coast of Yucatan) describe disorganized bands or loosely hierarchical kingdoms, either too peaceable to protect their own self-interest or too savage to be handled with anything but force, Cortés presents the peoples of the Mexican Plateau as a complex, differentiated, and even polite society. That description is not inaccurate, but earlier European writers had not scrupled about accuracy in describing the Carib or Maya as without civilization, and thus as needing the guiding hand of Spanish rule. The project of Cortés's *Cartas* is different: there the Mexica appear as potential subjects for Charles I on a par with the Dutch, the Navarrese, or the Andalusians, another jewel in the Spanish crown. An essential element of this portrayal is that, like those European people, the Mexica live in monumental cities made of stone.[19]

Cortés's first description of Tenochtitlan is a rare turn to lyricism by an author generally more concerned with account books, battle narratives, and apologetics. His depiction of the city's spatial layout is also, and more importantly, a portrait of its citizens, whom he wishes to represent as participating in complex forms of social organization for which the streets of Tenochtitlan provide a complex *bauplan*. Though this layout, as Cortés acknowledges, is in many respects strange, it can be made to "correspond" to the greatest cities of Old Spain in ways that make it legible to a European viewer. Cortés wants his readers to imagine it as a rich addition to King Charles's empire:

> This great city of Temochtitlan is seated on this salt lake, and from the mainland to the main body of the aforementioned city, on whatever side one wants to enter it, is two leagues. It has four entrances, all with pavement made by hand, and as wide as two cavalry lances. The city is as large as Seville and Cordoba.

> Esta gran ciudad de Tentixtitan está fundada en esta laguna salada, y desde la tierra firme hasta el cuerpo de la dicha ciudad, por cualquiera parte que quisieren entrar a ella, hay dos leguas. Tiene cuatro entradas, todas de calzada hecha a mano, tan ancha como dos lanzas jinetas. Es tan grande la ciudad como Sevilla y Córdoba. (Cortés, *Cartas*, 1994, 62)

If the point of the simile is to help European readers imagine a city they've never seen, Cortés's choice of *comparanda* rightly strikes us as bizarre. Given that Tenochtitlan is situated in a *"laguna salada,"* why not compare it to Venice instead? Amerigo Vespucci, after all, had done the same (and with less justification) in naming the newfound coast of Venezuela. Seville and Cordoba, by contrast, are set in a notoriously dry landscape only sparsely watered by the Guadalquivir.[20]

It would be fair to speculate that Cortés has in mind, and wants to remind us of, the place these towns occupy in a uniquely Spanish imaginary as the twin jewels of the Reconquista, two towns of exceptional size and wealth that, once conquered from Islamic rule, helped magnify the glory of the Castilian Crown in the century preceding its unification with that of Aragon. Cortés wants to suggest that Tenochtitlan might do the same for the unified crowns of Spain and the Holy Roman Empire—or has done it already, since by this point in his narrative Cortés has notionally converted the Mexica into Spanish subjects through the magic of the *requerimiento*. It should be noted that the Castilian armies took both Seville and Cordoba by surrender, not by assault; the Spaniards converted their Islamic monuments rather than destroying them.[21]

These cities offer Cortés a set of precedents according to which he can finesse the most sensitive point in his description of Tenochtitlan's urban space, namely, its organization around a monumental center devoted to what Cortés characterizes as idolatry. When he comes to discuss this aspect of the city, Cortés reemphasizes his earlier comparison between it and Seville:

> In this great city there are many mosques or houses of their idols, very beautiful buildings . . . there are at least forty very high and well-built towers, of which the largest has fifty tiers before one comes to the main body of the tower; the chief one is taller than the tower of the cathedral of Seville.

> Hay en esta gran ciudad muchas mezquitas o casas de sus ídolos de muy hermosos edificios . . . Hay bien cuarenta torres muy altas y bien obradas, que la mayor tiene cincuenta escalones para subir al cuerpo de la torre; la más principal es más alta que la torre de la iglesia mayor de Sevilla. (Cortés, *Cartas*, 1994, 64)

It is a well-rehearsed fact by now that Cortés described the grand religious buildings of Mexico as "mosques" (*mezquitas*). Cortés's own choice of words highlights an important aspect of his ethnographic technique in the *Cartas de Relación*. His evocation of a formerly Muslim Andalusian landscape, corresponding to a transfer of architectural vocabulary in detail, positions the Mexica as a people whom Spain can rule over.[22]

This form of *interpretatio* works to domesticate the Mexica in general and, in particular, a set of Mexica social practices organized around the city's temples that, by Cortés's own admission, struck Spanish observers as frightening and deeply strange. That most notorious of Aztec customs, human sacrifice, corresponded to European fantasies of New World savagery in ways that Cortés wanted to suppress and that later figures like Juan Ginés de Sepulveda, writing from a viewpoint yet more hostile to the natives, would accent. Neither the rituals involved in nor the divinities honored by Mexica sacrificial practices were understood by Cortés, who showed little interest in Mexica religion beyond the supposed identification between himself and a returning Quetzalcoatl. To attach all these practices to "*mezquitas o casas de idolos*" was to associate them with Islam, a form of non-Christian religious practice that Spaniards felt they knew well (although many of them, bizarrely, continued to regard it as polytheist until well into the modern period), and thereby to elide the difficulties presented by something truly new.[23]

Cortés's conventional invocation of mute wonder as a bar to description ("*no hay lengua humana*") obscures the descriptive work already done by the mere fact of lexical choice. If "mosque" seems like a poor match, at least according to our modern lights, for the step-pyramid temples of ancient Mexico, we should keep in mind that the comparison invoked an ideational and legal status that was far more important to Cortés's rhetorical project than any question of mere description. His comparison of the tower of Tenochtitlan's *templo mayor* to the grand cathedral of Seville points up the moral. Seville's cathedral was in fact a "converted" mosque—Christianized and transformed as a result of the Reconquista, but not destroyed. According to this model and the legal framework that went with it, the religious architecture of a conquered town became the king's property, not to be damaged and, a fortiori, not to be ruined.[24]

In this approach to describing Tenochtitlan, Cortés proceeded according to a conservationist script that was Spanish in its particulars but reflected general trends in Early Modern European thought. Ruins were made by barbarians; the "civilized" king, representing a society bound by laws, did not need to destroy what he conquered. By preserving it, he enriched and magnified his own kingdom. Architecture could serve—for Spaniard and Frenchman, for Christian and Turk—as a kind of trophy.

Why, then, did Cortés end by leveling to the ground a city that, by all indications, he had wanted to capture intact? Had the Mexica simply rejected the script of a civilized conquest, forcing Cortés to resort to more barbaric means? This was Cortés's view, to judge by a passage in the *Cartas* that seems—although we should always approach appearances in the *Cartas* with skepticism—to capture the moment at which Cortés loses all hope of taking the city without destroying it:

> Seeing that those of the city were rebels and showed such determination to defend themselves or die trying, I drew from this two conclusions: first, that we were going to get back little or none of the wealth that they had taken from us; and second, that they gave cause and forced us to destroy them totally. And from this last I had much anguish and it weighed me down in my soul, and I thought what tack I could take to terrorize them such that they would come to recognize their error and the harm they were going to receive from us. And I did nothing but burn and tear down the towers of their idols and their houses.

> Viendo que éstos de la ciudad estaban rebeldes y mostraban tanta determinación de morir o defenderse, colegí dello dos cosas: la una, que habíamos de haber poca o ninguna de la riqueza que nos habían tomado; y la otra, que daban ocasión y nos forzaban a que totalmente los destruyésemos. Y desta postrera

tenía más sentimiento y me pesaba en el alma, y pensaba qué forma ternía para
los atemorizar de manera que viniesen en conoscimiento de su yerro y del daño
que podían rescebir de nosotros. Y no hacía sino quemalles y derrocalles las
torres de sus ídolos y sus casas. (Cortés, *Cartas*, 1994, 140)

At last, Cortés commits himself to making ruins out of private and public
architecture alike. For him, this is a rough and lamentable means of bringing
the Mexica to confess their *yerro*—their mistake, a misdeed committed more
from ignorance than from malice. The *yerro* of the Mexica is twofold. First,
they have rebelled against a ruler whom they ought to have recognized as their
lawful king—Charles I, thanks to Cortés' earlier *requiremiento*—and, second,
they have shown a willingness to defend themselves to the death rather than
submit. The Mexica have gone astray from two different scripts: that of good
Spanish subjects and that of a defeated people. Cortés decides to ruin Tenochtitlan in order to remind its errant citizens of their proper roles in the ongoing
drama of conquest.

Like so many other moments of decision depicted in the *Cartas*, this passage is a post facto confection, designed to justify its author's course of action
in the eyes of a royal audience. Cortés has destroyed a city that he had earlier
described as one of the wonders of the earth and that should have belonged
to Spain. For both these losses, Cortés blames the inhabitants of Tenochtitlan
rather than himself. Indeed, he represents himself as having done everything
in his power to save the city, which he decides to destroy only when all other
avenues of correcting the *yerro* of the Mexica have been exhausted.[25]

This representation will ring false to even a moderately attentive reader of
the *Cartas de Relación*: already at what he depicts as his moment of decision,
Cortés has been burning down houses on the outskirts of Tenochtitlan for
weeks. There is no moment of crisis for Cortés, only an ever-intensifying cycle
of frustration and violence. But Cortés's imaginary self-justification speaks to
a real failure. It would have been better, not only for King Charles, but also for
Cortés and his men, if Tenochtitlan could have been taken without a fight, by
surrender, as Seville, Cordoba, and Granada had been taken. To have ruined
it instead is a mistake that neither Cortés nor anyone else will ever be able to
reverse. Often compared by his contemporaries to Alexander the Great, Cortés
has in this respect followed the Macedonian's trajectory all too exactly.[26]

I will not follow Cortés in blaming this failure on the obstinacy or, by impli-
cation, the stupidity of his Mexica victims. There is a school of modern his-

toriography that takes precisely this tack: writers like Anthony Pagden and Tsvetan Todorov have built causal explanations for Cortés's unlikely Mexican triumph that credit the conquistador with a kind of "semiotic mastery," a capacity for appropriating and manipulating alien ways of speaking or thinking, which is supposed to have given him an important advantage over his more naive Mexica victims. I want to argue instead that the ruination of Tenochtitlan shows the extent to which Cortés, despite his access to native translators and informants, was actually unable to enter into the discourse of Mexica culture on many particular points. Ruins were one such point: the sixteenth-century Mexica used and made ruins in ways that were critically different from those being worked out in contemporary Europe. Cortés was only dimly aware of the source of these difficulties, to which he tended to respond with violence.[27]

The argument I make throughout this book—that past societies had ways, distinct from our own, of understanding and making ruins—was anticipated in the 1970s and '80s by Mesoamericanists who stood face to face with a difficult architectural problem. Excavations underneath Mexico City had brought to light some of the urban fabric plowed under by the Spanish four centuries earlier. Stylistic and forensic examination revealed that some of the art recovered in these digs had not been produced in Tenochtitlan, but instead had been brought there from Tula or Teotihuacan. Since these cities stood dozens of miles distant from the Aztec capital, their relics were unlikely to have made it to Tenochtitlan by accident. It became clear to investigators that the Mexica had assigned special ritual and cultural value to these ancient objects. They had apparently discovered antiquarianism at about the same time as the Italian humanists.[28]

The materials transported to Tenochtitlan from Tula and Teotihuacan ranged from small jade pieces to larger monumental statuary and even stone blocks. Clearly, we can speak here not only of antiquarianism but also of spoliation. The rise and collapse of a Toltec proto-state centered around Teotihuacan in the eleventh and twelfth centuries had left that site and its satellite cities richly decorated but almost uninhabited. They were ready-made sources for the trappings of antiquity with which the Mexica, latecomers to the central valley, wanted to decorate their capital. For the Mexica, these sites had an originary value as sources of culture and especially of high culture. The Nahuatl name shared by Teotihuacan and Tula, *Tollan*, shares a root with another word, *toltecayotl*, which has been variously translated into English as "art," "artisanal skill," and even (as Miguel León-Portilla suggests) something like "civilization."[29]

Toltecayotl made ritual artifacts from a range of materials already (according to the Nahuatl lexicon) infused with divinity—gold, turquoise, jet, and, remarkably to a modern observer, small items that would now be characterized as archaeological finds. These "smoking stones" (to borrow terminology from the Mexica who helped compose the *Florentine Codex*, a massive compendium of indigenous knowledge produced in the mid-sixteenth century) could be identified, if one went in search of them near dawn, by the fog or mist that rose above their burial places. If one dug, one often found a fully formed or crafted artifact. That such stones were, to all appearances, regularly found not just near Tula and Teotihuacan but also some distance away from them involves no contradiction. For the Mexica, the Teotihuacan ruins and these smaller treasures were all alike material traces of the gods' historical presence on earth.[30]

Writings by Mexica authors in the generation after the Spanish conquest give us to understand that Tollan also had a historical value for the rulers and inhabitants of Tenochtitlan. There was the birthplace of the fifth sun, the one under which we now live, sustained by human sacrifice and destined to be ended by a world-destroying earthquake. Quetzalcoatl, the exiled god, had ruled there; the Mexica had passed through it in the course of their southward migration from Aztlan to the Central Plateau. For these reasons and others, genealogical connection with the Tolteca was an important source of legitimacy to the Mexica city-states that fought for supremacy in the region. Tenochtitlan (or at least its nobility) acquired such a connection through Acamapichtli, the first to rule the city after its eponymous founder, and a descendant (via Culhuacan) of the Toltec ruling line.[31]

At the height of their power, the Aztecs incorporated Tula—some thirty miles distant from Tenochtitlan—as an important ritual site within their growing empire. The rituals practiced there responded to and supported the myth-historical identity that the Mexica had constructed for this ruined city. At Tula, the temples not only honored important divinities like Quetzalcoatl but had actually been inhabited by them; these were the originals to which other temples metonymically referred, and the gods in some sense came closer.[32]

This helps explain an incident, reported by more than one Mexica chronicler, that took place shortly after the arrival of the Spaniards in Mexico. Cortés has presented Moteuczoma's representatives with Spanish bread, which is as strange to them as corn and potatoes were to contemporary Europeans.

Moteuczoma, the first to try it, calls it "*dulce y sabroso.*" Nevertheless, he has a scruple: "Esta comida, no es del infierno?" Such extra-worldly food, he concludes, should by rights belong to the gods. They burn a portion for Huitzilopochtli in what the chronicler Tezozomoc calls their "*gran cu del diablo,*" probably the structure now known as the Templo Mayor in Mexico City. Then, they send the remainder to Tula for Quetzalcoatl to taste. The priests there burn it and sacrifice quail over it, then offer up at the Temple of Quetzalcoatl. Much seems to hang on the outcome of this offering. Will the god accept it or not? When the messengers return home unscathed, Moteuczoma responds with relief:

> It's true that I took it for certain that those gods would have eaten you, but since it wasn't like that, they did not eat our foods either, they will have forgotten them, since it has been more than three hundred years since Quetzalcoatl went to heaven and hell. (Tezozomoc, *Cron.*, 401–402)

> Verdad que tenia por cierto que estos dioses os habían comido, pero pues no fue así, tampoco comieron de nuestras comidas, habranlas olvidado, que a más de trecientos años se fue Quetzalcoatl al cielo y al infierno.

Since Quetzalcoatl hasn't accepted the human offerings sent by Moteuczoma, he won't accept the offering of strange food either. It is true, as they say, that Quetzalcoatl has not ruled at Tula for three hundred years: the closeness of the gods has been withdrawn, an omen that later chroniclers like Tezozomoc will incorporate into teleological narratives that make the Spanish conquest seem inevitable. Moteuczoma's ruin-gazing has a something about it that resembles the melancholy attributed by Walter Benjamin to his baroque tragic heroes, who likewise come to conclude that there's nothing numinous about crumbling temples: a ruin is just a ruin.[33]

Tezozomoc's version of the story highlights a contradiction between the continued ritual significance of the ruined temple at Tula and an important element of Mexica military practice. For the Aztecs, there was more than one kind of war: some wars were for captives to satisfy the ever-intensifying sacrificial requirements of Tenochtitlan's ritual cycle, and some wars were for conquest. In the latter case, an army that had driven its opponents from the field would invade their city, take captives, and—most importantly—set fire to the city's main temple. This stylized act of ruination was what marked conquest as conquest—so much so that, in Aztec pictography, the glyph for "conquered town" was a temple with flames bursting out of it.[34]

Some postconquest sources associate the burning of captured temples with the defeat of the gods who had made their homes there and who would now be supplanted by Mexica deities. This claim might well be suspected of being a kind of *interpretatio Romana* that attempts to explain Mexica ritual practice on the basis of theological conceptions derived from the writings of those paradigmatic idolaters, the ancient Greeks and Romans. One would not need to look very far in Vergil, Livy, or Augustine for evidence that the gods were thought of as abandoning a city either in anticipation of or just after its capture by an enemy army. That said, some gods—in the form of sculpted objects or of priests or laymen who wore their costumes—certainly did "inhabit" the Templo Mayor of Tenochtitlan at some points on the ritual calendar. It seems likely that Aztec temple-burning worked to suppress this kind of activity in subject cities, and thus to undermine the social cohesion of subject peoples. A temple was many things to a community in the Valle de Mexico—landmark, *umbilicus mundi*, social center—but it was at least also a place where the gods put in their annual appearances. The postconquest Nahuatl word for them, *teocalli*, or "god's house," suggests as much.[35]

There is a striking dissonance between the Mexica use of ruination to drive away local gods and the simultaneous belief, with respect to Tula and Teotihuacan, that ruins could by their antiquity and historical meaning themselves become the gods' preferred dwelling places. Structurally, this dissonance bears comparison with one of the paradoxes that animated ancient Roman thought about ruins. Troy had to be ruined to liberate Aeneas's *pietas* for attachment to Italy, but then, as Horace and Lucan point out in their different ways, its ruins still exercised a certain claim on Roman loyalties. As we saw, this paradox came to a head when Rome's own ruination was in question. When they were surrounded by the Spaniards and their allies, all routes of escape and even supply of fresh water cut off, how did the residents of Tenochtitlan imagine that city's ruination then?[36]

These were conditions that Cortés had deliberately created, not primarily for strategic reasons but in order to send a message. He wanted to make the Mexica understand that they had been defeated, that they could no longer hope for a military victory: their only chance at survival was to surrender themselves and their city. To Cortés's endless frustration, the defenders of Tenochtitlan refused to receive this message. The reason may have been, as Inga Clendinnen argues, that the "script" for conquest among the Mexica had no place for sieges. I have already outlined this script, which began with a pitched battle in the field and ended with the destruction of a conquered city's temple. If Cortés had followed it—if he had attempted to impress upon the Aztecs that they had been conquered using signs they might have understood—he would have been compelled to start, rather than finish, by making ruins in a city that he wanted to save.[37]

Both Cortés, in the *Cartas*, and the soldier Bernal Díaz del Castillo, in his *Historia Verdadera*, record versions of a minor incident that reveals something of the mindset of the Aztecs in the last days of Tenochtitlan. In combat, at close quarters, the city's defenders are haranguing Cortés's native allies ("*nuestros amigos*," a phrase that would curdle with irony in the years to come):

> Those of the city, in order to give themselves courage when they saw such slaughter, told our allies that they [the allies] were doing nothing but burning and destroying what they themselves would have to come and rebuild, since if they [the Mexica] were the winners they [the allies] already knew that this had to happen; and if not, then they would have to do it for us. And it pleased God that they were right on this last point, except that they [the Mexica] were the ones who rebuilt it.

> Los de la ciudad, como veían tanto estrago, por esforzarse decían a nuestros amigos que no hiciesen sino quemar y destruir, que ellos se las harían tornar a hacer de nuevo, porque si ellos eran vencedores ya ellos sabían que había de ser ansí; y si no, que las habian de hacer para nosotros. Y desto postrero plugo a Dios que salieron verdaderos, aunque ellos son los que las tornan a hacer.
> (Cortés 1994, 155–156)

The attackers, these anonymous speakers say, are doing nothing but "*quemar y destruir*." They have shirked the real work of conquest, which should begin with man-to-man battles. Instead, they are destroying Tenochtitlan's housing stock. But far from terrorizing the Aztecs, as Cortés had hoped, the sight of their homes on fire hardly even upsets them, because they know that the very peoples who are working to destroy Tenochtitlan will have to come back to rebuild it after the fighting is over.[38]

In case of an Aztec victory, the subjects of their empire will be enslaved again and made to repair what they have wrecked. If the Spaniards win, though, the city will still need to be rebuilt. To rebuild it, the Spaniards will make slaves of their native allies just as surely as the Aztecs would have done. In either case—whether the Aztec Empire survives or not—Tenochtitlan will rise again. Barbara Mundy has recently shown how true this prediction turned out to be by demonstrating that important components of Tenochtitlan's spatial ordering persisted in the layout of Mexico City.[39]

Cortés claims that the Aztecs made their prediction *"por ezforzarse,"* to give themselves courage in the face of a Spanish campaign of terror. Probably this is wishful thinking on Cortés's part: he projects onto Tenochtitlan's defenders the emotions he had intended his ruination of the city to inspire. It's hard to see how the speech Cortés quotes could have counted as encouragement or bravura, especially since it fully acknowledges the possibility or even the likelihood that the Spanish will win. What the Mexica are expressing is rather a faith in the permanence of Tenochtitlan, an unwillingness to believe that a city so great could be permanently ruined. This faith, as Cortés himself concedes, is not misplaced.[40]

As Rome was for the Romans, so was Tenochtitlan for the Aztecs: a place, or at least an idea, that could not die. If it were ruined, it would have to be rebuilt. Could it have been conquered, intact, as Cortés had wanted to do? Perhaps, but certainly not by the means he employed. Always confident in his mastery of native languages and cultural practices, Cortés could not adopt—perhaps did not even suspect the existence of—a native discourse on cities and ruins that, for all its uncanny likeness to the European one, was not identical with it.

The destruction of Tenochtitlan was a firsthand experience with ruin-making that fit uncomfortably into the cognitive models offered by the culture of the European Renaissance, which equated ruin-making with barbarism. Whatever cultural advance the humanists might have believed themselves to have won over the "Goths" of a previous age, the Spanish in Mexico had proved themselves no less barbaric than these in their destruction of an architectural legacy that the earliest Spanish observers had placed on a par with that of the greatest cities in Spain. These events were a harbinger of darker things to come, and they provoked a literary response far different from the pose of antiquarian engagement taken by poets and historians face-to-face with the ruins of Rome.

If Cortés was the first to express regret at what he had done, he was far from the last. The theme runs like a red thread through the many histories of the conquest written in Spanish over the century to come. Faced with the choice of whether to excuse or to lament the destruction of Tenochtitlan, many authors did both: even for them, with national pride at stake, the destruction of such an ancient and magnificent city could not simply redound to Spain's credit. To see the same narrative repeated in Peru a decade later only reemphasized the tragedy of this reckless sacrifice, as the colonial administrator and historian Oviedo puts it, of whole populations at the altar of gold.[41]

For Oviedo, at the beginning of the "Spanish Century," the colonial game was still worth the candle. Those writing at the end of it knew for sure what Oviedo and his contemporaries had only begun to suspect: that the riches of the New World would end up impoverishing the nations that extracted them. Silver and gold mined from America had gone out of Spanish coffers as quickly as it had gone in, enriching Spain's trade partners but leaving Spain itself bankrupt, laboring under massive inflation. The sacrifice of whole nations on the idol gold had not even been successful: there was no gold left, but the peoples of the New World had still been destroyed. This, I think, is the historical perspective that lies behind Luis de Góngora's *Soledad Primera*, the greatest and most difficult literary artifact of the Spanish baroque.

The *Soledad Primera* has not been much studied in a colonial context. That it offers a commentary on the Spanish imperial project is, however, obvious from the outset, even if that commentary is not always easy to interpret. The opening lines of the poem,

> It was the flowering season of the year, in which the disguised thief of Europa
> (a half-moon the arms of his forehead, the sun all the illumination of his hair)

> Era del año la estación florida
> en que el mentido robador de Europa
> (media luna las armas de su frente,
> y el Sol todos los rayos de su pelo)   Góngora, *SP*, 1–4

are an obvious calque on the opening stanza of Camões's *Lusíadas*, the epic of Vasco de Gama's "conquest" of the Indies for Portugal. To be sure, Góngora is engaged in a poetic rivalry with the earlier author, substituting a perfectly crafted epyllion for Camões's baggy epic, but awareness of *aemulatio* gets us only so far in reading the allusion. If Camões's lines inaugurate Portuguese imperialism in the Indies, Góngora's reuse of them invites us to consider his own poem as marking the beginning of Spanish imperialism in those other Indies, the New World. Like all good allusions, however, this one reproduces its source text with a difference.[42]

In the *Lusíadas*, da Gama's ship of empire sails more or less smoothly; the storms it encounters only force it into strange ports in ways that advance the narrative of conquest. The *Soledad Primera*, by contrast, presents us with a ship that has already come to grief. Its lone survivor, clinging to a plank, is cast ashore in an unknown country. Scholars have tended to locate that country somewhere along the shores of the Mediterranean, but, given that the bulk of sixteenth-century Spanish shipwreck literature—a surprisingly fertile genre—is set in the New World, this narrative framing points us toward an American setting. Much the same thing could be said of the Soledad that Leo Marx said with considerable good sense of Shakespeare's *Tempest*: of course it is not set literally in the Americas; it might be set anywhere. But it is nonetheless clearly about an idea of a New World.[43]

To the extent that we can read it as a history of Spanish colonialism in parallel with Camões's triumphalist epic, I take the *Soledad Primera* to be offering something of a guided tour, post facto, of Spain's misdeeds and mistakes while simultaneously, through the bucolic trope of a castaway touring the unspoiled countryside, offering a counterfactual version of contact in which the "marvelous possessions" of Spain's New World colonies could have been kept marvelous by being left a little less possessed. It is in the context of this double project that we should read the poem's protagonist's short but rich encounter with a ruin.[44]

The shipwrecked sailor and his local guide are walking along a river. Just at the point where a mountain torrent meets the stream, "losing its pride and hiding its memory," the guide points out an almost indiscernible set of architectural remains:

> "These, which the trees now hardly permit to be towers," said the goatherd, with extreme displays of grief, "the nighttime stars were once the lanterns of their crenellations, when that which you see is rusted was clean steel."

> "Aquéllas que los árboles apenas
> dejan ser torres hoy," dijo el cabrero
> con muestras de dolor extraordinarias,
> "las estrellas nocturnas luminarias
>   eran de sus almenas,
> cuando el que ves sayal fue limpio acero."   Góngora, *SP*, 212–217

With "*muestras de dolor*," which recall both Cortés's feigned and Moteuczoma's real melancholy, the goatherd rebuilds in words a set of structures that we are unsure, on reflection, if he has ever seen standing. Their ruins, the work of human artifice, are indiscernible because they have come to be on a level with the nature that surrounds them. The goatherd goes on to develop this theme:

They lay flat now, and pious ivies dress their stripped stones, so that time understands how to give green flatteries to ruins and slaughters.

Yacen ahora, y sus desnudas piedras
   visten piadosas yedras,
   que a rüinas y a estragos
sabe el tiempo hacer verdes halagos.   Góngora, *SP*, 212–221

Even the fallen stones, which would form at least a minimal trace of the ruined structure, have begun to be reclaimed by *"piadosas yedras."* These ruins are fast approaching a kind of oblivion that Góngora seemingly also wants us to understand as a relief from the burden of history. The crumbling structures described by the goatherd encode not only their own destruction (*ruina*) but also the massacres (*estragos*) that accompanied this destruction and which the ruins memorialize. For this history, the encroaching ivy substitutes *"verdes halagos"*—green flattery. To reassimilate the ruined monument to nature is to forget—perhaps without any great psychological forcing—the crime that ruined it.[45]

Góngora, in his America of the mind, is employing a strategy that colonial Spanish observers also used, in Mexico, to suppress the ruins of buildings in whose destruction (and the massacres that had gone with that) they were indirectly implicated. When, for instance, Francisco Cervantes de Salazar, Spanish-born humanist and first rector of Mexico's first university, comes to discuss the Aztec temples "where countless men perished," he calls them not temples but hills—"*cierros*," although he then adds that they were made by hand. The figure is perhaps informed by the writer's knowledge that in a different cultural context the Maya of the Yucatan region really did assimilate their temples to mountains, but the point of the comparison is certainly not anthropological. What Cervantes de Salazar wants to do is efface the ruins of these temples and, in so doing, to obviate the question of who ruined them.[46]

Neither Góngora nor Cervantes de Salazar writes as a historian. We could draw a generic division between their literary "redescriptions" of ruined Mexica temples and the more directly documentary—we might even say "honest"—reports about these temples given by Spanish and especially by indigenous historiographers, who never sought to minimize Cortés's role in their destruction. If we did draw such a line, however, it would have to terminate by the middle of the eighteenth century. This was the moment when "history" proper, at least as a European project, began to efface the monuments of the Aztecs quite as zealously as any poet of the previous two centuries had done.

Cornelius de Pauw was, if not the first, at least the most influential advocate of the thesis that the Americans (preconquest, at least) had never built anything of note. This meant dismissing Cortés's (and others') firsthand reports about preconquest Tenochtitlan as exaggerations and outright lies. For instance, De Pauw demoted the "*prétendu château*" of the Aztec kings (as it appears in the *Cartas de Relación*) to a mere "*grange*," suggesting that Cortés the salesman had exaggerated the grandeur of this palace in order to impress his European sponsors. In defense of that reinterpretation, De Pauw offers a kind of *reductio ad absurdum*:

> So Hernán Cortés, not finding any suitable habitation in the whole capital of the state he had just conquered, caused to be built there, in haste, the manse which is there still; which should disabuse us about the exaggerated and extravagant representation one gives of that American city.

> ... aussi Fernan Cortés, ne decouvrant aucune habitation propre dans toute la capital de l'Etat qu'il venoit de conquerir, y fit-il construire, a la hâte, l'hôtel qui y subsiste éncore; ce qui doit nous désabuser sur la peinture outré et extravagante qu'on fait de cette ville Americaine. (de Pauw, *Recherches*, 1772, 256)

The representation of Tenochtitlan contained in Cortés's *Cartas de Relación* is not, for de Pauw, a report, but rather a "*peinture*." So false is this painting that, on de Pauw's construction, Cortés himself clumsily contradicts it by building a mansion of his own rather than moving into Moteuczoma's. A less polemical reader of the *Cartas* and Díaz del Castillo's *Historia Verdadera* would have realized that the reason Cortés did not occupy Moteuczoma's palace was that he had destroyed it himself.[47]

De Pauw was, however, polemical in the extreme. His 1771 *Recherches philosophiques sur les Américains* extracts the quintessence of 250 years of hostile reports about the Americas in order to frame that hostility as a thesis: every animal in America—including man—is weaker, smaller, damper, less perfect than its European counterpart. This is why, for him, there can be no civilization in the New World before its first contact with Europe. De Pauw is quite happy to employ a Spanish apologetic topos—the naturalizing or pastoralizing of Mexican ruins—in the service of a rhetorical project that is intended, among other things, to minimize the accomplishment of Spaniards in conquering the New World.[48]

The Abbé Raynal's *Histoire philosophique des deux Indes*, published a few years later, integrated this hostility into a historiographical scheme of truly grand explanatory scope and of such great attraction to Europeans that there are some who still defend it today. Raynal was an early exponent of a form of conjectural history that saw man's past as consisting of several universal and well-defined stages, and would remain influential throughout the long eighteenth century. On that model, all societies progressed up the same ladder, from nomadism to industrial civilization, acquiring at each stage a new suite of technologies. City-building, for Raynal as for many of his followers, went alongside agriculture, metal-working, and written language. Since the Aztecs (according to Raynal) lacked all three of these, they could not have had monumental cities either.[49]

Raynal acknowledges that there are ruins in Mexico, but he denies that these ruins imply that the Mexica had cities. His opponents see these ruins and reconstruct them, in their imagination, on the plan of those buildings "so pridefully described" by Cortés and the other conquistadors. Raynal, on the other hand, sees no reason to think that the greatest public and private buildings of Mexico looked any different before Cortés than after. They were then, as they are now, only "shapeless piles of stones stacked one upon the other." For Raynal, these ruins are not a trace of the past but its true image.[50]

The chasm that separates this way of looking at ruins from Petrarch's is almost too broad to be crossed. Where Petrarch uses ruins to revive the Roman past and bring it to bear on the present, Raynal denies the existence of any substantial difference between past and present: there's nothing to revive or reconstruct. For Petrarch ruins demand imaginative labor. Raynal is concerned to block any such labor and, as much as possible, to make ruins illegible. This is characteristic of Raynal's "enlightened" intellectual practice and his commitment to a stadial historiography for which the fact of Aztec civilization is inconvenient, but it also fits into a longer history of European denialism about New World ruins. Cortés's ruination of Tenochtitlan was no more compatible with Renaissance sensibilities than Tenochtitlan's very existence was with Raynal's, a few centuries later.

Ruins were a way for Renaissance writers to thematize their relationship with a past to which their mastery of letters gave them a certain privileged access. Across centuries, humanists could use ruins as a means of identifying themselves with civilized Rome as against a barbaric interregnum. Renaissance rulers used ruins similarly. Ruins mediated a possessive relationship between the present and the past; they territorialized claims of legitimacy stemming from dynastic inheritance or *translatio imperii*. Poets and princes alike dramatized their commitment to what ruins stood for by protecting them from further spoliation of the sort that they had suffered in an antecedent "dark age."

Tenochtitlan's destruction shows how this rubric could also turn ruins into a national embarrassment, if you made them yourself. The work that went into naturalizing American ruins over the next several centuries was a way of not thinking about them and especially of not thinking through what they implied about the people who had made them. As the passages I've cited from de Pauw and Raynal suggest, this intellectual practice worked to the detriment of the Mexica. The deletion of their former urban civilization refigured them as "savages," rather than the civilized near-peers Cortés describes in his *Cartas*. Well into the nineteenth century, however, the Nahuatl-speaking inhabitants of the Valle de Mexico were still each year performing plays, in a liturgical context, that reenacted and dramatized (under an allegory of the siege of Jerusalem) the destruction of Tenochtitlan. They, unlike their conquerors, were keeping the memory of ruination alive.[51]

It is an intriguing coincidence that Machiavelli's *Prince* should have appeared in print for the first time in 1532, the same year in which Francisco Pizarro was applying the most brutal of Machiavellian tactics to destroy the Inca Empire and bring an end to anything that Europeans would have recognized as civilization in the Americas. The synchrony is especially significant, given all that I've argued so far, because to my knowledge Machiavelli is the first Renaissance writer who positively recommends making ruins. In book 5 of *The Prince*, he draws quite different lessons from Roman history than his antecedents had done:

> The Romans, to hold Capua, Carthage, and Numantia, destroyed them, and they did not lose them. They wanted to hold Greece almost as the Spartans had held it, making it free, and leaving it its own laws, and this did not turn out for them, such that they were constrained to destroy many cities of that province in order to hold it, since in truth there is no sure way of possessing it other than ruination. And who becomes master of a city accustomed to live free, and does not destroy it, only waits for it to destroy him.

> I Romani per tenere Capua, Cartagine, e Numanzia, le disfecero, e non le perderono. Vollero tenere la Grecia quasi come la tennero gli Spartani, facendola libera, e lasciandole le leggi, e non successe loro; in modo che furono costretti disfare di molte città di quella provincia per tenerla, perché in verità non ci è modo sicuro a possederle, altro che la rovina. E chi diviene padrone di una città

consueta a vivere libera, e non la disfaccia, aspetti di essere disfatto da quella.
(Machiavelli, *Prin.* 5.6)

The conqueror of a free city, says Machiavelli, is positively constrained by self-interest to destroy it. This is verified by Roman experience in Greece and elsewhere, but more basically by a maxim of an almost Kafkaesque perversity: you can't lose a city that you've already destroyed yourself. This maxim, a striking inversion of Croesus's advice to Cyrus not to destroy Sardis, seems to end with the prince ruling over a kingdom of ruins. I think that Machiavelli purposely leaves as an open question how one can *tenere* something that is already *disfatto*.[52]

These lines could be taken as the charter for a change in European ways of warfare that was ongoing at the time of *The Prince*'s publication. Increasingly, sovereigns and generals saw ruin-making as a tactic, and not only for barbarians—although the soldiers who sacked Rome in 1527 were certainly so characterized by writers loyal to Italy and the Pope. Rome, as usual, survived mostly intact. The Wars of Religion were to inflict worse destruction on the cities and towns of Germany and France. In Europe, as in the Americas, advances in gunpowder and cannon technology made ruination faster and less laborious than it had ever been before.[53]

Perhaps, then—as readers have conventionally done—we should take this chapter of *The Prince* with reference to a European context only. On the other hand, as Machiavelli does not say but surely expects us to know, the Romans resettled Carthage, Capua, and Corinth with colonists after they had destroyed them.

Machiavelli thus offers a caustic commentary on Rome's self-conception as a homeland for the entire world. For Rome, too, attracting the loyalty of imperial subjects means destroying rivals. Histories of the Spanish Empire in Mexico have tended to see Cortés and other imperial agents as instrumentalizing that lesson. Chronology suggests, however—and I hope the foregoing pages have shown—that Cortés rediscovers it by accident. For him, as also perhaps for the Romans, ruination is a *pis aller*, a lazy man's way of cutting the Gordian knot posed by a population that does not want to be governed.

Epilogue

The Spanish destruction of Tenochtitlan (and the accompanying massacre of the city's inhabitants) has provided a paradigm for the modern making of ruins. Cortés in 1521 showed how to instrumentalize ruins at the intersection of warfare and the economy—a way to control territory and organize labor that has served elites well in the centuries since. In this sense, Mexico is everywhere now.[1]

Total war is a modern concept with plenty of historical antecedents. Still, the example of Tenochtitlan—with its straightforward emphasis on architectural destruction as a concomitant of slaughter—seems to have something special in common with the annihilation of Dresden, Hiroshima, and Sarajevo, among others. In each case, the destruction of a city is supposed to be an irrefutable argument for military defeat. In each case, the didactic value of ruination trumps concerns about architectural destruction and civilian casualties.[2]

Total war is only a special case of modern ruin-making. Less spectacular but more pervasive is the operation of the so-called spatial fix (of capital or of empire or of both). As the geographer and historian David Harvey describes it, the spatial fix is a two-stroke engine: first, addressing a crisis of overaccumulation by converting excess capital into built infrastructure, it then devalues that infrastructure to the point at which its abandonment appears justified. In recent decades, the globalization of the labor market has staged particularly dramatic instances of this second, devaluing movement in the cities of America's rust belt. On a smaller scale, the transformation of the technological habitus of shopping has led to the nationwide abandonment of shopping malls, which lie empty while nature reclaims them.[3]

Empire practices a spatial fix of its own, pursuing less direct but more pervasive forms of governance over subject peoples. When economic and cultural hegemony replaces direct political rule, the result is what the critic Ann Stoler calls "imperial debris": the architecture of imperial domination remains, even after the governors have gone back to the metropolis. More insidiously, too, imperial hegemons have benefitted by forcing their colonies to absorb imperialism's most damaging consequences. In this respect, the irradiated shacks on Bikini Atoll and the abandoned British prisons in Tasmania are ruins that bear comparison.[4]

Mexico again sets a precedent. Recall the debate between the Aztecs and their former subjects, now Cortés's allies, about who was going to rebuild Tenochtitlan once the Spanish had finished destroying it. In Cortés's account, that discussion ends with an ominous editorial note to the effect that the Aztecs were right to predict that someone was going to have to rebuild the city, but wrong about who that would be: not the Tarascans or the Tlatelolcans, but the Aztecs themselves. Cortés need not make explicit that they will build it for the Spaniards and not for themselves. This is understood: controlling territory also means controlling labor.

Whether we want to call this a precapitalist spatial fix or an adumbration of capitalist spatial fixes to come, we can still appreciate the exemplary function of this task in establishing Spanish dominance over the people and space of what would eventually be called Mexico. The conquistadors force their victims to build a new city as a way of demonstrating conquest but also of making conquest real; this work confirms, even as it enacts, Mexica servitude. If a task of this magnitude had not been to hand, Cortés would have had to invent one. His destruction of Tenochtitlan was thus a happy accident for the territorialization of the Spanish imperium.[5]

In many respects, we are still living out the script for ruin-making established by Cortés. Whether in Baghdad or in Detroit, empire and capital still use ruination to communicate their power to people who might otherwise want to contest it. In this sense, too, Mexico is everywhere. Why, then, does it remain invisible to us? How do we avoid thinking of ourselves—*qua*, and to the extent that we are, citizens of a nation state or beneficiaries of global capitalism—as making ruins?

The modern, archaeological suite of techniques for investigating ruins makes this task harder, not easier. One argument that emerges from the previous four chapters is that the sense of historical *distance* from ruins tends to increase as history unfolds. For the Greeks and Romans, ruins were practically contemporary, a potentiality latent in every urban development with which those responsible for making political decisions needed to reckon. In chapter 3, I suggest that early Islam—like Theoderic's Rome, a "late antique" civilization—had already assumed a postclassical orientation toward a corpus of ruins that stood on the other side of a chasm separating Islam from *jahiliyya*. By reinscribing contemporary ruins as belonging to the distant past, this postclassicism gave people a way of understanding ruin-production in medieval Islamic "modernity" as well.

The antiquarians of the European Renaissance pushed ruins still further into the past. For them, ruins (by the fourteenth century) not only came to signify an epochal break with the classical past; they were also (and at the same moment) becoming objects of "scientific" reconstruction, and, as such, also a means of producing knowledge about the past. This particular embedding in a machinery of knowledge production—an embedding that future generations of scholars were going to build upon rather than question—made ruins almost by definition archaeological and historically distant. So construed, the "present ruin" becomes a contradiction in terms.[6]

I am telescoping a long and complex transformation. Whatever the "pastness" of ruins after the fourteenth century, a writer like Volney could still, in 1791, muster them for a critique of contemporary social ills. "Every day," he writes, "I found along my route abandoned fields, deserted villages, cities in ruins. Often I came across ancient monuments, the wreckage of temples, palaces and fortifications; columns, aqueducts, tombs: and these sights turned my mind to reflecting on times past, and raised deep and melancholy thoughts in my heart." The ruins he is describing are in Syria, but they condemn an ancien régime that his native France shares with the Ottoman Empire. The particular monumental features that Volney enumerates—temples, palaces, aqueducts—tell us that his ruins date from Roman antiquity, but they still have a lesson to teach the revolutionary present. The Roman imperial trajectory that produced these ruins is one from which Europe still can, and should, turn aside.[7]

Even this tenuous point of contact between past and present, however, was to be largely severed by developments in classical scholarship over the next century. As the cultural historian Martin Thom has argued, the new classicism of the 1840s and after was a reactionary formation that wanted to neutralize the specter of the ancient republicanism that had motivated would-be reformers and revolutionaries since Rousseau. Numa Denis Foustel de Coulanges's *The Ancient City* is exemplary of the new trend: in it, Coulanges aims to show that ancient and modern cities differ radically in their function and structure in a way that discredits republican fantasies of restoring Roman or Athenian liberty to nineteenth-century France. To the extent that this trend has continued since then, ruins have been effectively neutralized in modern political discourse. They tell us about what other societies were like, but say nothing about how our own society might be.[8]

This is of course not to say that modernity has found no novel uses for ruins. Freud's famous description, in *Civilization and Its Discontents*, of the unconscious as a mental Rome, where selves and memories pile up and interrupt one another like buildings and eras, assumes an indexical relation between ruins and pastness. The adjustment with which Freud concludes the analogy—that in the unconscious, unlike in Rome, all the buildings coexist at once, entire and not ruined—is nothing if not an imagined realization of the antiquarian's dream, the ruin as evidentiary occasion for a total reconstruction.[9]

Near the end of his life, Freud returned to this imaginary figure in an essay written to accompany *Gradiva*, Wilhelm Jensen's fin-de-siècle novella of the archaeological imagination. The narrator of that text is a university antiquarian so committed to the project of reconstructing Rome that he can only experience his erotic fixation on the girl next door—who happens by chance to be traveling in Italy at the same time that he is—as the reanimation of an ancient statue, the *gradiva* (forward-walker) of the book's title. Freud's analytical contribution is to unpack the depth of this neurosis, which transfigured not only the narrator's experience of "love" but indeed his whole sexual identity and relationship to the world of reproduction. *Gradiva* is not only a name for a statue-type; it is also an obvious anagram of *gravida*, "pregnant."[10]

I bring all this up by way of suggesting that our modern way of thinking about ruins may *itself* be the kind of neurotic substitution/suppression that Freud used ruins to describe. We can think of ruins as icons of pastness in a way that stops us from seeing them as part of the present or as an omen of the future. Ruins have become a tourist experience that gains meaning via knowledge about historical context: the modern ruin-gazer wants to move smoothly from what ruins are to what they were. As Stoler puts it in summarizing the commonplace view of them, ruins "provide a quintessential image of what has vanished from the past and has long decayed." The physicality of ruins helps us forget how much of this image is a projection enabled by a histori-cizing apparatus inextricably connected to (if at a degree or two of remove from) scholarly archaeological research.[11]

The extent of that remove could be measured by a persistent tendency in popular culture—fiction and nonfiction alike—to associate ruins with catas-trophe. While academic scholarship is increasingly focused on the centuries-long processes that produce ruins, popularizing accounts still follow an older paradigm, according to which barbarians ruined Rome, climate change de-stroyed the cities of the Maya, and the eruption of Thera annihilated Cretan civilization—to cite three examples among many. For most people, what sep-arates present from past is still a catastrophic, punctual event and not a slow, long-term process.

These cultural patterns have had a decisive influence on the ways that we imagine (or fail to imagine) our own world falling into ruin. From *Planet of the Apes* to *Caesar's Column*, science fiction has made ruins into an objective correlative for the kind of catastrophe that turns our world upside down. In these works and many others, ruins are a starting point for a history of the future. What most past societies addressed within the bounds of historiogra-phy, we mainly express in a genre that almost definitionally traffics in the fictive and nonhistorical. We have no problem envisioning our cities in ruins; we have much more trouble confronting the fact that we may be ruining them ourselves, right now.[12]

Seen in this light, the Nazi architect Albert Speer's project for building a Berlin that would make a magnificent ruin becomes a parable. Speer designed the urban fabric of Nazi Berlin with an eye toward what his constructions would look like at the end of a thousand-year Reich. He was looking toward far-off future catastrophes at a time when attention to processes ongoing in the present would have been more instructive. In the 1930s, at the height of his professional activity, he could not have imagined that his monuments would lie in ruins a decade later, destroyed by allied bombs in a war that Germany itself had set off.[13]

Mexico is everywhere. We ignore this at our peril, because the effort it takes to suppress this knowledge sets bounds on our cultural imagination that, at the present moment, we can ill afford. In *The Great Derangement*, a collection of essays on the literature of global warming, Amitav Ghosh sug-gests that certain formal characteristics of bourgeois fiction and bourgeois ideology make these forms unsuited for thinking global transformation in an age when, nonetheless, we are obviously undergoing such a transformation in the form of climate change. Social uniformitarianism is the background assumption of a genre in which individual characters move against a stable background; instability at the level of "setting" is an identifying characteristic of obsolete genres (social realism) or marginal ones (science fiction).[14]

To this catalog of causes I would add our antiquarian and archaeological way of thinking with ruins. A ruin-producing catastrophe is always going to stand at some point in the distant future, because we lack the cultural equipment to think coherently about ruin-making as something that's going on in the present. Ned Beauman's 2013 novel, *The Teleportation Accident*, ends with a vision of the ruins of Los Angeles drowned by sea-level rise; it thus marks something of an exception to Ghosh's claim that serious fiction doesn't engage with climate change. But this novel is also an exception that proves the rule, since its time-travel ending caps a narrative set mostly in the 1940s and '50s. At the novel's conclusion, its antagonist gets teleported into the future, to the other side of a ruin-making catastrophe that, in his "native" historical period, is not yet imaginable.[15]

We have been taught to think of ruins as historical artifacts, relegated to the past by a catastrophic event. Instead, we should see them as processes taking place in a long present. In the preceding chapters, I have tried to sketch a new historiography of ruins that would proceed along just these lines. Ruination is a tactic in a social conflict that has been ongoing since the first cities were settled and that continues in the present. What capitalism has done to rust-belt cities like Buffalo, New Haven, and Detroit is a special case of an older phenomenon. Elites make ruins for their own convenience, in order to exploit their subalterns more effectively: a spatial fix, not just for capital, but for power in general.

Rome provides an obvious example. The parties who brought about Rome's ruination did not, for the most part, live in the city themselves. Some of them were busy fortifying villas in the countryside nearby; others had their dwellings as far away as Ravenna, Toulon, or Constantinople. The debate over Rome's future was one in which Rome's actual residents were largely without a voice. Even those prelates who had an interest in boosting the authority of the city's archbishop (and thus also, one might think, in preserving the city's special status) also had an interest in seeing parts of Rome crumble: the city whose preeminence they wanted to assert was on the opposite bank of the Tiber from the one that Theoderic wanted to preserve.

Powerful groups with otherwise conflicting interests could at least agree that Rome should be allowed to fall apart. As for the Ostrogoths, their opposition to this consensus made it easier for the Byzantines to defeat them militarily by co-opting local elites in a ruin-making project. Meanwhile, the people whose lives depended on Rome's built infrastructure had to make do with less—or leave town, which they did in droves, abandoning the civic past for a feudal future. No doubt many of them would have preferred to continue enjoying the privileges, economic and cultural, that Rome conferred even upon its poorest residents, but this choice was not theirs to make.

This self-determination was likewise denied to the citizens of Kufa, who had to watch Baghdad being built next door whether they liked it or not. They could condemn the new city (as in the hadith tradition, discussed in chapter 3), but they couldn't stop it from draining Kufa of wealth and resources. In the medieval Islamic world, too, the people who founded new cities to supplant old ones were, again, the rich and the powerful. Although a substantial class of scholars and merchants could move between Muslim cities without too much discomfort, there must have been multitudes left behind.

That ruination serves elite interests is the corollary to a principle that I state in my first chapter: territorial states make ruins. On the one hand, only a territorial state can muster the resources of several cities to prevent the habitation of one urban site long enough for it to fall to ruin. On the other hand, territorial states are also the only entities able to support urban populations on the scale of Rome or Baghdad. In both these ways, ruins are aftereffects of a statist model for extending and exerting power that began with the agricultural revolution and, as James Scott points out, has gone from anomaly to planetary norm over the past two thousand years.[16]

Summing up the current state of the art in physical anthropology, Scott locates the origin of urban settlements in a "caging effect": given the detrimental health effects of city living at the turn of the Neolithic, Earth's first urbanites must have been compelled by some factor beyond their control (warfare, agriculture, and religious ideology are the usual suspects) to swap hunter-gatherer or nomadic lifestyles for settlement in a city, a difficult tradeoff that involved giving up flexibility, good health, and a life of ease. Historians have begun to recognize that force and enslavement must have played important roles in recruiting workers to make this unequal exchange.

While early cities may thus have started out as foci for the subjugation of caged populations, one frequent outcome of urbanization was to give the people who had been thus caged a sense of their own collective power, which led to the development of governing institutions with a markedly popular character. Territorial states that developed on the basis of such cities came to see them as barriers to the exercise of more autocratic forms of state power on the part of governing or other elites. There were many ways for elites to work around or through these barriers; the most direct methods, as we have seen, resulted in the production of ruins.[17]

If Mexico is everywhere now, this should come as a corrective to our delusional faith that Mexico is always somewhere or some-when else. In fact—and this goes for ruin-making, too—we're right in the thick of it. Timothy Morton has described the agricultural revolution as a seven-millennia-long disaster: what looks like a process on the timescale of a human life looks like a catastrophe in geological time. Ruination is part of this process-catastrophe. We therefore cannot see ruins clearly without considering the deep historical structures that create them. One aim of my book has been to expose these structures. Our archaeological/antiquarian sense of ruins as belonging exclusively to the past is likewise a set of intellectual blinders that blocks us from seeing how ruins might also be emerging in the present. Another aim of my book has been to show how contingent the modern perspective is, and how little it corresponds to anything real about ruins. I have shown that earlier observers saw things differently; I want to conclude by inviting you to consider whether they might not have seen things more clearly, too.[18]

Prologue

1. Woodward 2003, 10ff. Acknowledgment of Thucydides as precedent, 202.
2. Schnapp 1997, 39–45.
3. Trigger 2006, 40–79.
4. Nationalist archaeologies: Trigger 2006, 20–25. Sahlins on the central importance of myths for self-understanding: Sahlins and Graeber 2017, 220.
5. For this framing of the "social construction" question, see Hacking 2000, 1–34. The Marx quotation comes from the opening page of "The Eighteenth Brumaire of Louis Bonaparte."
6. See esp. Harriet Flower's and Karl Hölkeskamp's contributions to Galinsky's *Memoria Romana*. For a discussion and comparison of that perspective with the one that I'll be adopting, see Ricoeur 2004, 216–232.

Chapter 1 · Athens: Democracy, Oligarchy, and Ruins in Classical Greece

1. For this reading of the revolt narrative, see Lang 1968, 31–32.
2. Initial exchange of harms between Europe and Asia: *Hist.* 1.1–5.
3. On revenge as a structuring element in the last half of the Herodotean narrative, see de Jong 2013, 274–277. Xerxes' revenge for Sardis: 6.96.7, 6.103.13, inter alia. On the personal character of apotisis, see, e.g., the dream oracle given to Hipparchus at *Hist.* 5.56.1:

τλῆθι λέων ἄτλητα παθὼν τετληότι θυμῷ:
οὐδεὶς ἀνθρώπων ἀδικῶν τίσιν οὐκ ἀποτίσει

And compare Immerwahr 1956, 249–252. For a more extensive treatment of Herodotus's "metaphysics" of tisis, see Lateiner 1980.

4. Relevant "paired" usages of ἱρὰ: 6.9.18, 6.13.12, 6.25.6, 6.96.7, 8.33.1, 8.109.16. Many nonpaired occurrences of the term may be most intelligibly interpreted in this light, among which are 6.103.13, 7.8.31, and 8.140.8. In Athens, which is the city about whose built infrastructure we know the most, it would be difficult to name a "public" building from the classical period that was not also ἱερόν in the sense of being dedicated to a god. The Acropolis, of course, but also the theater of Dionysus, the law courts on the Areopagus and elsewhere, and the Prytaneion were all divine property. Even the agora, where the boule assembled, was dotted with temples and other infrastructure devoted to the worship of the gods (Papazarkadas 2011, 17–91). This is not to say that any of these buildings played a primarily religious part in civic life, but only to point out that dedication to a divinity was a prevalent idiom for establishing the "public" (as opposed to private) character of buildings. And not only of

buildings: one is reminded in this connection of the sacred olive trees, known to us from a speech of Lysias, which could not be rooted up even though they were often on private property (*Lysias* 7.1–3). Nothing leads us to think that these trees had any kind of ritual use; to designate them as ἱερόν simply meant to remove them from the realm of private ownership. This reading would seem to follow from Polignac's thesis as to the ritual origins of the *polis* (Polignac 1995, 1–13) and Seaford's arguments regarding the early history of "public property" in Greece (Seaford 2004, 96–110).

  5. Altars to Zeus and Athena: Mikalson 1987, 83.

  6. On the narrative function of Xerxes' revenge drive, see Baragwanath 2008, 245–247.

  7. A Persian base on the Areopagus: οἱ δὲ Πέρσαι ἱζόμενοι ἐπὶ τὸν καταντίον τῆς ἀκροπόλιος ὄχθον, τὸν Ἀθηναῖοι καλέουσι Ἀρήιον πάγον, ἐπολιόρκεον τρόπον τοιόνδε: ὅκως στυππεῖον περὶ τοὺς ὀιστοὺς περιθέντες ἅψειαν, ἐτόξευον ἐς τὸ φράγμα (*Hist.* 8.52.1). For the Areopagus's "conservative valence" at the time of the Persian Sack, see *Ath. Pol.* 23.1–3, although it bears noting that things might have changed by Herodotus's time: Hall 1990, 326. The exiles: *Hist.* 8.54. A belated and dramatic apology on the Great King's part? If so, he makes a notably inappropriate casting decision.

  8. For a different standpoint on the "correctness" of Themistocles' interpretation, see Robertson 1987. However, a positivist approach is probably inappropriate for reading Greek oracles, especially ones embedded in the narrative of Herodotus; Barker (2006, 14–23) highlights the extent to which these interpretive debates are staged by Herodotus as indices of "Greekness" in general and of democratic socialization in particular.

  9. For this narrative, see *Hist.* 4.150–161 with Dougherty 1998. The island Plataea: *Hist.* 8.151.2–3.

  10. For a summary of the ancient evidence on this point, see Momigliano 1944. *Ath. Pol.* 27.1–5 is explicit in connecting the full development of Athenian democracy to thalassocracy. Herodotus's views on this form of power are not as jaundiced as Thucydides' will turn out to be (Kopp 2016, pp. 141–144), but even the latter author grants the distinctively democratic character of Athens' maritime empire: Thuc. *Hist.* 8.67.

  11. This was essentially the practice of Athens with regard to Melos (Thuc. *Hist.* 5.117) and Aegina (2.27): both cities were emptied of inhabitants, then resettled by an Athenian kleroukhy. This was effective only as long as Athens maintained its mastery of the sea; toward the end of the war, both sites were reoccupied by their initial inhabitants (or, in the case of Melos, what was left of them); Aegina was eventually used by the Lacedaemonians as a base from which to try to blockade Athens itself. On the Greek system of "partial conquests" and "partial sovereignties," see Vlassopoulos 2007, 192–196.

  12. *LSJ* s.vv. Writing about Pausanias, Jacob Isager has already drawn attention to the difficulties surrounding the translation of this word: Isager 2009, 208–210.

  13. In Thucydides, cf. 6.76.2 and 8.24.3. Isocrates (20.9.6 and 4.37.4, inter alia), Demosthenes (18.183.5 and 19.39.7, inter alia) and of course Herodotus (1.76.8 and 1.155.11, inter alia) are three other prose authors who use *anastatos* in this transferred sense, as referring not to populations that have been removed but to the city or region from which those populations have been removed. Like Thucydides, Herodotus sometimes uses the word in its direct sense as well (e.g., 1.97.4).

  14. In some limited sense, the *polis* can be said to have begun as a kind of fortification at an extremely early date (Hansen 2006b, 41–43; cf. Weber 2013 [1924], 163–166). On Weber's account, the *polis* starts off in a position to dominate its *chora*; Hansen, on the other hand, emphasizes that *poleis* usually formed in mainland Greece through a combination and amalgamation of already existing authority centers scattered across the hinterland (Hansen 2000, 51–54). In either case, at least for all historical formations that were not colonies, the *polis* always has these two sides: a political center and an agrarian hinterland, between which

citizens move in a way that justifies considering these cities under the heading of what Weber calls an *Ackerbürgerstadt* (Vlassopoulos 2007, 124–127). Central places as necessary gathering points for hinterland inhabitants: Horden and Purcell 2000, 108–115.

For a discussion of the economic functions of the classical *polis* vis-à-vis its hinterland and its population, see Salmon 1999, 147–167. See also Ober 2010, 15ff. Hansen, following Horden and Purcell's revisionist stance toward the population dynamics of ancient cities, suggests that an extremely populous central polis is actually a prerequisite for increasing population density in the *chora*, as more efficient systems of redistribution and increased local demand permit the super-exploitation of rural areas by surplus population (Hansen 2006b, 65ff.). So the polis could persist without the *chora*—perhaps, as Athens did, by developing a *"chora* abroad" in the Black Sea—but the *chora*, at least at population levels in the range that Hansen suggests, could not have done without the polis. Cf. Thucydides' claim (*Hist.* 1.10) that the Spartans still live in widely distributed villages, τῷ παλαιῷ τῆς Ἑλλάδος τρόπῳ (in the ancient fashion of Hellas).

15. Megara Hyblaea: Herod. *Hist.* 7.156, with Thuc. *Hist.* 6.49 and Hansen 2006b, 43. Rhodes: Strabo *Geog.* 14.2.7–9, with Hansen 2003, 84b.

16. On Sparta's position within its hinterland, see J. Hall 2000, 75–80. On the variegated history of Messene, see Luraghi 2008, passim, but esp. 124–132.

17. For violence and paranoia in Spartiate-Helot relations, see Cartledge 2013,151–153. Cartledge 1985, 41ff., situates this response with respect to the helots of Messene in particular. Cartledge concludes (46) by postulating that a latent *polis*-identity was the deciding factor in the Messenians' eventually successful revolt from Spartan domination.

18. On this "colonization" and its place in Herodotus, see Hartog 1988, 115–118. For an attempt to reconstruct the events in question, see Cook 1937 and compare with the archaeologically informed revisions of Sartre 2009, 35–44. Compare the derivation of *ereipion* to that of Latin *ruina* or Arabic *hadam*.

19. Mirroring effect: Hartog 1988, 331ff.; cf. Redfield 1985.

20. On the Scythians' great *nomos*, see Hartog 1988, 34–60, and Payen 1997, passim. For this reading of the *Histories*, see, e.g., Said 2002 and Immerwahr 1956, 249. The cyclical "rise and fall" of cities has seemed to many readers to be a kind of tragic dimension of the text, if not indeed an absolute Herodotean "historical law."

21. For the parallel between Scythian mobility and the Athenian naval strategy, see Hartog 1988, 50.

22. Isoc. *Arch.* 78.

23. Deliberation and the *eph' hemin*: Arist. *EN* 1112a–1113a. Athenians were not impassive in the face of "natural disasters," but their responses were most strongly articulated at an individual level: the Great Plague, e.g., leaves a mark in the archaeological record as occasioning ritual dedications (Thompson 1981, 347–348). Thucydides (2.47.4) confirms this orientation with respect to the "natural" catastrophe about which written evidence is most forthcoming. He records that an indirect form of public deliberation took place with respect to an oracle (2.54); following the argument of Eidinow (2007), I take this deliberation to have been "about" the assignment of blame for the plague rather than the organization of a collective response.

24. Finley 1973, 15, for the conventional date, 454, of the transfer of the treasury, and 25 for an estimate of the cost of erecting the Parthenon. For a diachronic study of public building in Athens that suggests how extraordinary, at least on a quantitative level, the Periclean building program really was, see Salmon 1999, 196. For a possible testimonium of the ancient debate, see Plut. *Per.* 12.1–2.

25. For a synoptic treatment of Thucydides' interest in what we would now call archaeology, see Cook 1955, 266–270. Cook's attempt to reconstruct the face of Mycenae as Thucydides would have seen it forces us to ask why the historian should have been so disappointed with

the size and scale of a city that, if it was not exactly thriving, could still boast a few impressive architectural monuments.

26. For a treatment of the *opsis/dunamis* divide in Thucydides that pays close attention to its archaeological dimension, see Hedrick 1995, 69–73, and cf. Ober 1993, 93, and for the salience of this distinction to Thucydides' narrative technique, see Greenwood 2006, 38ff. On the problem of *dunamis*, compare, for instance, the distinction between territory and military power posed by Pericles at 1.143. Compare 1.144, 2.43 and 4.126, inter alia. 2.41.4 may be taken as complicating this point, especially since the passage is in obvious dialogue with Thucydides' own conjectures at 1.10: μετὰ μεγάλων δὲ σημείων καὶ οὐ δή τοι ἀμάρτυρόν γε τὴν δύναμιν παρασχόμενοι τοῖς τε νῦν καὶ τοῖς ἔπειτα θαυμασθησόμεθα, καὶ οὐδὲν προσδεόμενοι οὔτε Ὁμήρου ἐπαινέτου οὔτε ὅστις ἔπεσι μὲν τὸ αὐτίκα τέρψει, τῶν δ᾽ ἔργων τὴν ὑπόνοιαν ἡ ἀλήθεια βλάψει, ἀλλὰ πᾶσαν μὲν θάλασσαν καὶ γῆν ἐσβατὸν τῇ ἡμετέρᾳ τόλμῃ καταναγκάσαντες γενέσθαι, πανταχοῦ δὲ μνημεῖα κακῶν τε κἀγαθῶν ἀίδια ξυγκατοικίσαντες (With great signs and not indeed leaving our power unevidenced, by those now living and those to come hereafter we shall be marveled at, and we shall need no Homer to praise us or any such who pleases with words for the present, but the truth wounds the pride of the deeds he described; but rather by our daring we have made all the land and sea passable for us, and we have set up monuments everywhere of good and evil). But, strikingly, and despite a metaphorical vocabulary that seems to gesture toward actual buildings and monuments (μνημεῖα, ξυγκατοικίσαντες), Pericles seems to be referring here to Athens' legacy in a historical record: he is speaking of its accomplishments, its conquests, and the extent of its empire, rather than of its built infrastructure. Pericles would seem to be ratifying his author's own elevation of the historian over both the poet and the ruin. Pericles' reference to Athens' abandonment: Thuc. *Hist.* 1.144: "Let wailing be made, not for land and buildings, but for men; for men acquire these, not these men." On Thucydides' "public bias," see Crane 1996, 25. For Pericles' hostility to the luxury practices of great houses, see Plut. *Vit. Per.* 16.5. Compare Ober 2010, 273–274, with Pericles' program of public employment as described at Plut. *Vit. Per.* 12.3–5. On Pericles' anti-oligarchic partisanship, and the fiscal appropriations that stemmed from it, see Plut. *Vit. Per.* 11

27. For Thucydides' "tragic history," see originally Cornford 1907, 239–243.

28. Thucydides 1953, 260 ff. See also Rabel 1984; Foster 2010, 34–36; Ober 1993, 93–94.

29. Hornblower 1987, 96; and see 97ff. for further discussion. On this query, see Marshall Sahlins's elaboration in the introduction to his *Apologies to Thucydides*: "The problem is not simply Thucydides' taken-for-granted attitude toward the culture whose history he was writing; it is rather his presumption that the culture didn't matter" (Sahlins 2004, 2–3). For an alternative interpretation, see Luraghi 2000.

30. For a fairly standard narrative of the history of tragedy at Athens, see Cartledge 2002, 22–24. For discussion of the invasion trope in tragedy, see Griffin 1998, 51. Griffin introduces the trope in the context of a larger argument, that tragedy seems to give no bright-line advice or ideology for the management of an empire such as the Athenians had or were acquiring when the plays he discusses were produced—a claim that, in turn, is supposed to militate against larger claims, like those made in Goldhill 1987, 58–76, about the civic and collective functions of the genre. But the plays under discussion, as I hope to show, do indeed speak to and through anxieties of the polis as a whole; the absence in a play of a legible and positive ideological program cannot be taken to mean, as Griffin takes it, that a play does not engage with civic ideologies. Points of contact between Thucydides and tragedy have long been observed. Cornford notes that, while he often borrows what we might call, following Hayden White, a tragic emplotment, Thucydides stays well clear of tragedy's spectacular effects (Cornford 1907, 242). We might, along with Emily Greenwood, rather describe the Thucydidean use of visuality and spectacle as filmic, and as relying for its effectiveness on cuts between diverse

points of view, a device that of course was alien to Athenian tragedy (Greenwood 2006, 19–41).

31. Eur. *And.* 11. 1–15, with the remarks of duBois, 2008, 147ff.

32. On the monumentality of Troy's smoking ruins, see Aesch. *Ag.*, 636–680. Cf. Eur. *Tro.* ll. 1325–end.

33. On the question of Athens' "just deserts," see, e.g., *CAH²*, vol. 6, 27–29; Scott 2009, 11–12; and Schwenk 2013, 8–10. But of course there were those in Athens at the time who seem to have expected better; see Lys. 12.69ff. One reason that cities had previously not been subject to the sort of treatment they often received during the Peloponnesian War is, doubtless, that the Greeks had always preferred to fight around cities or to take them by sudden attack or betrayal; siege warfare involving the kind of machinery that might conclude a siege in a span shorter than an Iliadic ten years was practically unknown to the ancient Greeks. For a structural hypothesis that explains these and other developments in the conduct of warfare during the Peloponnesian war, see Ober 1985, 31ff., and cf. Gomme 1945, 16ff.

34. There is more to Erianthus' proposal than a stereotypically Theban hatred of Athens. From a strategic point of view, Thebes could expect to become the arbiter of central Greece after Athens' removal, and moreover the city's χώρα, which had been butting up against the borders of Attica for some time, could be expected to swallow up many of Athens' newly "liberated" suburbs. Thus, perhaps, Erianthus' otherwise excessive insistence that the land around Athens be redesignated as pasturage: not only might such usage keep Athens from being resettled, as were many of the sites it had ruined, but the advantage of new grazing lands would fall, for the most part, to Boeotian shepherds (Schwenk 2013, 10); cf. Lysias 15.3.

35. I thank Emily Greenwood for this insightful suggestion. Compare *Hellenica* 2.2.20, where, it should be noted, Xenophon says nothing about this incident, or even about Lysander's renegotiation of the treaty. He reports only the reasoning of the Gerousia, which would not enslave Athens on account of the service it had done to Greece in the Persian Wars. We may find this argument, coming as it does out of the kind of patriotic rhetoric typical of the popular Athenian oratory that Plato mocked in the *Menexenus*, less convincing even than Plutarch's proffered explanation. But if these historical puzzles ever troubled the Athenians themselves, we have no evidence of it. Cf. also Plut. *De Gloria Ath.* 1 and esp. 5. The trope of Euripides as cultural savior was one that Plutarch employed elsewhere: Plut. *Nic.* 29. Plutarch's reading strikes me as more appropriate to a Roman discourse about ruins than a Greek one, for reasons I discuss in the next chapter. For the use of φέρω in Plutarch to mean "bear a child," see Wyttenbach 1843, s.v. "φέρω." Both the Loeb (1916) and Budé (1964) translations take Ἀγρότειραν to refer to a state of abandonment and physical ruination, though it could of course also refer to the house of Atreides' savage history. The ambiguity, in this instance, could be applied to Athens as well, either historically, as referring to the city's conduct during the last stages of the recent war, or proleptically, as giving a mournful vision of a future city inhabited only by wild animals.

36. Lysias 2.37, in Todd 2007. For his dependence on Herodotus, see Frangeskou 1999, 323, and note particularly the verbal echoes uniting Lysias's speech to that of the Athenians at Herod. *Hist.* 9.27. When orators mention ruins from the Persian Wars, they do so in an antiquarian way, which only obliquely gestures toward the moment at which those ruins were created.: Aesch. *Tim.* 182 and Lyc. *Leoc.* 80–82.

37. Isoc. *Pac.* 105.

38. Compare Isoc. *Paneg.* 69.10 (πρὸς μίαν μὲν πόλιν κινδυνεύσειν), *Evag.* 68.5 (ἀντὶ τοῦ τὴν ἤπειρον πορθεῖν περὶ τῆς αὐτῶν κινδυνεύειν ἠναγκάσθησαν), and *Pac.* 37.6 (περὶ ἀνδραποδισμοῦ κινδυνεύειν), inter alia.

39. Tamiolaki 2013; for the Plutarch passage in question, see n22 above. For the general tenor of this "class conflict," see Ober 1993, 94–95.

40. For common modes of wealth concealment in Classical Athens, see Christ 2006, 191ff.; and compare Ober 1989, 194–196, which gives a judicious assessment of the extent to which wealthy citizens could expect to conceal the magnitude of their riches. This game of concealment should be understood as part of the mass/elite negotiations classically discussed by Ober 1989, esp. 305ff.

41. Arist. *Pol.* 1311a14, *Ath. Pol.* 16.3

42. Panic in the agora: Dem. *Cor.* 168–172. On Thebes, see Munn 2013, 104 and Hornblower 1983, 263–266. On the effects of the ruination of Thebes, see *CAH*² 6, 852: "By and large the prevailing mood in Athens was pacific, particularly after the destruction of Thebes."

43. Plut. *Alex.* 13.1, *Phoc.* 17.3.

44. For tyrannical and oligarchic use of ruination, see Arist. *Pol.* 1311a10ff. and *Ath. Pol.* 16.1ff. on the identification of Phocion's party as optimate; for Demetrius's role within that party, see Nepos *Vit. Phoc.* 3.1. Athens' refusal to surrender the orators: Plut. *Vit. Phoc.* 17.4–5; on Phocion's earlier unpopularity, 7–8.

45. This documentary citation is typical of the speech as a whole, an idiosyncratic oration that Danielle Allen characterizes as needing to establish by antiquarianism the authority it loses by straying from the democratic norms of oratory—in, as Allen says, an oligarchic direction (Allen 2000, 25–27), but Allen's implicit identification of oligarchic ideology with Platonic political theory is surely subject to debate.

46. The epigraphic version: Tod, *Greek Historical Inscriptions*, p. 204; for Cartledge's most recent account, see Cartledge 2013, 29ff. Other scholarship that rejects the Lycurgan version of the oath: *CAH*², vol. 5, 314–315; Siewert 1972, 106–108. Scholarship that accepts it: Dinsmoor 1934, 158; Baron 1966, 604; Boersma 1970, 44 and n432, for a listing of the scholarship in support of this oath's authenticity; Wittenburg 2012, who adduces (804) a passage of Plutarch's *Life of Pericles* (17.1) he believes shows that the oath in its augmented form was known to Pericles; but the passage at best would show that Plutarch accepted Lycurgus's version of the oath. In fact, the list at Plut. *Vit. Per.* 17.1 seems to show exactly the opposite of what Wittenburg would like it to: it gives both the rebuilding of temples and the provisions of the Plataean Oath as separate items, suggesting that the latter did not include the former.

One final testimony in favor of the authenticity of the oath as Lycurgus gives it appears in Cicero's *De Re Publica*, book 3: "Post autem cum Persis et Philippus qui cogitavit, et Alexander qui gessit, hanc bellandi causam inferebat quod vellet Graeciae fana poenire; quae ne reficienda quidem Grai putaverunt, ut esset posteris ante oculos documentum Persarum sceleris sempiternum" (3.9.12–17) (Thereafter Philip, who had the idea, and Alexander, who brought it to execution, put forth this casus belli against the Persians, that they wanted to avenge the temples of Greece, which the Greeks indeed thought ought not to be rebuilt, so that they could serve for their descendants as an eternal monument to the crimes of the Persians). There seems little reason to doubt that Cicero is here describing something like the Plataean Oath as Lycurgus gives it. The wording of the purpose clause is, however, close enough to Lycurgus's—and far enough from the simple syntax of the oath in its inscriptional form—to suggest that the version presented in *Against Leocrates* was probably what Cicero had in mind. Scholars arguing in favor of the historicity of the clause it records have wisely ignored this passage, which does not, in the final analysis, attest an independent tradition.

47. Boersma 1970, 44. On this "*Rachegedank*," see Bloedow 2003 and, among ancient sources, Isoc. *Paneg.* 184–187 and Arr. *Anab.* 2.14, purportedly containing the contents of an earlier letter. In both of these texts, for reasons I discuss below, the ruins of Athens are passed over in discreet silence. The notion of a "revenge motive" for waging war on Persia—which became fundamental for later historical narratives of Alexander's invasion—was, as Bloedow shows, already present *in nuce* among the writings anti-Persian and Panhellenic Athenians prior to 330.

48. Alexander as philosopher-king (in both antiquity and in modern scholarship: Bosworth 1996, 2–4. Plutarch's two essays on the "fortune of Alexander" are exemplary in this connection, e.g., the remarks ascribed to Zeno (*Mor.* 329a–d), which make Alexander into a stoic sage. It was this "philosophical" and benevolent character of the conquests that could seem so hard to square with the violent and even barbaric procedures through which they were carried out and secured: Bosworth 1996, 133–165. For an interpretation of the ruinations of Thebes and Persepolis with reference to Alexander's "barbaric soul," and for an attack on recent attempts to depict them as matters of policy, see Bloedow and Loube 1997. On the contemporary propaganda value of burning Persepolis, two theories (broadly speaking) have been advanced. On the one hand, it seems possible that Persepolis could have been "sacrificed" to satisfy a Greece that was then in revolt (Badian 1994, 267–268, slightly modifying an earlier presentation of the same argument that Borza 1972, 244, endorsed, with some qualifications). On the other hand, such a wanton act of destruction could have been intended to terrorize the Greeks themselves, who had already seen Thebes leveled to satisfy Alexander's temper.

49. The Medism of Alexander I: e.g., Herod. *Hist.* 8.136. Persepolis itself remained ruined until the present, a site that post-Achaemenid dynasties treated, with almost ritual reverence, as justifying any act of vengeance against the Greeks and then the Romans (Kosmin 2018, 206–210).

50. The version of the story on which I've been reporting so far belongs to the so-called vulgate tradition (Borza 1972, 233–235). As usual, the major exception to the vulgate account is Arrian, who makes no mention of any hetaera: Arr. *An.* 3.18.11–12. The ambiguities and cavils in Plutarch's account don't necessarily point to this alternate version: other "vulgate" narratives, e.g., Dio. Sic. 17.70–73, also express doubts about whether the firing of such a great city could really have happened "by accident." Contemporary historians have tended to prefer Arrian's clearer and apparently less anecdotal account (Hammond 1992, but cf. Bloedow and Loube 1997). It should be noted, however, that Arrian's account contains obvious signs of a "literary" elaboration: compare the objections offered there by Parmenio to those that Croesus suggests to Cyrus against the pillage of Sardis in Herodotus (*Hist.* 1.89).

51. On ruination as a matter of successor-king policy, see Kosmin 2018, 183ff.

Chapter 2 · Rome: Ruins and Empire in the Late Antique World

1. Rutilius: *De reditu* 414: "Cernimus exemplis oppida posse mori." Lucretius: e.g., *DRN* 2.1144–1145: "Sic igitur magni quoque circum moenia mundi / expugnata dabunt labem putrisque ruinas." Seneca: "Mundo quidam minantur interitum et huc universum, quod omnia divina humanaque complectitur, si fas putas credere, dies aliquis dissipabit et in confusionem veterem tenebrasque demerget: eat nunc aliquis et singulas comploret animas; Carthaginis ac Numantiae Corinthique cinerem et si quid aliud altius cecidit lamentetur, cum etiam hoc quod non habet quo cadat sit interiturum" (Sen. *Ad Pol.* 1). Gregory Woolf rightly emphasizes that Roman cities, too, are in the long run surprisingly resilient against disaster: few are the cities ruined by the Romans during their imperial expansion that don't get rebuilt by the mid-third century CE (Woolf 2020, 403). What I wish to emphasize in the following pages is the inverse of that phenomenon, the power of the Roman Empire to keep cities on even prime sites ruined for centuries.

2. For Carthage and Numantia, see Oros. *Adv. Pag.* 5.1.5–7: "An forte aliud tunc Carthagini uidebatur, cum post annos centum uiginti, quibus modo bellorum clades modo pacis condiciones perhorrescens, nunc rebelli intentione nunc supplici bellis pacem, pace bella mutabat, nouissime miseris ciuibus passim se in ignem ultima desperatione iacientibus unus rogus tota ciuitas fuit? cui etiam nunc, situ paruae, moenibus destitutae, pars miseriarum est audire quid fuerit. edat Hispania sententiam suam: cum per annos ducentos ubique agros

suos sanguine suo rigabat inportunumque hostem ultro ostiatim inquietantem nec repellere poterat nec sustinere, cum se suis diuersis urbibus ac locis, fracti caede bellorum, obsidionum fame exinaniti, interfectis coniugibus ac liberis suis ob remedia miseriarum concursu misero ac mutua caede iugulabant, quid tunc de suis temporibus sentiebat?" Fulgentius of Carthage gives a parallel case showing that Orosius's point of view was not unique, especially among Carthagians: *De aet.* 11.

3. Machiavelli: see pp. 112–113. Roman power ruined Corinth (146 BCE), Carthage (146 BCE), and Jerusalem (70CE), then rebuilt and repopulated each of them with colonists (in 49 BCE, 44 BCE, and 136 CE, respectively.) The dates are approximate, since Roman colonies weren't built in a day, and we should not suppose that the "new" cities were entirely populated by settlers from Italy: Woolf 2016. Orosius's remarks about the magnitude of Carthage should be read with a grain of salt, since the Roman city probably grew to be more populous under the Antonines than it had been at its peak before the Punic Wars. However, Orosius is probably correct in absolute terms about fifth-century Carthage.

4. Hor. *Ep.* 1.11.7–10:

Scis Lebedus quid sit: Gabiis desertior atque
Fidenis uicus; tamen illic uiuere uellem,
oblitusque meorum, obliuiscendus et illis,
Neptunum procul e terra spectare furentem.

Killgrove and Tykot 2018 gives a summary of the archaeological evidence supporting Horace's judgment.

5. *AUC.* 1.29.2; *AUC.* 1.30.1. On the sack of Alba as a parallel to the fall of Troy in the Roman epic tradition, see Keith 2016.

6. Cic. *Tusc.* 3.12.53: "Karthaginienses multi Romae servierunt, Macedones rege Perse capto; vidi etiam in Peloponneso, cum essem adulescens, quosdam Corinthios. Hi poterant omnes eadem illa de Andromacha deplorare: 'Haec omnia vidi . . . ,' Sed iam decantaverant fortasse. Eo enim erant voltu, oratione, omni reliquo motu et statu, ut eos Argivos aut Sicyonios diceres, magisque me moverant Corinthi subito aspectae parietinae quam ipsos Corinthios, quorum animis diuturna cogitatio callum vetustatis obduxerat." For studies showing the growth of Italian *municipia* during the High Empire, see Woolf 2002, 385, and associated bibliography.

7. App. *Rom.* 8.132. For Republican treatments of Rome's Trojan origins, see Gruen 1992, 6–51. Cato the Elder narrated a version of this legend in his *Origines*: e.g., Serv. ad *Aen.* 1.5–6. Ennius's *Annales* also began with the fall of Troy, although Ennius treated this at rather less length than did Virgil.

8. Momigliano 1975, 22–25.

9. On Roman self-insertion in the Athenian landscape, see Arafat 1996, esp. 12ff. and 169–184, and compare Paus. 1.18.4. It is a characteristic, and pointed, bit of Pausanian irony that neither the Roman nor the Thracian ever gets named in his text. "Voluntary" rededications of Athenian public infrastructure: e.g. (and always controversially), the dedication of the Theater of Dionysius (Arafat 1996, 155) and the Parthenon (Beard 2010, 71ff.) to Nero. Roman-era "conquests" of Athens: e.g., Livy *Per.* 81 and Habicht 1997, 307–314; on Caesar's easy conquest of Athens, Habicht 1997, 352, and on Augustus's occupation, 364. On the survival of Athenian civic institutions, see Chamoux 2001, 165–73; for a concise chronology of this later period, see Habicht 1997, 366–369. On restrictions to the "independent sovereignty" of Athens and of Greek poleis in general, see Carlsson 2010, 71.

10. Livy (*AUC* 1.1) suggests that Aeneas may have made a (treacherous) separate peace with the Greeks, an insinuation picked up and magnified by Servius's commentary on the

passages just cited. For a more modern reading that echoes these concerns, see Coluccio Salutati's *De tyranno*, 5.7, in Salutati 2014b.

11. Primary sense of "ruo": Lewis and Short, s.v. "Ia." For the pre-Latin history of the word, see Ernout and Meillet 1951, s.v.

12. Virgilian elaboration of the *urbs capta* motif: Paul 1982. Enargeia in book 2: Rossi 2004, 17–30. Vision of Venus: *Aen.* 2.589–633. Venus's apparition follows immediately after the Helen episode, a section of the text that is thought by many, if not most, modern critics to be spurious (for the problem and associated bibliography, see Peirano 2012, 242–263); it is possible that the author of the Helen episode was responding to a perceived "doubling" or confusion in the narrative; equally, the Helen episode may have replaced something that would have made sense of this apparent pleonasm.

13. On the memory-jogging power of this death *ante ora parentum*, see O'Sullivan 2009, esp. 448–453. The evidence that finally convinces Anchises: *Aen.* 2.679–691.

14. The apologetics may have been necessary given Homer's representation of Aeneas in the *Iliad*: Morgan 1955. Aeneas's penchant for flight: e.g., *Il.* 5.305ff.

15. On the nature of the commentary on the *Aeneid* being offered here, see Feeney 1984. On *pietas* in the abstract and its ideological function in attaching Augustus to the Caesarian heritage, see Ramage 1985. On the problems involved in "apotheosizing" a living emperor, see, e.g., Jenkinson 1974. On the transferred apotheosis in *Carm.* 3.3., see Cole 2001, 77–78.

16. On what changed in Roman governance with the coming of Augustus, see Syme 2002, 339–508. On the closing of the horizon of possibility for the "recovery" of the pre-Augustan republic, see Gowing 2005, 120–131. On the factive continuity of the Roman *res publica*, something that is evident even in the lexical choices made by imperial historians, see Flower 2010, 1–5, and Gowing 2005, 28ff. On what changed in Roman governance with the coming of Augustus, see Syme 2002, 339–508.

17. Caesar's visit to Troy is in many respects an explicit calque of Xerxes' visit to the same site in Herodotus: *Hist.* 7.42–44.

18. For a Vergilian precedent for this transposition of Roman "family tree" language into the real, see Gowers 2011. Family tree language in Lucan: e.g., 8.692, 9.89.

19. On Camillus's legendary status as a Roman builder, see Cornell 2000. On Camillus as paradigm for Augustus in Roman historiography, see Gaertner 2008. On the *Casa Romuli* as a sacred site in Augustan Rome, see, e.g., Cass. Dio 53.16.5.

20. Cf. Kraus, 1994, 6–7.

21. Spencer 2005. For a review of the historiographical sources for Nero's architectural program, see Perkins 1956.

22. On archaeological evidence for damage done by the sack of 410, see Kulikowski 2007, 179. and Lanciani 1903, 57–61. Those who suffered most were those with the most to lose: most evidence of early fifth-century destruction is restricted to the aristocratic houses on the Aventine (Lanciani 1903, 57–61). Then again, a modern-day historian might wonder if Lanciani is not too hasty in blaming this destruction on the Goths. The burning of these aristocratic establishments could well have followed accidentally, upon their abandonment after the sack.

23. Psychological impact: Sarris 2011, 42–43; Ward-Perkins 2005, 41–44. Among the ancient texts that reflect this interpretation are Aug. *De Exc. Urb.* 2.3, Soc. *Ecc.* 355b–c, and Paul. Diac. 12.13.3–4. On the emergence of "local romanities" that co-opted the empire's financial base, see Brown 1981, 125–128 and Brown 2012, 392–400.

24. Aug. *De Exc. Urb.* 6.6: "An putatis civitatem in parietibus deputandam? Civitas in civibus est, non in parietibus. Denique si diceret Deus Sodomitis, Fugite, quia incensurus sum locum istum: nonne magnum meritum eos habere diceremus, si fugerent, si flamma de caelo

descendens moenis parietesque vastaret? Nonne Deus pepercerat civitati, quia civitas migraverat, et perniciem illius ignis evaserat?"

25. Aug. *CD* 1.3.

26. Among the anti-Christian readings of Rutilius, Dufourcq 1905, 488–492, and Courcelle 1948 are exemplary in placing Rutilius directly in dialogue with Christian contemporaries such as Augustine.

27. Passages: *DRS* 1.167–176 (Rufius Volusianus), 207–216 (Palladius), 267–276 (Valerius Messala), 417–428 (Rufius Volusianus again), 467–474 (Albinus), 493–510 (Victorinus), 542–558 (Protadius), 577–596 (Lachanius, the poet's father), and 599–614 (Lucillus). Several of these figures are known to us from other contemporary sources, particularly the correspondences of Symmachus and Sidonius Apollinaris.

28. On Symmachus's techniques for preserving an aristocratic network in the face of his own preference for the countryside and the increasing difficulties of travel in the late fourth century CE, see Salzman 2004, 81–94. On Paulinus's place in a post- or extraurban network of extremely broad scope, see Brown 1972, 210–212.

29. For a more in-depth study of this allusory chain, see Squillante 2005, 173–198, and, for a treatment that emphasizes Rutilius' dependence on Ovid, Fo 1989, 52. Tissol 2002 offers a full account of Homeric/Ovidian double allusions in the poem. Vergil is another important source of language and allusive content for Namatianus, and on this basis it has sometimes been argued that Aeneas is one of the poet's identificatory avatars: e.g., Wolff 2005, 68, and Clarke 2014, passim.

30. Alessandro Fo (1989, ad loc.) suggests that Rutilius's language in these lines creates an effect of temporal blurring that evokes "*lunghi spazi di tempo*"—perhaps those stretching between Rutilius, Livy's Camillus, and Rome's original cabin builder, Romulus. For the foundational and agrarian resonances of *casa* to which I believe Rutilius is referring here, see *Thesaurus Linguae Latinae*, s.v. IB.

31. Recent readings of *De reditu* as propaganda: e.g., Cameron 2010, 211; Sarris 2011, 50–51.

32. For this allusion, see "laeta boum passim campis armenta videmus / caprigenumque pecus nullo custode per herbas" (*Aen.* 3.220–21). "We saw happy beasts and cattle throughout the fields, and goat-creatures wandering without a goatherd in the grass." Cf. Castorina ad loc.

Namatianus's allusion, and possibly its Vergilian associations, are mediated by a passage near the beginning of Lucan's *Bellum Civile*: "At nunc semirutis pendent quod moenia tectis / urbibus Italiae lapsisque ingentia muris." Blurring of land and sea boundaries in *de Reditu*: Clarke 2014. On the development of new trade patterns adapted to the degradation of Roman infrastructure and political power, see Whittaker 1993, item XIII, esp. 178ff. On shifting settlement patterns, see O'Donnell 2008, 266ff.; cf. Cass. *Var.* 8.29, a plea for the erstwhile inhabitants of Parma to reoccupy the city they had abandoned for the comparative safety of the nearby hills: "Dignum est, ut libenti animo faciatis quod iuberi pro urbis vestrae utilitate cognoscitis." On infrastructural breakdown as cause of decay in other forms of built infrastructure, see O'Donnell 2008, 366ff.; Lanciani 1901, 139–142. An exemplary narrative appears at Paul. Diac. *Hist. Lang.* 3.23.

33. On imagined communities, see Anderson 1983, 39–44. In the present case, the hierarchy of elite and subaltern that Anderson points out as a key ideological element in the formation of national consciousness would appear to be reversed: it is among the loftiest Roman elites, not the masses, that a "national consciousness" seems to emerge. This counterintuitive class inversion is, as we have seen and will see, typical of ruin-making situations.

34. Lanciani 1903, 77–90. O'Donnell (2008, 260–270) makes a similar claim. Woolf 2020 notes that this is the period when Roman population statistics hit rock bottom, reduced perhaps a hundredfold from its peak of one million under the Julio-Claudians (393).

35. For the history of Theoderic's conquest and his claim to kingship, see Moorhead 1987, and on the valence of the term *rex* in this context, see esp. 39–40. For the Amal dynasty in general, see Sarris 2011, 102–121. For Theoderic's building program in its Roman dimensions, see fundamentally Fauvinet-Ranson 2006. On the importance of Gothic identity and Gothic self-identification in fifth-century Italy, see Amory 1997, 50–58. Scholars dubious of Cassiodorus's claims about the effectiveness of Gothic administration: Lafferty 2010, 28–29; Brown 1984, 110ff. Ward-Perkins (2005, 74ff.) suggests, astutely, that Gothic "romanizing" propaganda was also directed against other post-Roman states in Europe, by comparison to whom the Ostrogoths could claim a "higher degree of civilization."

36. For Bjornlie's characterization of the ex post facto editing of this collection, see Bjornlie 2013, 198–205.

37. This evaluation of Theoderic holds good even from a Byzantine perspective: Procopius, *Hist.* 3.5–8.

38. Cass. *Var.* 3.51; O'Donnell 2008, 139ff.; Brown 1984, 12ff.

39. Ward-Perkins 1985, 19–30. For a treatment of the chronological debates surrounding the confiscation of temple estates, see Cameron 2010, 39–51. For Julian's intervention, see *Liber Pont.* 34, with Ambr. *Ep.* 18.38; for a treatment of the chronological debates surrounding the confiscation of temple estates, see Cameron 2010, 39–51. For a concise statement of Dey's argument, see Dey 2015, 127–130.

40. Restorations by Theoderic: Cass. *Var.* 1.6, 25; 2.27, 35, 36, 37; 3.29; 4.31, 51. Religious endowments under Theoderic: *Liber Pont.* 53. Epigraphic evidence reveals that Theoderic did, in fact, dedicate a number of Arian churches; all of these were in Ravenna, however, and seem to have been built with the royal comitatus in mind (O'Donnell 2008, 73, with Johnson 1988).

41. Exemplary here are St. Ambrose's arguments against the restoration of the Ara Victoriae in the Senate, *Epist.* 17–18. His contention there that churches do much of the duty of temples, but without state funding or involvement, strikes me as typical; if we were attempting to describe the institutional transformation that resulted from Christianity's conquest of the commanding heights of imperial power, we might call it a "privatization" of the holy. These claims were bound to win sympathy from a cash-strapped emperor, and not only for religious reasons. Endowments of land and wealth are a constant companion of new church construction in the *Liber Pontificalis*. Consider, too, the effectiveness of shrines for reestablishing lines of patronage and power in a world where political change was beginning to make the old hierarchies obsolete (Brown 1981, 94–105).

42. Cass. *Var.* 4.51.1–3. Cf. Fauvinet-Ranson 2006, 133–141. On this rhetorical tendency in the *Variae*, see Brenk 1987, 107.

43. Devecka 2016. On the post-Roman fate of aristocracies in the West—somewhere between assimilation, emigration, and extermination—see Sarris 2011, 72–73, alongside Wormald 1976, 217–226. Wormald goes on (225) to suggest, in a way that is very compatible with my own argumentation, that one of the factors in the eventual disappearance of the Italian aristocracy may have been competition for "recruitment" from episcopal and monastic establishments.

44. For earlier imperial policy toward ruins, see, e.g., *Nov. Divi Maioriani* 4, with Lanciani 1901, 28ff. Likewise, *Cod. Theod.* 10.2.1, a rescript of 378 CE that stipulates preventative measures to be taken against ruination: "Rationales vel ordinarii iudices earum domorum, quas procuratorum nequitia vel rationalium negligentia labi patitur in ruinas, insituant auctionem hastis habitis ex licitatione currente" (Rational or ordinary judges shall set up an auction, announced in the usual way, of those houses that, either because of their owners' wretchedness or the officials' unconcern, have begun to fall into ruin). *Nov. Maioriani* 4.1, which permits the use of materials from buildings "quod nullo modo reparari viderimus posse" (which we have seen cannot be repaired by any means) comes closest to Theoderic's position.

45. On *decus* in the *Variae*, see, e.g., Cass. *Var.* 1.6, 25, 28; 2.35, 36; 3.9, 31, inter alia, with Fauvinet-Ranson 2002, 231–240, and 2006, 197ff. And consider the stern words with which Cass. *Var.* 3.31 begins: "Quamvis universae rei publicae nostrae infatigabilem curam desideremus impendere et deo favente ad statum studeamus pristinum cuncta revocare, tamen Romanae civitatis sollicitiora nos augmenta constringunt, ubi quicquid decoris impenditur, generalibus gaudiis exhibetur. pervenit itaque ad nostram conscientiam suggestione multorum, quae prava non potest dissimulare commissa, plura in praeiudicio urbis Romanae detestabiles praesumptores assumere, ut cui nos summum adhibere desideramus studium, dolum patiatur iniustum."

46. Cass. *Var.* 3.10.2: "Ideo magnitudini tuae praesenti ammonitione declaramus, ut marmora, quae de domo Pinciana constat esse deposita, ad Ravennatem urbem per catabolenses vestra ordinatione dirigantur." On the palace, see Wood 2007, 252ff.

47. Shrinkage as survival strategy: Woolf 2020, 406.

48. This strange letter has received more than its share of scholarly attention lately. See most recently Bjornlie 2013, 314–318, recapitulating the conclusions of an earlier (2009) article that reads the letter as just suggested and places it in the context of Cassiodorus's personal apologetics after the end of the Gothic regime in Italy; see also La Rocca 2010.

49. Procopius, *Hist.* 7.36–40, with the commentary of Kaldellis (Procopius, 2014).

50. Procopius, *Hist.* 8.22.

Chapter 3 · Baghdad: Postclassical Ruins and the Islamic Cityscape

1. Ibn Khaldun 1967, 263–275.

2. I borrow this term from Marshall Hodgson's path-breaking *The Venture of Islam*, where "Islamicate" fills the need for a term that embraces the whole range of cultural forms that emerge in lands where Islam is the majority religion, without implying that these cultural forms are themselves "religious" (Hodgson 1974, 1–13). Though I take to heart the objections raised against this language by Shahab (Ahmed 2017, 120ff.), I have continued to employ it as a term of convenience that gives me room to elaborate how an "Islamic discourse" (a more nuanced theoretical term that Ahmed himself prefers: e.g., 129) forms around ruins.

3. "Arguments in stone": see Carver 1993, viii. On the evolution of elite mobility as an ideal, which may have preceded its development as a reality, see Juynboll's treatment of "talab al-ʿilm": Juynboll 1983, 66ff. For elite and general mobility in the medieval Islamicate World, see Rosenthal 2007, 35–37.

4. Very few of the historical details surrounding Islam's foundation and early spread are vouched for unambiguously by the Qur'an itself; our information on these scores comes from later narrative or anecdotal sources, sources that postdate the life of Muhammad by centuries but which have generally been assumed to contain accurate information about sixth- and seventh-century Arabia that was preserved in an oral tradition. Crone and Cook 1977; Hawting 2006; Wansbrough 2006, inter alia.

5. Evidence in the Qur'an: Al-Azmeh 2014, 432–448.

6. For this translation of *kharab* in a Qur'anic context, see Penrice 2011, s.v.

7. For Qur'anic citations throughout this chapter (and, where relevant, the next two), I have used the Sahih International translation, adjusting orthography in accord with the conventions followed in the body of my text.

8. The suras containing or making explicit reference to these pericopes are 7, 9, 10, 11, 12, 14, 15, 17, 21, 22, 23, 25, 28, 29, 30, 32, 38, 40, 43, 69, 89, and 91.

9. On the narrative structure and formulaic status of these narratives, see Neuwirth 2006, 105–106.

10. Of the twenty-one suras containing circumstantially detailed accounts of the so-called

Arab Prophets and the destruction of their communities, only sura twenty-two (al Hajj) postdates the Meccan period. The remainder are spread unevenly throughout Noldeke's three Meccan periods, the distribution showing some weighting toward the end of Muhammad's time in Mecca.

11. Al-Azmeh points out that the Qur'an, by *al-A'rab*, generally means Bedouins or non-city-dwelling Arabians (al-Azmeh 2014, 362). As he goes on to say, the Qur'an regards these groups with intense suspicion.

12. On the textual history of Qur'anic anti-urbanism see Crone 1994. Compare the hypothesis of Wolf 1951, which locates this anti-urbanism within a particular set of tribal polemics. On القَلَى, see Penrice 2011, q.v.

13. On the so-called first hejira, see Bowersock 2017, 70ff. This story has the weight of tradition behind it, but the tradition is a late one and (in detail, at least) may stem from eighth-century attempts to "explain" the Qur'an rather than from external evidence. On the etymological connections of hejira, see al-Jallad 2017.

14. Whether or not one accepts the historical identity of archaeological sites like Mada'in Salih with the ruined cities of the Qur'an (as, e.g., Gibb 1962), these were surely read and narrativized as monuments to impiety very early in the Islamic tradition. On the pre-Islamic tribe (not city) of Thamud, see Bowersock 1983, 90ff., and Hoyland 2001, 68–69. For evidence of the persistence of this ethnic identity after the Roman annexation of Nabatea, see *Notitia Dignitatum* 28 and 34, with analysis by Shahîd 1984, 29.

15. Invitation to "read" ruins as trope in the Qur'an: 12:108, 35:44, 40:21, and 47:10, inter alia. On traditional interest in locating these "lost cities," see Wheeler 2006, 41–42. Qur'an-inspired identifications of, and narratives about, such sites are likely to differ substantially from the conclusions of modern archaeologists: Hoyland 2001, 223–224.

16. For a framing of the problem, see Gibb 1962, 269–270. For the charges embodied in the phrase *asatir al-awalin*, see Dundes 2003, 1–14.

17. The so-called Arabian prophets of the Qur'an have a shadowy presence in pre-Islamic poetry as well (al-Azmeh 2014, 290). Since (despite later claims to the contrary) that poetry seems to have been transmitted orally, it would be wrong to take these adumbrations of the Qur'anic narrative *asatir* in the literal sense of the word.

18. For the intra-Semitic origins of the root, see Jeffery 2007, s.v. I am comparing Islamic antiquarianism with that of medieval Europe as (charitably) represented by Schnapp 1997, 74ff. "Ahistoricity" of the Qur'an, with a history of the discussion: Donner 1998, 80ff. The example from al-Tabari: *Hist.* 4: 88–95. For a historiographical comparison with the narrative techniques favored by Judaeo-Christian scriptures, see MacAuliffe 2006.

19. This point is admirably well-established for Mecca in particular by Crone 1987.

20. For this revisionist account of "tribalism" in pre-Islamic Arabia, see Crone 1986 (and cf. Clastres 1989).

21. For the political milieu, see Bowersock 2012 (passim, but esp. 21–48). For Nabatea, an exemplary case of secondary state-formation followed by absorption, see Bowersock 1983. The Nabateans began to settle in villages legible to a Hellenic audience after contact with Antigonus in the early third century BCE; by 106 CE, Nabatea had become a Roman province.

22. For this broad-brush description of the pre-Islamic social order in Arabia, see Donner 1981. Donner rightly notes (11) that settled populations have always been demographically superior to nomadic ones in that region.

23. The contrast between Greek and Arabian *polis*-societies: Hansen 2002, 241–248. Cf. Wheatley 2001, 24ff., on the pre-Islamic city as refuge from nomadic depredation or oppression.

24. Sells 1989, 2–3; Irwin 1999, 55–56. City as locus of "non-legitimate domination": Weber 1978, 2012ff. Cultural prestige of the Bedouin in medieval Islam: Lapidus 1969, 106ff. In the

linguistic and grammatical traditions: Versteegh 2014, 107–125. As an orienting metaphor in early Islamic political thought: Crone 2004, 20–23.

25. On *qarya*, see (for MSA) Wehr 1979, s.v., and (for Sabaic) Beeston et al. 1982, s.v. For the mythic history of Iram as a lost city of the sands, see Edgell 2004 and below, p. 87.

26. Wheatley 2001, 32. The main contribution of Hijazi cities to the future of Islamic urbanism, as Wheatley puts it, is a "paradigm for ordering institutional and group actions at all levels of society." This was especially true of Medina, where the house of the prophet became a prototype of the Friday Mosque, which was to serve a similar central role in later urban spaces: AlSayyad 1991, 153. For a critique of some older claims that cities are "necessary" to Islamic practice, see, e.g., Lapidus 1969. Destruction of cities in Perso-Byzantine wars: Sarris 2011, 250–255. Peaceful takeover of cities by Muslims: Wheatley 2001, 57.

27. Al-Baladhuri 2013, 165ff. Thus al-Baladhuri, not too much later in the *Futuh*: وحدثني حفص بن عمر العمري قال: حدثني الهيثم بن عدي الطائي قال: أقام المسلمون بالمدائن واختطوها وبنوا المساجد فيها) (168) The evidence as to the pre-conquest layout of Ctesiphon is not consistent in every respect, but is unanimous in describing the site as a cluster of more or less separate cities: el-Ali 1968, 424–433. Muslims continued to dwell in al-Mada'in through the end of the thirteenth century, at least: el-Ali 1968, 419–420. Original layout of Kufa: Massignon 1935.

28. Pious treatment of the companions of Muhammad: Juynboll 1983, 48–50. Use of ersatz building materials in early Kufa: Wheatley 2001, 47. This interpretation of Kufa's ground plan: AlSayyad 1991, 55–56.

29. For a history of the linkage between cities and civilization as mytheme, see Thom 1995, 142–184. On its development as an element of canonical "stadial" history, see p. 111. For a more recent and historically sensitive elaboration of the same theme, see Flannery and Marcus 2014, 341ff. For a developed critique of this "city-centered" view of civilization, see Crone 1986.

30. On Hira and its Christian population, see Hoyland 2001, 82 and, more fully, Shahîd 1971. Postconquest taxation: Abū Yūsuf and al-Kurashi 1969. To see this application of the Qur'anic *jizya* as a matter of conjuncture rather than nomothesis is an especially plausible thesis, given the trouble that even the earliest commentators had making sense of the passage in question (Q 9:29): Kister 1964, with associated bibliography.

31. Grabar 1987, 43–71; al-Muqaddasi 2005, 88, 99–100. Spoliation of churches: AlSayyad 1991, 84; al-Muqaddasi 2005, 81. Modern scholars have taken the inscription on the inside of the Dome of the Rock as an explicit testimony to the building's "supersessionist" intent: Bloom and Blair 1997, 29–31. Note too that the Dome of the Rock is supposed, in Islamic tradition, to have replaced an earlier wooden structure: Bowersock 2017, 46. On the integration of Umayyad monuments into Roman urban fabrics, *pace* Kennedy's (1985) much-repeated claim that the Muslims turned broad avenues into crowded *suqs*, see Dey 2015, 213ff.

32. General spoliation of Mada'in: El-Ali 1968, 421 and Ibn Hawqal 1939, 244: وقد نقل عامة ابنيتها الى بغداد

33. For the multiform character of this rivalry, see Crone 2014b, 160–177.

34. Other versions of the story: Bier 1993, 61–62. For the interpretation given here, see Lassner 1970, 128ff.

35. Innovation rather than imitation as dominant mode of early Islamic art: Grabar 1987, 72–98. On the architectural pattern of the 'Iwan, see Bier 1993, and compare Grabar 1987, 133–168.

36. Late Roman spoliation: see pp. 59–60.

37. The Pyramids: al-Maqrizi 1959, 184, with Selden, 2013. The Cisterns of Malga: Ibn Khaldun 1967, 265. According to this schema, one characteristic feature of early Islamic spoliation is that what it tears down is as important as, if not indeed more important than,

what it raises up. Late antique spoliators in Rome, as we saw, were largely indifferent to the nature of the buildings from which they took their stones, and this was reflected in legal strictures that regarded all ruins—also indifferently—as belonging to a "classical" past in which the meanings of individual structures were usually lost. Islamic interest in reading the functional "meaning" of despoiled buildings thus represents an innovation as against Greco-Roman practices: here, for the first time, we find architecture intersecting with a form of historiography.

38. Kufa: al-Muqaddasi 1906, 115. For al-Muqaddasi as a geographer of decay, see Wheatley 2001, 101–122.

39. Or *al-basratan*: Yaqut 1866, 636. On the functional positions of Kufa and Basra, see alSayyad 1991, 47, with Wheatley 2001, 87–91. On the sawad and the role of the ʿIraqi urban system in exploiting it, see Morony 1984, 126–164.

40. For the history of Kufa during the period of the first and second fitnas, see Hodgson 1974, 210–221. For Ali's sojourn in Kufa and eventual assassination there, see al-Tabari 1990a, v. 21.

41. For the founding of Wasit, see al-Baladhuri 1916, 175ff. On Wasit's contribution to undermining the positions of Kufa and Basra, see Wheatley 2001, 88. On Hajjaj's motives for founding Wasit, see Djaït 1986, 316–317.

42. On the social background and propaganda techniques of the ʿAbbasid revolutionaries, see Sharon 1983, 17–48, now with the remarks of Crone 2014b, 160–167.

43. For this situation of the founding of this city within the ideological context of the Abbasid revolution, see Gutas 1998, 17–20.

44. Al-Muqaddasi 1906, 113 and 115.

45. For this tradition, see also al-Muqaddasi 1906, 120. Because Sufyan ath-Thawri (716–778 CE), the famous Kufan hadith transmitter, occurs as the last common link in most of the *isnad*s that support this tradition, Juynboll has argued that it should be traced to Kufa and probably to Sufyan's lifetime, either just before or just after the building of Baghdad (Juynboll 1983, 208ff.). If Juynboll is right, then this text seems to offer a "native" response to Baghdad's incursion on the ʿIraqi scene.

46. The intertext is with the Qurʾanic narrative of Qarun (Korah), a Jewish rebel against Moses whose rebellion the Qurʾan ascribes to a desire to show off his wealth and build great houses (Q 28:76–82). As punishment for this, God causes him to sink underneath the earth:
فَخَسَفْنَا بِهِ وَبِدَارِهِ ٱلْأَرْضَ فَمَا كَانَ لَهُ مِن فِئَةٍ يَنصُرُونَهُ مِن دُونِ ٱللَّهِ وَمَا كَانَ مِنَ ٱلْمُنتَصِرِينَ.

47. The semantic range of *jabbar*: Wehr 1984, q.v., with Crone 2003, 17 and Lewis 1991, 103n30.

48. Constantine's foundation of Constantinople as a "bestitute" for Rome: *Anonymus Valesianus* 1.6 and Zosimus, 2.51–54 with Alfoldi 1947.

49. Al-Khatabi 1971, 73: ينبأنا ابراهيم بن مخلد القاضي قال ينبأنا اسماعيل بن على الخطبي قال: سقط رأس القبة الخضراء ابي جعفر المنصور التي في قصره بمدينته يوم الثلاثاء لسبع خلون من جمادى الآخرة سنة تسع وعشرين وثلاثمائة، وكان ليلتئذ مطر عظيم ورعد هائل وبرق شديد، وكانت هذه القبة تاج بغداد و علم البلد ومأرة من مآثر بني عباس عظيمة. For a survey of Baghdad's ruined neighborhoods, see al-Muqaddasi 1906, 120.

50. Al-Muqaddasi's praise of Jerusalem: al-Muqaddasi 1906, 155ff. Evidence for transfer of loyalties to Fatimids: 177. The dossier for this and associated bibliography: Wheatley 2001, 67. Jerusalem would fall under Fatimid control about a century after al-Muqaddasi's death, shortly before suffering a brutal sack at the hands of European crusaders.

51. This would be a fruitful starting point, too, for modern historians who want to follow Fowden 2013 and al-Azmeh 2014 in integrating Islam into the world of late antiquity.

52. The nature of the book: al-Qadi al-Qudaʾi 2013, 7–9.

53. Goitein 1969, 87–88. The explanation offered by Goitein for this phenomenon— namely, that Islamic patterns of collective ownership created a kind of tragedy of the com-

mons in which, if some tenants of a house were unable or unwilling to pay for maintenance and upkeep, the rest would likewise withdraw their support and move elsewhere—may or may not be correct. For an alternative interpretation of Goitein's evidence as reflecting shifts in the real estate market, see Costello 1977, 14.

54. For the salience of ruins to the practice (and not just the theory) of *zuhd*, see *Encyclopedia of Islam*, https://brill.com/view/package/eio, accessed July 2018, s.v. "ascetics and asceticism."

55. On the placement and function of this figure in the pre-Islamic *qasida*, see Irwin 2000, 15–16.

56. Al-Buhturi, *Siniyya* 1–47, with Arberry 1965, ad loc.

57. Five days' riding: al-Buhturi, *Sinniya*, in Arberry 1965, 48–49.

58. For this capacious sense of what counts as an "Islamic discourse," see, e.g., Ahmed 2017, 304.

59. Those claiming this kind of authority for esoteric wisdom are, in a sense, following the authorial tradition of the Hermetic corpus, which speaks throughout of a noesis that cannot be fully represented, let alone improved upon, by human beings (Fowden 1993, 119–127). Hamori 1971 reads the story of the City of Brass in a way that establishes an allegorical unity between architectural and intellectual traditions.

60. Al-Tha'labi 1954, 126–127: ان رجلا يقال له عبد الله بن قلابة خرج في طلب إبل له قد ضلّت, فبينما في
بعض صحارى عدن في تلك الفلوات اذ وقع على مدينة عليه حصن حول ذلك الحصن قصور عظيمة وأعلام طوال, فلما
دنا منها ظنّ أن فيها من يسأله عن إبله فلم ير فيها احدا ولا داخلا ولا خارجا فنزل عن ناقته. وعقلها وسل سيفه ودخل من
باب الحصن فاذا هو ببابين عظيمين لم يرفي الدنيا اعظم منهما ولا اطول واذا خشبهما من أطيب عود وعليهما نجوم من
ياقوت أصفر وياقوت أحمر ضووُها قد ملأ المسكان, فلما فتح احد البابين فاذاهو بمدينة لم ير الاعون مثلها . . . ثم انه
حمل من لؤلؤها وبنادق المسك والزعفران ولم يستطع ان يقلع من زبرجدها

61. Ibn Khaldun, 1967, 17–18.

Chapter 4 · *Tenochtitlan: Preservationism and Its Failures in Early Modern Mexico*

1. For the significance of this terminological turn, see Marcus 1992. Her argument that the designation "early modern" refers to a period that anticipates the problems of modernity and after is one that I follow in this chapter.

2. Works that focus almost exclusively on more recent ruins: Woodward 2003, Boym 2001, and Ginsberg 2004, inter alia.

3. The full passage, from Cyriac's diary for the period of July 31 through August 2, 1444: "Ad Plinius deinde, ille Naturalis Historiae conditor diligentissimus, ea in parte qua ingenua et nobiliora mundi opera commemorat, quom hoc praecipuum existimasset opus, in principio inquit: 'Durat et Cyzici delubrum, in quo filum aureum commissuris omnibus politi lapidis subiecit artifex,' et reliqua. Cuiusce vero positi fili latitudinem et concavitatem vidimus, et eam ipsam atque alia pleraque eiusdem eximiae aedis insignia diligenter inspecta metitaque hisce quoad licuerat describendum atque stilo defingendum curavimus. Sed heu quantum ab illo deformem revisimus, quod antea bis septem iam annis exactis perspeximus; nam tunc XXX et unam columnas erectas vidimus extare, nunc vero unam de XXX manere et partim epistilii destitutas cognovi. Sed et quae integrae fere omnes inclitae parietes extabant, nunc a barbaris magna quidem ex parte diminutae soloque collapsae videntur. Sed enim insigni suo et mirabili in frontispicio eximia deum et praeclarissima illa de marmore simulacra Jove ipso optimo protectore suaeque eximiae celsitudinis patrocinio inlaesa tutantur et intacta suo fere prisco splendore manent." For more on this visit, see Ashmole 1956. Cf. Cyriac's *Diary* 3.40, statuary and buildings at Paros "magna ex parte longinqua vetustate et cultorum ignavia hominum defectas soloque obrutas" (generally wrecked and leveled to the ground by long age

and the worthlessness of the men who dwelt around). The Pliny passage which Cyriac recalls (in slightly different form than the modern *textus receptus*) is *NH* 36.22.98.

4. My reconstruction of the background here depends upon Scalamonti's narrative of Cyriac's first visit to Cyzicus: *Vit. Kyr.* 81. On Cyriac's ambiguous relationship with the Ottoman government, cf. *Ep.* 8.2. For the links drawn by Renaissance writers between contemporary Turks and ancient Goths or Vandals as bringers of ruin, see Bisaha 2004, 43–93 and esp. 58ff. On the "barbarian" genealogies supplied by European Renaissance writers for the Turks, see Meserve 2008, 16–26. The Turks' supposed lack of respect for urban architecture as a figure for their nomadism: Meserve 2008, 72.

5. I cite this anecdote from Finkel 2006: "A land was previously in the realm of Islam. After a while the abject infidels overran it, destroyed the colleges and mosques, and left them vacant. They filled the pulpits and galleries with the tokens of infidelity and error, intending to insult the religion of Islam with all kinds of vile deeds, and by spreading their ugly acts to all corners of the earth." Could the land be reconquered, in violation of a peace treaty, without prejudice to the Sultan's good faith? "Yes, for the Sultan of the people of Islam to make peace with the infidels is legal only when there is a benefit to all Muslims. When there is no benefit, peace is never legal. When a benefit has been seen, and it is then observed to be more beneficial to break it, then to break it becomes absolutely obligatory and binding" (Finkel 2006, 159). For the extent of the territories claimed by this figure, see, e.g., Finkel 2006, 159ff. and Braudel 1972, 729ff. For an interesting testimony of a diplomat named Lopez as to the Turks' use of ruins to lend irredentist justification to military expeditions, see Braudel 1972, 1079.

6. Hui's "ruinaissance" is a period in which poets are able to use ruins to think the relations between antiquity and an emerging modernity in multiple registers: Hui 2017, 52ff. Barkan's approach to archaeology as something not only recuperative but also, in an Early Modern setting, generative has also guided my approach in this chapter: Barkan 1999, esp. 273ff.

7. The motif is especially prominent in Old English poetry (on which, see Hume 1976). For the general distinction between medieval and Early Modern modes of ruin-gazing, see Schnapp 1997, 106. For a gloss on this passage that highlights its literary modernity by contrast with its apparently medieval subject matter, see Baron 1966, 109. *De saec.* 27.5–12: "Et, ne longius queramus exempla, ponamus ante oculos hanc regiam urbem, gloriosam patriam tuam atque meam, que, ne fallor, 'tantum inter alias caput extulit urbes quantum lenta solent inter viburna cypressi,' ut ille ait. Ascendamus consecratum pio cruore beati Miniatis ab Arni sinistra ripa colliculum aut antiquarum Fesularum bicipitem montem vel aliquod ex circumstantibus promuntoriis unde per sinus omnes completius videri possit nostra Florentia. Ascendamus, precor, et intueamur minantia menia celo, sidereas turres, immania templa, et immensa palatia, que non, ut sunt, privatorum opibus structa, sed impensa publica vix est credibile potuisse compleri, et demum vel mente vel oculis ad singula redeuntes consideremus quanta in se detrimenta susceperint. Palatium quidem populi admirabile cunctis et, quod fateri oportet, superbissimum opus, iam mole sua in se ipso resedit et tam intus quam extra rimarum fatiscens hiatibus lentam, licet seram, tamen iam videtur nuntiare ruinam. Basilica vero nostra, stupendum opus, cui, si unquam ad exitum venerit, nullum credatur inter mortales edificium posse conferri, tanto sumptu tantaque diligentia inceptum et usque ad quartum iam fornicem consummatum, qua speciosissimo campanili coniungitur, quo quidem nedum pulcrius ornari marmoribus sed nec pingi aut cogitari formosius queat, rimam egit, que videatur in deformitatem ruine finaliter evasura, ut post modicum temporis resarciendi non minus futura sit indiga quam complendi. Quot autem et qualia civium habitacula quotque palatia intestini dissidii civica pestis absumpsit! Quot tum studiosa, tum fortuita consumpserunt incendia! Quot vetustate in se ipsa (tanta est violentia temporis)

corruerunt! Quot mox sunt, si paulum expectaveris (paululum enim est quicquid tempore mensuratur si ad eternitatis immensitatem retuleris), peritura! Ex quo, postquam in rebus quas inter mortalia aut perpetuas aut diutinas reputamus in nostris oculis tot future resolutionis cernimus detrimenta, quid est de ceteris omnium consensu fragilioribus iudicandum!"

8. For the Ciceronian framing of the debate staged in *De seculo*, see Lombardo 1982 and, more recently, the introduction to Salutati 2014.

9. For Petrarch's own involvement in the avowedly restorationist (Musto 2003, 45ff.) revolutionary activity surrounding Cola di Rienzo, see Cosenza 1913.

10. Santi and Castiglione, *Lettera*, sec. 4: "Però parve che il tempo come invidioso della gloria de' mortali, non confidandosi pienamente delle sue forze sole, si accordasse con la fortuna e con li profani e scellerati barbari, li quali alla edace lima e venenato morso di quelli aggiungessero l'empio furore e il ferro e il fuoco, e tutti quelli modi che bastavano per ruinarla."

11. The strictly nationalist interest evinced in these invasions by a Bruni (*History of the Florentine People* 1.40–79, esp. 76), a Machiavelli (*HF* 1.1–5) or a Salutati (e.g., *Reply* 157) should not be mistaken for an anticipation of the problematic of "decline and fall" as it was to be articulated in later centuries: Bowersock 1996, 30. The examples just cited all show how this interest was presentist in its engagement with a contemporary situation in which the major Italian city-states did not enjoy a political independence consonant with their emerging sense of cultural autonomy: Pocock 2005, 156–176.

12. *HPF* 1.75: "Denique quotcumque ex variis barbarorum diluviis superfuerant urbes per Italiam, crescere atque florere et in pristinam auctoritatem sese in dies attollere." Orosius: see pp. 38–39.

13. On ruins as a locus for antiquarian explorations in the Renaissance, see Findlen 1998, 95–96. Cyriac of Ancona: see above. Buondelmonti: *Liber* 1–2. Biondo Flavio: *Italia Illustrata*, 1.8. For a treatment of the historian/antiquarian contrast with particular reference to Biondo, see Hay 1958, 97–99. Biondo's "Hyginus" is presumably Hyginus Gromaticus (fl. c. 100 CE), but the text on which Guido Presbyter based his claims has been lost, if it ever existed. On Biondo's mode of citation here, and on his deployment of "postclassical documents" in general, see Hay 1958, 110ff. Ruins as artifacts: Barkan 1999, 124–135; Karmon 2011, 90ff.; Burkhardt 1954, 133–137. Machiavelli's "ruin itinerary," *HF* 1.5: "Hanno, oltre di questo, variato il nome non solamente le provincie, ma i laghi, i fiumi, i mari e gli uomini; perche la Francia, l'Italia e la Spagna sono ripiene di nomi nuovi e al tutto dagli antichi alieni; come si vede, lasciandone indrieto molti altri, che il Po, Garda, l'Arcipelago sono per nomi disformi agli antichi nominati; gli uomini ancora, di Cesari e Pompei, Pieri, Giovanni e Mattei diventorono."

14. For Bruni's work in the service of the Florentine chancery, see Baron 1966 201ff. For an excellent and unprejudiced discussion of fifteenth-century genre crossing between historiography and antiquarianism, see Grafton 2007, 91–93, esp. n.42. Here Grafton is expanding upon, and nuancing, the classical account of his teacher Arnaldo Momigliano, for which see esp. Momigliano 1990, 169–173.

15. For the secular character of the Renaissance as a period of state agglomeration, see Braudel 1972, 657–663. For continental Spain as an "empire," see Elliott 1963, 41–44 with Elliott 1992.

16. For an analytical treatment of Spanish imperial historiography, see Pocock's dissection of Mexia's *Historia Imperial y Cesarea*: Pocock 2005, 239–357. Translatio imperii: 247; Lupher 2003, 47ff. Renaissance Spanish reception of Italian culture: Morales 1792. One obvious avenue of transmission for the ideas discussed here would have been Jacopo Sannazaro's *Arcadia*, a formative influence behind the poetry of Spain's *Siglo de Oro*, which mourns the Spanish capture of Naples by comparing that city to a ruined Pompeii: Sannazaro 1806, 184,

and 189–190. respectively. Restoration work in Rome, as elsewhere, helped provide political legitimacy: as Karmon (2011) puts it, "Preservation of the past was inseparable from the right to govern Rome" (51). For a discussion of the limits, terms, and direction that characterized this kind of critique, see Barkan 1999, 36–40. Papal restrictions on spoliation: Lanciani 1900, 180–197. Ottoman conservation in Istanbul: Inalcik 1969, 248–249. On Cordoba, see Ecker 2003, 113–141, and Briones 1996, 149–152. On Carlos V's preservation efforts generally, see Brothers 1994, 79–81. On Seville, see Briones 1996, 199ff. For this citation, and for much of my information about Renaissance Spanish preservationism, I am indebted to David Karmon. His own forthcoming essay on this topic contains a fuller exposition.

17. At the earliest, European knowledge of the American *tierra firme* dates from Columbus's return to Spain after his fourth voyage, in November 1504; Cortés had departed for Hispañola some months earlier. On Cortés's difficult legal and rhetorical position, see Elliott's introductory essay in Cortés 2001, which also gives a sense of Cortés's limited intellectual formation.

18. Glory: Agamben 2009, 197–259. On the ideal of a universal monarchy, see Montesquieu 1891, 12–34; and in the Spanish context Pimentel 2000, with whom I agree in seeing this dream as a *longue durée* feature of Spanish politics and thought through the eighteenth century.

19. For these observations, see Gerbi 2010, 97–98.

20. For Vespucci's Venetian comparison, see Gerbi 2010, 37. Cortés, indeed, knew Venice well enough by reputation to set the provinces of Mexico in comparison with it—but the grounds of the comparison are political, not chorographic. Of Tlascalteca, he writes that "la orden que hasta ahora se ha alcanzado que la gente della tiene en gobernarse es casi como las señorías de Venecia y Génova o Pisa, porque no hay señor general de todos" (The public order that it has achieved at present that the people follow in governing themselves is almost like that of the principalities of Venice and Genoa or Pisa, since there is no general lord over all.) (Cortés 1994, 41).

21. On the *requerimiento* as an incantation creating Spanish subjects, see Greenblatt 1991, 97–98. On its use by Cortés, see Zavala 1981. For the glorifying effects of the completion of the Reconquista, see Elliott 2006, 45–48.

22. Clendinnen 1991b, 89ff.; Grafton 1992, 89. In much the same way, for instance, Cortés could use particularly European political terminology, for example, "vasallo," to make the same point (Clendinnen 1991b, 73). Some architectural examples: Cortés describes the houses of the natives of Yucatan as "pequeños y bajos, muy amoriscados" (small and short, much in the Moorish fashion); he adds that they have "mesquitas y adoratorios y sus andenes todo a la redonda muy ancho, y allí tienen sus ídolos que adoran" (mosques and chapels and their shape is round, very wide, and there they have their idols which they worship) (Cortés 1994, 21). Beginning his voyage inland toward Tenochtitlan, Cortes leaves "la ciudad de Cempoal, que yo intitulé Sevilla" (the city of Cempoal, which I called Seville) (32). Examples in this line could be multiplied. A more subtle, but perhaps more revealing instance: the Tlaxcaltecas wear "albornices," or burnouses, the customary cloak of Andalusian and North African Muslims (45). Stephen Greenblatt has aptly characterized this initial act of perception— a "taking possession" at the level of consciousness—as "the imagination at work" (Greenblatt 1991, 22). For some of the "literary" techniques by which explorers before Cortés remade the New World, see Grafton 1992, 75–85; and, for a broader account of the problem of "comprehension" that faced Europeans encountering the New World in the early sixteenth century, see Elliott 1970, 13–27. On the long tail of this debate in European science, see Gerbi 1973, passim, and esp. 28–29. Comparison as a mode of European description: Elliott 1970, 18–19; Greenblatt 1991, 7–8; Lockhart 1999, 81–97.

23. The relevant indigenous accounts of the *Noche Triste* are collected in León-Portilla 2007, 83–90. European misunderstandings of Islamic theology: Tolan 1999. On Cortés's

rewriting of Aztecs as Muslims, see Pagden's remarks in Cortés 2001, 62ff.; on the political and cultural resonance of Cortes's vocabulary for describing New World architecture, see Hamann 2008, 816–818.

24. Briones 1996, 199ff. *Siete Partidas* VII.xxv.1 ("pero en las villas de los Christianos no deben haber los Moros mezquita . . . et las mezquitas que habien antiguamente deber seer del rey, et puedelas el dar a quien quisiere.")

25. The *quinto real*: Elliott 2006, 169. Cortés's consistent concern with financial profit and loss in the *Cartas*: Gerbi 2010, 90ff.

26. Burning the suburbs of Tenochtitlan: e.g., del Castillo 2010, 57.3–4. As, for instance, only a few paragraphs before the passage just cited: "Por el real de la calzada, donde yo estaba, habíamos quemado con los bergantines muchas casas de los arrabales de la ciudad" (from the encampment on the highway, where I was, we had burnt with the brigantines many houses on the outskirts of the city) (Cortés 1994, 139). And Cortés's harried attempts to reduce some of Tenochtitlan's neighbors during his siege of the capital seem to have ended with those cities' complete destruction (132–135). Comparisons between Cortés and Alexander: e.g., del Castillo 2010, 69 and 124, where Alexander's mistreatment of his troops offers a *negative* precedent. After the fall of Tenochtitlan, the Alexander example switches valences: 164 and 206.

27. At Cortés 2001, 55, Pagden cites with approval the more extensive argument for this claim at Todorov 1984, 98–123.

28. Hamann 2002 outlines the cultural meaning of "ancient" objects for the Mexica, as well as providing a review of earlier bibliography on this topic. López Lúján 2014 offers an updated perspective, informed by recent excavations at the Templo Mayor complex in Mexico City.

29. For the relationship that the Mexica ideated between themselves and these ruined cities, see Nichols 2013. The philological remarks just offered on *toltecayotl* owe much to Léon-Portilla 2012, 79.

30. For an in-depth discussion of these "divine materials," see Bassett 2015, 90ff. Sahagun's informants discuss "smoking stones" on 406–407 of the *Florentine Codex*, bk. 11.

31. This account is based on that offered at Léon-Portilla 2012, 150–160; but see Kockelman 1997 for a note of caution on the role of postconquest Spanish filters in shaping the received narrative.

32. On Quetzalcoatl's tenure at Teotihuacan, see Graulich 1981, 47–48.

33. The aim of the rite seems to be to test whether "Quetzalcoatl"—that is, Cortés—has returned from the underworld after a long exile; Motenczoma recurs to a markedly "classical" cultural site in order, it would seem, to prevent the return of the past. On the structural relation "absent Quetzalcoatl" / "present (king of) Tenochtitlan," see Clendinnen 1991b, 27, and Wolf 1962, 122ff. Benjamin on ruins as a locus of the melancholy in Baroque tragedy: Benjamin 1998, 66–167.

34. Clendinnen 1991a, 78; for an illustration, see Conrad 1984, 54, fig. 9. On the importance of preconquest temples (and, postconquest, their erstwhile platforms) for civic identity, see Lockhart 1999, 105–112.

35. *Teocalli*: Karttunen 1992, s.v. God-objects in the Templo Mayor: Bassett 2015, 128–129. On Roman thinking about the local habitations of the gods, see Ando 2009, 120–148. On the place of temples within the Aztec sacred economy more generally, see Conrad 1984, 13–15; Wolf 1962, 69ff.

36. The paradox: see pp. 10–11.

37. For this important observation—which entirely overturns the thesis of Todorov 1984—see Clendinnen 1991a. By the end of the siege, the city's defenders "ya tenían tan pocas casas donde poder estar que el señor de la cibdad andaba metido en una canoa con ciertos prencipales, que no sabían qué hacer de sí" (Cortés 1994, 161); "had so few houses by then in

which they could be, that the ruler of the city went around in a canoe with certain chiefs, who had no idea what to do with themselves." But what the Spaniards had done was still nothing more, to the Aztecs, than "*quemar y destruir*" (155).

38. Compare del Castillo, *VH* 74: "Pues a nuestros amigos los tlaxcaltecas, si muchos vituperios nos decían a nosotros, más les decían a ellos; y que los tendrían por esclavos para sacrificar y hacer sus sementeras, y tornar a edificar sus casas que les habíamos derrocado, y que las habían de hacer de cal y canto labradas, y que su Uichilobos se lo había prometido."

39. Mundy 2015, 73–113.

40. In the end, Mexica and Tlaxcalans alike were forced to rebuild the ruined city. For a history of Spanish corvée levees in the New World context, see Owensby 2008, 12–20. The so-called New Laws, passed in the late 1540s, notionally transformed what had been a system of outright slavery to one that recruited native Mexicans for corvée labor; but it was a long time before these laws began to be effectively enforced, and, even then, autonomous Amerindian communities often had to fight at law against local Spanish or Creole overlords whose conceptions of corvée obligations ran toward servitude (141ff.). For an economic analysis of this transition, see Wolf 1962, 189ff.

41. Quoted in Gerbi 2010, 367; see also Gerbi's more extensive discussion of this phenomenon in Oviedo, in Gerbi 2010, 361–368.

42. For the allusion, see Beverly's commentary in Góngora 1980, *ad loc*. Camões's opening:

Era no tempo alegre, quando entrava
no roubador de Europa a luz febeia,
quando um e o outro corno lhe aquentava,
e Flora derramava o de Amalteia.   (*Lus*. 2.72, ll.1–4)

On the *Lusíadas* as a "victor's epic," see Quint 1993, 32ff.

43. Thus Marx: "Of course, the play is not literally set in America; although Shakespeare is nowhere explicit about the location of the 'uninhabited island,' so far as he allows us to guess it lies somewhere in the Mediterranean off the coast of Africa. For the dramatist's purpose it might be anywhere. Nevertheless, it is almost certain that Shakespeare had in mind the reports of a recent voyage to the New World" (1964, 34). It is perhaps of significance in this connection that *The Tempest* (1611) and *Soledad Primera* (1616) were close contemporaries. For the debate about where to locate the Soledades see, e.g., Beverley 1973, 233–248; Crawford 1939, 347–349; and Wardropper 1962, 178–181. Precisions of geography could add little to, and might take much away from, a poem whose main attraction lies, by its author's own account, in "speculating through the darkness of the work" (Góngora, *Epist*. 1.65–67, in Osuna Cabezas 2009). On this passage of the *Soledades*, see Góngora y Argote and Beverley 1980 ad loc., and for an unmistakable reference to Columbus, see *Soledad Primera*, 413ff. On the shipwreck literature of the Spanish Golden Age (of which Cabeza de Vaca's *Naufragios* is a well-known example), see Gerbi 2010, 246–247.

44. On the function of rhetoric in creating such "marvelous possessions," see Greenblatt 1991, 60–85. By the late sixteenth century, such rhetoric was losing its effect and producing what we might call an "enchantment gap." Compare the remarks of José de Acosta, writing not long before Góngora: "Knowledge of and speculation about natural things, especially if they are notable and strange, incites a natural pleasure and delight in refined minds, and information about foreign customs and history too, with its novelty, pleases." Acosta 1792, dedication. "The new world has already ceased to be new"; Acosta, *proemio*. On Spanish disappointment with the New World, see Clendinnen 1991a, 90ff.; Lockhart 1992, 124. Wolf (1962, 202ff.) treats this "disappointment" as resulting from the intrusion of the Spaniards into a Mesoamerican cycle of expansion and decline. On this narrative, the "peripheral" colonial possession would appear to have pulled the imperial masters into its own orbit.

45. *"Halago"* should be differentiated from *"lisonja,"* which unambiguously indicates interested flattery and translates the similarly unambiguous Lat. *adulatio* (see Nebrija's 1492 *Diccionario Latino-Español*, s.v. "adulatio"). For a closely parallel use of *halago* as a figure for climbing ivy, see Quevedo's sonnet "Esta yedra anudada que camina," l. 6. For the etymological equation between *"strages"* and *"estragos,"* see, e.g., Nebrija, s.v. "strages."

46. *Dialogo* III, p. 64: "Has de saber, sin embargo, otra cosa no menos digna de ser sabida, y es que había otros cerros mucho más altos que éste, hechos a mano, y de que aún existen algunos. Subiase por escalones de piedra hasta el remate, que era una placeta; y en ella, como reses en un rastro, sacrificaban y ofrecían a los idolos victimas humanas, sacándoles primero el corazón. Y ésto es notorio que no acostumbraban hacerlo solamente cada año, sino casi cada mes; en cuyo genero de sacrificio, cosa apenas creíble, perecieron innumerables hombres." For indigenous assimilation of pyramids to mountains, see Stone 1992. Remarkably, Salazar goes on a few pages later to cite Egyptian parallels for the Aztecs' hieroglyphic script (Cervantes de Salazar 1963, 66). His calling the Aztec temples *cerros* rather than *pyramides* thus needs to be regarded as a conscious choice. For the historical expansion of the place of human sacrifice in Aztec cult, and for some suggestions as to its scale at the turn of the sixteenth century, see Conrad 1984, 29–44 and Clendinnen 1991a, 90ff.

47. For a sense of de Pauw's theoretical aims and practices, see Pocock 2008, 176–180. The place of de Pauw in the development of conjectural history: Potofsky 2002. De Pauw's approach had much in common with the more fully developed "stadial" models of Scottish Enlightenment figures like Ferguson and Smith; the major difference between their positions was that de Pauw also maintained that the racial inferiority of America's natives was what had prevented them in the past, and what would prevent them in the future, from achieving a "civilized" level of progress. This line of thinking intersects with his rejection of American ruins in his long-winded and viciously racist dismissal of Inca Garcilaso de la Vega (Pauw 1772, 186–193).

48. For de Pauw's anti-American polemic and the powerful influence this would exercise on subsequent debates over the natural and political history of the New World, see Gerbi 1973, 80–85.

49. Stadial theory in enlightenment histories of the New World: Pocock 2008, 205–210, 284ff.

50. Raynal 1781, 367: "La region qui nous occupe [read: Mexico], offre-t-elle de ces magnifiques ruines? Il doit donc passer pour demontré que les édifices publics et particuliers, si orgueilleusement décrits, n'étoient que des amas informes de pierres entassées les unes sur les autres; que la célèbre Mexico n'étoit qu'une bourgade formée d'une multitude de cabanes rustiques repandues irregulièrement sur un grand éspace; et que les autres lieux, dont on a voulu exalter la grandeur ou la beauté, étoient encore inferieurs à cette première des cités."

51. The play: Sell and Burkhart 2012, 243–280. Other echoes of Tenochtitlan's destruction in Nahuatl theater: Lara 2004, 91–110.

52. Croesus's advice: Herod. *Hist.* 1.88.

53. On the importance of these developments for the emergence of "modern" cities, see Arnade 2013.

Epilogue

1. For this idea, see Geuss 2017, 292.

2. The place of urban ruination in total war: Hewitt 1987. For a comparative treatment of the three cities mentioned, see Shaw 2004.

3. The best summary account of spatial fixing is Harvey 2001, 21–26.

4. "Imperial Debris": Stoler 2008. Bikini Atoll: Stoler 2008, 203. Tasmanian ruins: Hughes 1988, 400.

5. Mundy 2015, 2–5.

6. Trigger 2006, 8off.

7. Volney 1791, 1–2: "Chaque jour, je trouvais sur ma route des champs abandonnés, des villages désertés, des villes en ruines. Souvent je rencontrais d'antiques monuments, des débris de temples, de palais et de forteresses; des colonnes, des aqueducs, des tombeaux: et ce spectacle tourna mon esprit vers la méditation des temps passés, et suscita dans mon coeur des pensées graves et profondes."

8. Thom 1995, 100–102.

9. Freud 1989, 17–19.

10. Jensen and Freud 1993.

11. Stoler 2008, 194.

12. Page 2008.

13. Hell and Schönle 2010, 186.

14. Ghosh 2017, 19–25.

15. Beauman 2013, 36off.

16. Scott 2017, 219–220.

17. Nicholls 2008.

18. Morton 2016, 22–23.

Abrams, Philip. *Historical Sociology*. Ithaca, NY: Cornell UP, 1982.

Abrams, Philip, and E. A. Wrigley. *Towns in Societies*. Cambridge: Cambridge UP, 1978.

Abu-Lughod, Janet L. *Before European Hegemony: The World System A.D., 1250–1350*. New York: Oxford UP, 1989.

Abū Yūsuf Yaʿqūb, and al-Kurashi Yahyā ibn Ādam. *Abū Yūsuf's Kitāb Al-Kharāj*. Translated by A. Ben Shemesh. Leiden: Brill, 1969.

Acosta, José de. *Historia natural y moral de las Indias: en que se tratan las cosas notables del cielo, elementos, metales, plantas y animales de ellas; y los ritos, ceremonias, leyes, gobierno y guerras de los Indios*. Madrid: P. Aznar, 1792.

Aeschylus. *Persae*. Edited by M. L. West. Stuttgart: Teubner, 1991.

———. *Septem quae Supersunt Trageodiae*. Edited by D. Page. Oxford: Clarendon P, 1957.

Agamben, Giorgio. *What Is an Apparatus? and Other Essays*. Meridian, Crossing Aesthetics. Stanford, CA: Stanford UP, 2009.

Ahmed, Shahab. *What Is Islam? The Importance of Being Islamic*. Princeton: Princeton UP, 2017.

Aitken, Ellen Bradshaw. *Between Magic and Religion: Interdisciplinary Studies in Ancient Mediterranean Religion and Society*. Lanham, MD: Rowman & Littlefield, 2001.

Al-Azmeh, A. *The Emergence of Islam in Late Antiquity*. Cambridge: Cambridge UP, 2014.

Al-Baladhuri, A. *Futuh al-Buldan*. Beirut: Dar al-Nashr lil-Jamiʾin, 1916.

Alcock, Susan E. *Graecia Capta: The Landscapes of Roman Greece*. Cambridge: Cambridge UP, 1993.

Alfoldi, A. "On the Foundation of Constantinople: A Few Notes." *Journal of Roman Studies* 37 (1947): 10–16.

Al-Jallad, A. "Marginal Notes on: ASWS 73—the root HGR in pre-Islamic Arabic." http://aljallad.nl/marginal-notes-on-asws-73-the-root-hgr-in-pre-islamic-arabic/, accessed 11/22/2017.

Al-Khaṭīb al-Baghdādī. *Tarikh Baghdad*. Beirut: Dar al-Kitab al-ʿArabi, 1966.

Allen, Danielle S. "Changing the Authoritative Voice: Lycurgus's "Against Leocrates." *Classical Antiquity* 19, no. 1 (2000): 5–33.

Allison, June W. *Power and Preparedness in Thucydides*. Baltimore: Johns Hopkins UP, 1989.

———. " 'Axiosis,' the New Arete: A Periclean Metaphor for Friendship." *Classical Quarterly* 51, no. 1, new ser. (2001): 53–64.

Al-Maqrizi. *Kitab al-khitat*. Cairo: Maktabat Ihya al-ʿUlum, 1959.

Al-Muqaddasī, S. "Ahsan ut-Taqasim fi Maʾrifat ul-Aqalim." *Bibliotheca Geographorum Arabicorum*. Edited by M. J. de Geoje. Leiden: Brill, 1906.

Al-Qāḍī al-Quḍāʾi. *A Treasury of Virtues.* Translated by Tahera Qutbuddin. New York: New York UP, 2013.

AlSayyad, Nezar. *Cities and Caliphs: On the Genesis of Arab Muslim Urbanism.* Contributions to the Study of World History, no. 26. New York: Greenwood, 1991.

Al-Tabarī. *Tārīkh al-Ṭabarī: tārīkh al-rusul wa-al-mulūk,* vol 1. Cairo: Dar al-Maʿarif, 1960.

———. *The History of Al-Tabari.* Vol. 21, *The Victory of the Marwanids, A.D. 685–693/A.H. 66–73,* translated by M. Fishbein. Albany: State U of New York P, 1990a.

———. *The History of Al-Tabari.* Vol. 39, translated by H. Kennedy. Albany: State U of New York P, 1990b.

Al-Thaʿlabi, A. *Qisas al-Anbiyaʾ.* Cairo, 1954.

Alston, R. "Seeing Caesar in Ruins: Toward a Radical Aesthetic of Ruins." *European Review of History* 18, no. 5–6 (2012): 697–716.

Amemiya, Takeshi. *Economy and Economics of Ancient Greece.* Routledge Explorations in Economic History 33. London: Routledge, 2007.

Amory, Patrick. *People and Identity in Ostrogothic Italy, 489–554.* Cambridge: Cambridge UP, 1997.

Anderson, Benedict. *Imagined Communities: Reflections on the Origin and Spread of Nationalism.* New York: Random House, 1983.

Anderson, Perry. *Passages from Antiquity to Feudalism.* London: NLB, 1974.

Ando, Clifford. "Decline, Fall, and Transformation." *Journal of Late Antiquity* 1, no. 1 (2008): 31–60.

Anghiera, Pietro Martire dʾ. *De rebus oceanicis et novo orbe decades III.* Cologne: apud Geruinum Calenium, 1574.

Arafat, K. W. *Pausanias' Greece: Ancient Artists and Roman Rulers.* Cambridge: Cambridge UP, 1996.

Arberry, A. *Arabic Poetry: A Primer for Students.* Cambridge: Cambridge UP, 1965.

Aristotle. *Atheniensium Respublica.* Edited by F. G. Kenyon. Oxford: Oxford UP, 1920.

———. *Politica.* Edited by W. D. Rose. Oxford: Oxford UP, 1957.

Arnade, P. "Carthage or Jerusalem? Princely Violence and the Spatial Transformation of the Medieval into the Early Modern City." *Journal of Urban History* 39, no.4 (2013): 726–748.

Ashmole, B. "Cyriac of Ancona and the Temple of Hadrian at Cyzicus." *Journal of the Warburg and Courtauld Institutes* 19, nos. 3/4 (1956): 179–191.

Aston, Margaret. "English Ruins and English History: The Dissolution and the Sense of the Past." *Journal of the Warburg and Courtauld Institutes* 36, no. 1 (1973): 231–255.

Attridge, H. "The Messiah and the Millennium: The Roots of Two Jewish-Christian Symbols." In *Imagining the End: Visions of Apocalypse from the Ancient Middle East to Modern America,* ed. Abbas Amanat and Magnus t. Bernhardsson, 90–105. London: I. B. Tauris, 2002.

Augustine. *De Civitate Dei Libri XXII.* Vol. 1, edited by B. Dombart. Leipzig: Teubner, 1877.

Bachvarova, Mary R., Dorota Dutsch, and Ann Suter, eds. *The Fall of Cities in the Mediterranean: Commemoration in Literature, Folk-Song, and Liturgy.* Cambridge: Cambridge UP, 2016.

Badian, Ernst. "Agis III: Revisions and Reflections." In Worthington, *Ventures into Greek History,* 258–292.

Badiou, Alain. *Being and Event.* London: Continuum, 2005.

Bakker, Egbert J. "The Making of History." In Bakker, de Jong, and van Wees, *Brill's Companion to Herodotus,* 1–32.

Bakker, Egbert J., Irene J. F. de Jong, and Hans van Wees, eds. *Brill's Companion to Herodotus.* Leiden: Brill, 2002.

Baragwanath, Emily. *Motivation and Narrative in Herodotus.* Oxford: Oxford UP, 2008.

Barkan, Leonard. *Unearthing the Past: Archaeology and Aesthetics in the Making of Renaissance Culture.* New Haven, CT: Yale UP, 1999.

Barker, Elton. "Paging the Oracle: Interpretation, Identity, and Performance in Herodorus' History." *Greece & Rome* 53, no.1 (2006): 1–28.

Barnwell, P. S. *Emperor, Prefects, and Kings: The Roman West, 395–565.* London: Duckworth, 1992.

Baron, Hans. *The Crisis of the Early Italian Renaissance: Civic Humanism and Republican Liberty in an Age of Classicism and Tyranny.* Rev. ed. Princeton, NJ: Princeton UP, 1966.

Barthes, Roland. *A Lover's Discourse: Fragments.* New York: Hill & Wang, 1978.

Bassett, M. H. *The Fate of Earthly Things: Aztec Gods and God-Bodies.* Austin: U of Texas P, 2015.

Beard, Mary. *The Roman Triumph.* Cambridge, MA: Harvard UP, 2007.

———. *The Fires of Vesuvius.* Cambridge, MA: Harvard UP, 2010.

———. *The Parthenon.* Wonders of the World. Rev. ed. Cambridge, MA: Harvard UP, 2010.

Beard, Mary, John North, and Simon Price. *Religions of Rome.* Vol. 1. Cambridge: Cambridge UP, 1998.

Beauman, N. *The Teleportation Accident.* London: Bloomsbury, 2013.

Beeston, Alfred, Felix Landon, Mahmud Ali Ghul, Walter W. Müller, and Jacques Ryckmans. *Sabaic Dictionary: English-French-Arabic.* Leiden: Peeters, 1982.

Benjamin, Walter. *The Origin of German Tragic Drama.* Translated by John Osborne. Reprint, London: Verso, 1998.

Benson, C. "The Dead and the Living: Some Descriptions of the Ruins and Relics of Rome Known to the English." In *Urban Space in the Middle Ages and the Early Modern Age,* ed. Albrecht Classen, 147–182. Berlin: De Gruyter, 2009.

Beverley, John R. "Soledad Primera, Lines 1–61." *MLN* 88, no. 2 (1973): 233–248.

Bier, L. "The Sasanian Palaces and Their Influence in Early Islam." *Ars Orientalis* 23 (1993): 57–66.

Bisaha, Nancy. *Creating East and West: Renaissance Humanists and the Ottoman Turks.* Philadelphia: U of Pennsylvania P, 2004.

Bjornlie, M. Shane. "What Have Elephants to Do with Sixth-Century Politics?" *Journal of Late Antiquity* 2, no.1 (2009): 143–172.

———. *Politics and Tradition between Rome, Ravenna and Constantinople: A Study of Cassiodorus and the* Variae. Cambridge: Cambridge UP, 2013.

Blanks, David R., and Michael Frassetto, eds. *Western Views of Islam in Medieval and Early Modern Europe.* New York: Palgrave Macmillan, 1999.

Bloch, Marc Léopold Benjamin. *Land and Work in Mediaeval Europe: Selected Papers.* Harper Torchbooks. New York: Harper & Row, 1969.

Bloedow, E. "Why Did Philip and Alexander Launch a War against the Persian Empire?" *Antiquité Classique* 72 (2003): 261–274.

Bloedow, E., and H. Loube. "Alexander the Great 'Under Fire' at Persepolis." *Klio* 79, no. 2 (1997): 341–353.

Bloom, Jonathan, and Sheila Blair. *Islamic Arts.* London: Phaidon, 1997.

Boardman, John. *The Greeks Overseas.* Pelican Books. Baltimore: Penguin Books, 1964.

Boardman, John, Jasper Griffin, and Oswyn Murray, eds. *The Oxford History of Greece and the Hellenistic World.* Oxford: Oxford UP, 1986.

Bodel, John, and Saul M. Olyan, eds. *Household and Family Religion in Antiquity.* Ancient World Comparative Histories. Malden, MA: Blackwell, 2008.

Boersma, Johannes Sipko. *Athenian Building Policy from 561/0 to 405/4 B.C.* Scripta Archaeologica Groningana. Vol. 4. Groningen: Wolters-Noordhoff, 1970.

Borza, E. "Fire from Heaven." *Classical Philology* 67, no. 4 (1972): 233–245.

Bosworth, A. B. *Alexander and the East: The Tragedy of Triumph.* Oxford: Clarendon P, 1996.

Bowersock, G. W. *Roman Arabia.* Cambridge, MA: Harvard UP, 1983.

——. "The Vanishing Paradigm of the Fall of Rome." Bulletin of the American Academy of Arts and Sciences 49.8 (1996): 29–43.

——. *The Crucible of Islam.* Cambridge, MA: Harvard UP, 2017.

——. *Empires in Collision in Late Antiquity.* Waltham, MA: Brandeis UP, 2002.

Bowes, Kimberly Diane. *Private Worship, Public Values, and Religious Change in Late Antiquity.* Cambridge: Cambridge UP, 2008.

Boym, Svetlana. *The Future of Nostalgia.* New York: Basic Books, 2001.

Brandolini, Aurelio Lippo. *Republics and Kingdoms Compared.* Edited and translated by James Hankins. Cambridge, MA: Harvard UP, 2009.

Braudel, Fernand. *The Mediterranean and the Mediterranean World in the Age of Philip II.* New York: Harper & Row, 1972.

Brenk, Beat. "Spolia from Constantine to Charlemagne: Aesthetics versus Ideology." *Dumbarton Oaks Papers* 41 (1987): 103–109.

Briones, Antonio Luis Ampliato. *Muro, orden y espacio en la arquitectura del renacimiento andaluz: Teoría y práctica en la obra de Diego Siloe, Andrés De Vandelvira y Hernán Ruiz II.* Seville: Consejería de Obras Públicas y Transportes, 1996.

Brothers, Cammy. "The Renaissance Reception of the Alhambra: The Letters of Andrea Navagero and the Palace of Charles V." *Muqarnas XI: An Annual on Islamic Art and Architecture* 11 (1994): 79–102.

Brown, Peter Robert Lamont. *The World of Late Antiquity, AD 150–750.* History of European Civilization Library. New York: Harcourt Brace Jovanovich, 1971.

——. *Religion and Society in the Age of Saint Augustine.* London: Faber & Faber, 1972.

——. *The Making of Late Antiquity.* The Carl Newell Jackson Lectures, 1976. Cambridge, MA: Harvard UP, 1978.

——. *The Cult of the Saints: Its Rise and Function in Latin Christianity.* Haskell Lectures on History of Religions, new ser., no. 2. Chicago: U of Chicago P, 1981.

——. *Through the Eye of a Needle.* Princeton: Princeton UP, 2012.

Brown, Truesdell Sparhawk. *Gentlemen and Officers: Imperial Administration and Aristocratic Power in Byzantine Italy, AD 554–800.* Rome: British School at Rome, 1984.

Bruni, Leonardo. *History of the Florentine People.* Vol. 1, edited and translated by James Hankins. Cambridge, MA: Harvard UP, 2001.

Buondelmonti, Cristoforo de', and Charles Du Fresne Du Cange (sieur). *Christoph.Bondelmontii, Florentini, Librum insularum archipelagi.* Apud G. Reimer, 1824.

Burckhardt, Jacob. *The Civilization of the Renaissance in Italy: An Essay.* The Modern Library of the World's Best Books 32. New York: Modern Library, 1954.

Burke, Edmund M. "The Economy of Athens in the Classical Era: Some Adjustments to the Primitivist Model." *Transactions of the American Philological Association (1974–)* 122 (1992): 199–226.

Calpurnius Siculus. *The Eclogues.* Edited by C. H. Keene. London: Bristol Classical Press, 1996.

Cameron, Alan. "Rutilius Namatianus, St. Augustine, and the Date of the *De Reditu*." *Journal of Roman Studies* 57, no. 1/2 (1967): 31–39.

——. *The Last Pagans of Rome.* New York: Oxford UP, 2010.

Camões. *Lusíadas.* Edited by M. de Faria e Sousa. Lisbon: Imprensa Nacional, 1972.

Caner, Daniel. *Wandering, Begging Monks: Spiritual Authority and the Promotion of Monasticism in Late Antiquity.* The Transformation of the Classical Heritage 33. Berkeley: U of California P, 2002.

Carlsson, Susanne. *Hellenistic Democracies: Freedom, Independence and Political Procedure in*

Some East Greek City-States. Historia-Einzelschriften. Vol. 206. Stuttgart: Franz Steiner Verlag, 2010.

Cartledge, Paul. "Rebels and Sambos in Classical Greece: A Comparative View." *History of Political Thought* 6, no.1/2 (1985): 16–46.

———. *Sparta and Lakonia: A Regional History, 1300–362 BC*. 2nd ed. London: Routledge, 2002.

———. *After Thermopylae: The Oath of Plataea and the End of the Graeco-Persian Wars*. Oxford: Oxford UP, 2013.

Cartledge, Paul, Paul Millett, and Stephen Todd, eds. *Nomos: Essays in Athenian Law, Politics, and Society*. Cambridge: Cambridge UP, 1990.

Carver, M. O. H. *Arguments in Stone: Archaeological Research and the European Town in the First Millennium*. Oxford: Oxbow Books, 1993.

Casas, Bartolomé de las, and André Saint-Lu. *Brevísima relación de la destruición[sic] de las Indias*. Bogota: C. J. M. Rios, 1813.

Cassiodorus. *Cassiodorus Senatoris Variae*. Edited by T. Mommsen. Berlin: Weidman, 1894.

Casson, Lionel. *Travel in the Ancient World*. Baltimore: Johns Hopkins UP, 1994.

Castillo, Bernal Díaz Del, and Henry R. Wagner. "Notes on Writings by and about Bernal Díaz Del Castillo." *Hispanic American Historical Review* 25, no. 2 (1945):199–211.

Cervantes de Salazar, Francisco. *México en 1554, y Túmulo imperial*. Colección "Sepan Cuantos . . . ," no. 25. México: Editorial Porrúa, 1963.

Chamoux, François. *Hellenistic Civilization*. Malden, MA: Blackwell, 2001.

Charles-Edwards, T. "Law in the Western Kingdoms between the Fifth and the Seventh Century." In *CAH²*, vol. 14. Cambridge: Cambridge UP, 2001

Christ, M. R. "Theopompus and Herodotus: A Reassessment." *Classical Quarterly* 43, no. 1, new ser. (1993): 47–52.

———. *The Bad Citizen in Classical Athens*. Cambridge: Cambridge UP, 2006.

Clarke, Jacqueline. "The Struggle for Control of the Landscape in Book 1 of Rutilius Namatianus." *Arethusa* 47, no.1 (2014): 89–107.

Classen, Albrecht, ed. *Urban Space in the Middle Ages and the Early Modern Age*. Vol. 4. Berlin: De Gruyter, 2009.

Clastres, P. *Society against the State: Essays in Political Anthropology*. Translated by R. Hurley. New York: Zone, 1989.

Clendinnen, Inga. *Ambivalent Conquests: Maya and Spaniard in Yucatan, 1517–1570*. Cambridge Latin American Studies 61. Cambridge: Cambridge UP, 1987a.

———. *Ambivalent Conquests; Maya and Spaniard in Yucatan, 1517–1570*. Cambridge: Cambridge UP, 1987b.

———. *Aztecs: An Interpretation*. Cambridge: Cambridge UP, 1991a.

———. "'Fierce and Unnatural Cruelty': Cortés and the Conquest of Mexico." *Representations*, no. 33 (1991b): 65–100.

Cochrane, Charles Norris. *Christianity and Classical Culture: A Study of Thought and Action from Augustus to Augustine*. London: Oxford UP, 1957.

———. *Thucydides and the Science of History*. New York: Russell & Russell, 1965.

Cole, Spencer. "The Dynamics of Deification in Horace's Odes 1–3." In Aitken, *Between Magic and Religion*, 67–91.

Collins, R. "The Western Kingdoms." In *CAH²*, vol. 14, 112–134. Cambridge: Cambridge UP, 2001.

Connell, William F. *After Moctezuma: Indigenous Politics and Self-Government in Mexico City, 1524–1730*. Norman: U of Oklahoma P, 2011.

Connely, J. *The Parthenon Enigma*. New York: Knopf, 2014.

Conrad, Geoffrey W. *Religion and Empire: The Dynamics of Aztec and Inca Expansionism*. New Studies in Archaeology. Cambridge: Cambridge UP, 1984.

Conte, Gian Biagio. *Latin Literature: A History*. Baltimore: Johns Hopkins UP, 1994.

Cook, J. M. *The Persian Empire*. London: J. M. Dent, 1983.

Cook, R. "Amasis and the Greeks in Egypt," *Journal of Hellenic Studies* 57, no. 2 (1937): 227–237.

———. "Thucydides as Archaeologist." *Annual of the British School at Athens* 50 (1955): 266–270.

Cornell, T. C. "The City of Rome in the Middle Republic (c. 400–100 BC)." In Coulston and Dodge, *Ancient Rome*, 42–60.

Cornelius Nepos. *Cornelii Nepotis quae Exstant*. Edited by H. Malcovati. Turin: Paravia, 1944.

Cornford, Francis Macdonald. *Thucydides Mythistoricus*. London: E. Arnold, 1907.

Cortés, Hernán. *Cartas De Relacíon*. Edited by M. Alcala. Mexico, D.F.: Editorial Porruas, 1994.

———. *Letters from Mexico*. New Haven, CT : Yale Nota Bene, 2001.

Cosenza, M. E. *Francesco Petrarca and the Revolution of Cola di Rienzo*. Chicago: U of Chicago P, 1913.

Costello, V. F. *Urbanization in the Middle East*. Cambridge: Cambridge UP, 1977.

Coster, Charles Henry. "Christianity and the Invasions: Two Sketches." *Classical Journal* 54, no. 4 (1959): 146–159.

Coulston, Jon, and Hazel Dodge, eds., *Ancient Rome: The Archaeology of the Eternal City*, 42–60. Barnsley, UK: Oxbow Books, 2000.

Courcelle, Pierre. *Histoire littéraire des grandes invasions Germaniques*. Paris: Hachette, 1948.

Courtney, E. *Commentary on the Satires of Juvenal*. London: Athlone Press, 1980.

Crane, Gregory. *The Blinded Eye: Thucydides and the New Written Word*. Greek Studies: Interdisciplinary Approaches. Lanham, MD: Rowman & Littlefield, 1996.

———. "The Case of Plataea." In *War and Democracy*, ed. C. McCann and B. Strauss, 127–160. New York: Sharpe, 2001.

Crawford, J. P. Wickersham. "The Setting of Góngora's Las Soledades." *Hispanic Review* 7, no. 4 (1939): 347–349.

Crone, Patricia. "The Tribe and the State." In Mann and Hall, *States in History*, 446–478.

———. *Meccan Trade and the Rise of Islam*. Princeton: Princeton UP, 1987.

———. "The First-Century Concept of 'Hiǧra.'" *Arabica* (1994): 352–387.

———. *God's Rule: Government and Islam*. New York: Columbia UP, 2004.

———. *Pre-Industrial Societies: Anatomy of the Pre-Modern World*. London: OneWorld, 2014a.

———. *The Nativist Prophets of Early Islamic Iran: Rural Revolt and Local Zoroastrianism*. Cambridge: Cambridge UP, 2014b.

Crone, Patricia, and Michael Cook. *Hagarism: The Making of the Islamic World*. Cambridge: Cambridge UP Archive, 1977.

Culican, William. *The Medes and Persians*. Ancient Peoples and Places. Vol. 42. New York: Praeger, 1965.

Dalby, Andrew. *Empire of Pleasures: Luxury and Indulgence in the Roman World*. London: Routledge, 2000.

Davis, Mike. *Dead Cities and Other Tales*. New York: New Press, 2003.

———. *City of Quartz: Excavating the Future in Los Angeles*. London: Verso, 2006.

De Jong, I. "Narratological Aspects of the Histories of Herodotus." In *Herodotus: Volume 1: Herodotus and the Narrative of the Past*, ed. Rosaria Vignolo Munson, 251–290. Oxford: Oxford UP, 2013.

Del Castillo, Bernal Díaz. *Historia verdadera de la conquista de la Nueva España*. Vol. 2. Cambridge: Cambridge UP, 2010.

Deleuze, Gilles. *The Fold: Leibniz and the Baroque*. Minneapolis: U of Minnesota P, 1993.

De Ligt, Luuk, and Laurens E. Tacoma. *Migration and Mobility in the Early Roman Empire*. Leiden: Brill, 2016.

De Ste. Croix, G. E. M. *The Class Struggle in the Ancient Greek World: From the Archaic Age to the Arab Conquests.* London: Duckworth, 1981.

Devecka, Martin. "White Elephant Gifts: Classicism in Ostrogothic Policy and in *Variae* 10.30." *Journal of Late Antiquity* 9, no. 1 (2016): 195–217.

Dey, Hendrik. *The Afterlife of the Roman City.* Cambridge: Cambridge UP, 2015.

Diamond, Jared. *Collapse: How Societies Choose to Fail or Succeed.* New York: Penguin, 2008.

Dill, Samuel. *Roman Society in the Last Century of the Western Empire.* London: Macmillan, 1898.

Dinsmoor, William Bell. "The Date of the Older Parthenon." *American Journal of Archaeology* 38, no. 3 (1934): 408–448.

Djaït, H. 1986. *Al-Kūfa, Naissance de la ville Islamique.* Paris, Maisonneuve et Larose, 1986.

Donner, F. *The Early Islamic Conquests.* Princeton, NJ: Princeton UP, 1981.

———. *Narratives of Islamic Origins: The Beginnings of Islamic Historical Writing.* Vol. 14. Westerham, UK: Darwin P, 1998.

Dougherty, Carol. "It's Murder to Found a Colony." In Kurke and Dougherty, *Cultural Poetics in Archaic Greece,* 178–198.

Dover, Kenneth James. *Greek Popular Morality in the Time of Plato and Aristotle.* Oxford: Blackwell, 1974.

duBois, P. *Slaves and Other Objects.* Chicago: U of Chicago P, 2008.

Dufourcq, F. "Rutilius Namatianus contre Saint Augustin." *Revue d'Histoire* 10 (1905): 488–492.

Dundes, A. *Fables of the Ancients? Folklore in the Qur'an.* Lanham, MD: Rowman & Littlefield, 2003.

Easterling, P. E. *The Cambridge Companion to Greek Tragedy.* Cambridge: Cambridge UP, 1997.

Ecker, Heather L. "The Conversion of Mosques to Synagogues in Seville: The Case of the Mezquita De La Judería." *Gesta* 36, no. 2 (1997): 190–207.

———. "The Great Mosque of Córdoba in the Twelfth and Thirteenth Centuries." *Muqarnas* 20 (2003): 113–141.

Edgell, H. "The Myth of the 'Lost City of the Arabian Sands.'" *Proceedings of the Seminar for Arabian Studies* 34 (2004): 105–120.

Edwards, C. "Imagining Ruins in Ancient Rome." *European Review of History* 18, no. 5–6 (2012): 645–661.

Eidinow, Esther. *Oracles, Curses, and Risk among the Ancient Greeks.* Oxford: Oxford UP, 2007.

Eisenstadt, S. N. *The Political Systems of Empires.* London: Free Press of Glencoe, 1963.

El-Ali, Saleh Ahmad. *Al-Madā'in and Its Surrounding Area in Arabic Literary Sources.* Turin: Giappichelli, 1968.

Elliott, John H. *Imperial Spain: 1469–1716.* 2nd ed. New York: Penguin Books, 1963.

———. *The Old World and the New, 1492–1650.* The Wiles Lectures, 1969. Cambridge: Cambridge UP, 1970.

———. *The Revolt of the Catalans.* Cambridge: Cambridge UP, 1984.

———. *Spain and Its World, 1500–1700: Selected Essays.* New Haven, CT: Yale UP, 1989.

———. "A Europe of Composite Monarchies." *Past & Present* 137 (1992): 48–71.

———. *Empires of the Atlantic World: Britain and Spain in America, 1492–1830.* New Haven, CT: Yale UP, 2006.

Ellis, Linda, and Frank L. Kidner, eds. *Travel, Communication and Geography in Late Antiquity: Sacred and Profane.* Aldershot, UK: Ashgate, 2004.

Elson, C., and P. Covey, eds. *Intermediate Elites in Pre-Columbian States and Empires.* Tucson: U of Arizona P, 2006.

Empson, William. *Some Versions of Pastoral*. A New Directions Paperbook 92. New York: New Directions, 1974.

Ernout, Alfred, and Antoine Meillet. "Dictionnaire étymologique de la langue latine: Histoire des mots." Paris: Klinsieck, 1951.

Euripides. Euripidis *Fabulae*. Vol. 2, edited by J. Diggle. Oxford: Oxford UP, 1981.

——. *Electra*. Classical Texts. Warminster, UK: Aris & Phillips, 1988.

——. *Helen*. Edited by W. Allen. Cambridge: Cambridge UP, 2008.

Evans, J. A. S. "The Oracle of the 'Wooden Wall.'" *Classical Journal* 78, no. 1 (1982): 24–29.

Fauvinet-Ranson, Valerie. "Les valeurs ideologiques de la parure monumentale des cites en Italie chez Cassiodore." In *Ideologie et valeurs civiques dans le monde romain*, ed. H. Inglebert, 231–240. Paris: Picard, 2002.

——. *"Decor civitatis, decor Italiae": Monuments, traveaux publics et spectacles au VIe siècle d'après les 'Variae' de Cassiodore*. Bari: Edipuglia, 2006.

Feeney, Denis C. "The Reconciliations of Juno." *Classical Quarterly* 34, no.1 (1984): 179–194.

Fentress, Elizabeth. *Cosa V: An Intermittent Town, Excavations, 1991–1997*. Ann Arbor: U of Michigan P, 2003.

Ferrari, G. "The Ancient Temple on the Acropolis at Athens." *American Journal of Archaeology* 106, no. 1 (2002): 11–35.

Ferrari, M. "Spigolature Bobiesi." *Italia Medioevale e Umanistica* 16 (1973): 1–14.

Findlen, Paula. "Possessing the Past: The Material World of the Italian Renaissance." *American Historical Review* 103, no. 1 (1998): 83–114.

Finkel, Caroline. *Osman's Dream: The History of the Ottoman Empire*. New York: Basic Books, 2006.

Finley, M. *The World of Odysseus*. New York: Random House, 1954.

——. *Aspects of Antiquity; Discoveries and Controversies*. New York: Viking Press, 1968.

——. *The Ancient Economy*. Berkeley: U of California P, 1973.

Flannery, Kent. *The Creation of Inequality: How Our Prehistoric Ancestors Set the Stage for Monarchy, Slavery, and Empire*. Cambridge, MA: Harvard UP, 2012.

Flannery, Kent, and Joyce Marcus. *The Creation of Inequality: How Our Prehistoric Ancestors Set the Stage for Monarchy, Slavery, and Empire*. Cambridge, MA: Harvard UP, 2012.

Flavio, Biondo. *Italy Illuminated*. Vol. 1, edited and translated by Jeffrey A. White. Cambridge, MA: Harvard UP, 2005.

Flower, Harriet I. *Roman Republics*. Princeton NJ: Princeton UP, 2010.

Fo, Alessandro. "Ritorno a Claudio Rutilio Namaziano." *Materiali e discussioni per l'analisi dei testi classici* 22 (1989): 49–74.

Foster, E. *Thucydides, Pericles, and Periclean Imperialism*. Cambridge: Cambridge UP, 2010.

Foucault, Michel. *The Order of Things: An Archaeology of the Human Sciences*. New York: Vintage Books, 1973.

——. *The Archaeology of Knowledge*. Translated by A. M. Sheridan Smith. New York: Routledge, 2005.

Fowden, G. *The Egyptian Hermes: A Historical Approach to the Late Pagan Mind*. Princeton, NJ: Princeton UP, 1993.

——. *Before and after Muhammad: The First Millennium Refocused*. Princeton: Princeton, NJ: PrincetonUP, 2013.

Frangeskou, Vassiliki. "Tradition and Originality in Some Attic Funeral Orations." *Classical World* (1999): 315–336.

Freud, Sigmund. *The Basic Writings of Sigmund Freud*. Translated by A. A. Brill. New York: Modern Library, 1938.

——. *Civilization and Its Discontents*. New York: Norton, 1989.

Gaertner, Jan Felix. "Livy's Camillus and the Political Discourse of the Late Republic." *Journal of Roman Studies* 98 (2008): 27–52.

Galinsky, K., ed. *Memoria Romana*. Ann Arbor: U of Michigan P, 2014.

Galtung, Johan, Tore Heiestad, and Erik Rudeng. "On the Decline and Fall of Empires: The Roman Empire and Western Imperialism Compared." *Review (Fernand Braudel Center)* 4, no. 1 (1980): 91–153.

Gebhardt, E., and M. Dickle "The View from the Isthmus, BC. 200–44." *Corinth* 20 (2003): 261–278.

Geertz, Clifford. *The Interpretation of Cultures*. New York: Basic Books, 1973.

Gerbi, Antonello. *The Dispute of the New World: The History of a Polemic, 1750–1900*. Rev. ed. Pittsburgh: U of Pittsburgh P, 1973.

———. *Nature in the New World: From Christopher Columbus to Gonzalo Fernández de Oviedo*. Translated by Jeremy Moyle. Pittsburgh: U of Pittsburgh P, 2010.

Geuss, R. *Changing the Subject*. Cambridge, MA: Harvard UP, 2017.

Ghosh, A. *The Great Derangement*. Chicago: U of Chicago P, 2017.

Giardina, A. *Cassiodoro politico*. Rome: L'Erma di Bretschneider, 2006.

Gibb, H. "Pre-Islamic Monotheism in Arabia." *Harvard Theological Review* 55.4 (1962): 269–280.

Gibbon, Edward. *Memoires of Edward Gibbon, Written by Himself*. London: Routledge & Sons, 1891.

Gilhus, I. *Animals, Gods, and Humans: Changing Attitudes to Animals in Greek, Roman, and Early Christian Ideas*. London: Routledge, 2006.

Ginsberg, Robert. *Aesthetics of Ruins*. Amsterdam: Rodopi B.V., 2004.

Godelier, Maurice. *Rationality and Irrationality in Economics*. New York: Monthly Review Press, 1973.

———. *The Mental and the Material: Thought, Economy and Society*. London: Verso, 2011.

Goffart, Walter. "Zosimus, the First Historian of Rome's Fall." *American Historical Review* 76, no. 2 (1971): 412–441.

———. *Rome's Fall and After*. Hambledon, UK: Continuum, 2003.

———. "Salvian of Marseille, *De gubernatione dei* 5.38–45 and the 'Colonate' Problem." *Antiquité Tardive* 17 (2009): 269–288.

Goguey, D. *Les animaux dans la mentalité Romaine*. Brussels: Latomus. 2003.

Goitein, S. D. "Cairo: An Islamic City in Light of the Geniza Documents." In Lapidus, *Middle Eastern Cities*, 80–97.

Goldhill, S. "The Great Dionysia and Civic Ideology." *Journal of Hellenic Studies* 107 (1987): 58–76.

Gomme, A. W. *A Historical Commentary on Thucydides*. Oxford: Clarendon P, 1945.

Góngora y Argote, Luis de. *Soledades*. Edited by John Beverley. Madrid: Ediciones Cátedra, 1980.

Gowers, Emily. "Trees and Family Trees in the *Aeneid*." *Classical Antiquity* 30, no. 1 (2011): 87–118.

Gowing, Alain M. *Empire and Memory: The Representation of the Roman Republic in Imperial Culture*. Cambridge: Cambridge UP, 2005.

Grabar, O. *The Formation of Islamic Art: Revised and Enlarged Edition*. New Haven, CT: Yale UP, 1987.

———. *Islamic Art and Beyond*. Burlington, VT: Aldershot, 2006.

Grafton, Anthony. *New Worlds, Ancient Texts: The Power of Tradition and the Shock of Discovery*. Cambridge, MA: Harvard UP, 1992.

———. *What Was History? The Art of History in Early Modern Europe*. Cambridge: Cambridge UP, 2007.

Graulich, M. "The Metaphor of the Day in Ancient Mexican Myth and Ritual." *Current Anthropology* 22.1 (1981): 45–60.

Greenblatt, Stephen. *Marvelous Possessions: The Wonder of the New World.* Chicago: U of Chicago P, 1991.

Greenblatt, Stephen, and Giles Gunn, eds. *Redrawing the Boundaries: The Transformation of English and American Literary studies.* New York: Modern Language Association of America, 1992.

Greene, Molly. *A Shared World: Christians and Muslims in the Early Modern Mediterranean.* Princeton, NJ: Princeton UP, 2000.

———. *Catholic Pirates and Greek Merchants.* Princeton, NJ: Princeton UP, 2010.

Greenwood, Emily. *Thucydides and the Shaping of History.* Classical Literature and Society. London: Duckworth, 2006.

Griffin, Jasper. "The Social Function of Attic Tragedy." *Classical Quarterly* 48, no. 1, new ser. (1998): 39–61.

Griffith, Mark. "Brilliant Dynasts: Power and Politics in the 'Oresteia.'" *Classical Antiquity* 14, no. 1 (1995): 62–129.

Gruen, Erich S. *Culture and National Identity in Republican Rome.* Ithaca, NY: Cornell UP, 1992.

———. *Diaspora: Jews amidst Greeks and Romans.* Cambridge, MA: Harvard UP, 2004.

Guevara, Antonio de. *Marco aurelio con el Relox de principes.* Madrid: por Juan Cromberger, 1537.

Gutas, D. *Greek Thought, Arabic Culture: The Graeco-Arabic Translation Movement in Baghdad and Early 'Abbasid Society.* London; Routledge, 1998.

Habicht, Christian. *Athens from Alexander to Antony.* Cambridge, MA: Harvard UP, 1997.

Hacking, Ian. *The Social Construction of What?* Cambridge, MA: Harvard UP, 2000.

Haenel, G., and J. Sirmond, eds. *Novellae constitutiones imperatorum Theodosii II, Valentiniani III, Maximi, Maiorani, Severi, Anthemii.* Bonn: Adolphus Marcus Verlag, 1844.

Hall, J. "Sparta, Lacedaimonia, and the Nature of Perioikic Dependency." In *Further Studies in the Ancient Greek Polis,* ed. P. Flensted-Jensen, 75–91. Berlin: Franz Steiner Verlag, 2000.

Hall, L. "Ephialtes, the Areopagus, and the Thirty." *Classical Quarterly* 40, no. 2 (1990): 319–328.

Hallenbeck, Jan T. *Pavia and Rome: The Lombard Monarchy and the Papacy in the Eighth Century.* Transactions of the American Philosophical Society. Vol. 72, pt. 4, 1982. Philadelphia: American Philosophical Society, 1982.

Hamann, B. "The Social Life of Pre-sunrise Things: Indigenous Mesoamerican Archaeology." *Current Anthropology* 43.3 (2002): 351–382.

———. "Chronological Pollution: Potsherds, Mosques, and Broken Gods before and after the Conquest of Mexico." *Current Anthropology* 49, no. 5 (2008): 803–836.

Hammond, N. "The Narrative of Herodotus VII and the Decree of Themistocles at Troezen." *Journal of Hellenic Studies* 102, no. 1 (1982): 75–93.

———. "The Archaeological and Literary Evidence for the Burning of the Persepolis Palace." *Classical Quarterly* 40, no. 2 (1992): 358–364.

Hamori, A. "An Allegory from the Arabian Nights: The City of Brass." *Bulletin of the School of Oriental and African Studies, University of London* 34 (1971): 9–19.

Hankins, James. "The 'Baron Thesis' After Forty Years and Some Recent Studies of Leonardo Bruni." *Journal of the History of Ideas* 56, no. 2 (1995): 309–338.

Hansen, Mogens Herman, ed. *A Comparative Study of Six City-State Cultures: An Investigation.* Copenhagen: Kgl. Danske Videnskabernes Selskab, 2002.

———. "95 Theses about the Greek 'Polis' in the Archaic and Classical Periods. A Report on the Results Obtained by the Copenhagen Polis Centre in the Period 1993–003." *Historia: Zeitschrift für Alte Geschichte* 3 (2003): 257–282.

——. *The Shotgun Method: The Demography of the Ancient Greek City-State Culture*. The Fordyce W. Mitchel Memorial Lecture Series. Columbia: U of Missouri P, 2006a.

——. *Polis: An Introduction to the Ancient Greek City-State*. Oxford: Oxford UP, 2006b.

Hardie, Philip R. *Virgil's Aeneid: Cosmos and Imperium*. Oxford: Clarendon P, 2003.

Hartog, François. *The Mirror of Herodotus*. Translated by Janet Lloyd. Berkeley: U of California P, 1988.

Harvey, David. *The Limits to Capital*. Chicago: U of Chicago P, 1982.

——. *The Urbanization of Capital: Studies in the History and Theory of Capitalist Urbanization*. London: Verso, 1985.

——. *Spaces of Capital: Towards a Critical Geography*. London: Verso, 2001.

Harvey, Susan Ashbrook, and David Hunter, eds. *The Oxford Handbook of Early Christian Studies*. Oxford Handbooks in Religion and Theology. Oxford: Oxford UP, 2008.

Haverfield, Francis. *Ancient Town-Planning*. Oxford: Clarendon P, 1913.

Hawting, G. R., ed. *The Development of Islamic Ritual*. Burlington, VT: Aldershot, 2006.

Hay, D. "Flavio Biondo and the Middle Ages." *Proceedings of the British Academy* 45 (1958), 97–127.

Hedrick, C. "Thucydides and the Beginnings of Archaeology." In *Methods in the Mediterranean: Historical and Archaeological Views on Texts and Archaeology*, ed. D. Small, 45–90. Leiden: Brill, 1995.

Heidel, W. A. "A Note on the Agamemnon of Aeschylus." *American Journal of Philology* 55, no. 2 (1934): 153–166.

Hell, Julia. "Katechon: Carl Schmitt's Imperial Theology and the Ruins of the Future." *Germanic Review: Literature, Culture, Theory* 84, no. 4 (2009): 283–326.

——. "Imperial Ruin-Gazers." In Hell and Schönle, *Ruins of Modernity*, 169–192.

Hell, Julia, and Andreas Schönle, eds. *The Ruins of Modernity*. Durham, NC: Duke UP, 2010.

Herodotus. *Herodoti Historiae*. Edited by Carolus Hude. Oxford: Clarendon P, 1927.

Hewitt, K. "The Social Space of Terror: Towards a Civil Interpretation of Total War." *Environment and Planning D: Society and Space* 5, no .4 (1987): 445–474.

Hodgson, M. G. S. *The Venture of Islam: Conscience and History in a World Civilization*. Vol. 1. Chicago: U of Chicago P, 1974.

Hogan, J. "The Axiosis of Words." *Greek, Roman and Byzantine Studies* 21, no. 2 (1980): 139–150.

Hopkins, K. "Economic Growth and Towns in Classical Antiquity." In *Towns in Societies*, ed. P. Abrams and E. Wrigley, 35–78. Cambridge: Cambridge UP, 1978.

Horden, Peregrine, and Nicholas Purcell. *The Corrupting Sea: A Study of Mediterranean History*. Oxford: Blackwell, 2000.

Hornblower, Simon. *The Greek World, 479–323 BC*. Classical Civilizations. London: Methuen, 1983.

——. *Thucydides*. Baltimore: Johns Hopkins UP, 1987.

——. *A Commentary on Thucydides*. Oxford: Clarendon P, 1991.

Hoyland, Robert G. *Seeing Islam as Others Saw It: A Survey and Evaluation of Christian, Jewish, and Zoroastrian Writings on Early Islam*. Princeton, NJ: Darwin P, 1997.

——. *Arabia and the Arabs: From the Bronze Age to the Coming of Islam*. London: Routledge, 2001.

Hsu, W. "Central Place Theory and City Size Distribution." *Economic Journal* 122, no. 563 (2012): 903–932.

Hughes, Robert. *The Fatal Shore: The Epic of Australia's Founding*. New York: Vintage Books, 1988.

Hume, K. "The 'Ruin Motif' in Old English Poetry." *Anglia-Zeitschrift für englische Philologie* 94 (1976): 339–360.

Humphreys, S. C. "Public and Private Interests in Classical Athens." *Classical Journal* 73, no. 2 (1977): 97–104.

Hunter, Virginia J. "Thucydides, Gorgias, and Mass Psychology." *Hermes* 114, no. 4 (1986): 412–429.

———. *Policing Athens: Social Control in the Attic Lawsuits, 420–320 B.C.* Princeton, NJ: Princeton UP, 1994.

Ibn Hawqal. *Kitab surat al-ard.* Leiden: Brill, 1939.

Ibn Khaldūn. *The Muqaddimah: An Introduction to History.* Princeton, NJ: Princeton UP, 1974.

Immerwahr, H. "Aspects of Historical Causation in Herodotus." *Transactions of the American Philological Association* 87 (1956): 241–280.

———. "Ergon: History as a Monument in Herodotus and Thucydides." *AJP* 31, no. 3 (1960): 261–290.

Inalcik, Halil. "The Policy of Mehmed II toward the Greek Population of Istanbul and the Byzantine Buildings of the City." *Dumbarton Oaks Papers* 23/24 (1969): 229–249.

Inca Garcilaso de la Vega. *The Incas.* Edited by A. Gheerbant. Translated by M. Jolas. New York: Avon Books, 1961.

Irwin, R. *Night and Horses and the Desert: An Anthology of Classical Arabic Literature.* New York: Harry N. Abrams, 1999.

———. *The Arabian Nights: A Companion.* London: I. B. Tauris, 2000.

Isaac, Benjamin H. *The Invention of Racism in Classical Antiquity.* Princeton, NJ: Princeton UP, 2004.

Isager, Jacob. "Destruction or Depopulation of Cities in Pausanias: Nikopolis, Aetolia, and Epirus." *Proceedings of the Danish Institute at Athens* 6 (2009): 201–215.

Isocrates, B. G. Mandilaras, ed. *Opera Omnia.* Vol. 2. Leipzig: Teubner, 2003.

Jacobs, Jane. *Cities and the Wealth of Nations.* New York: Vintage, 1985.

Jacobsen, Thorkild. *The Harps That Once . . . : Sumerian Poetry in Translation.* New Haven, CT: Yale UP, 1997.

Janan, Micaela Wakil. *The Politics of Desire: Propertius IV.* The Joan Palevsky Imprint in Classical Literature. Berkeley: U of California P, 2001.

Jeffery, Arthur. *The Foreign Vocabulary of the Qurʾān.* Leiden: Brill, 2007.

Jenkinson, J. Richard. "Sarcasm in Lucan i. 33–66." *Classical Review* 24, no. 1 (1974): 8–9.

Jensen, Wilhelm, and Sigmund Freud. *Gradiva/Delusion and Dream in Wilhelm Jensen's Gradiva.* Los Angeles: Sun and Moon Press, 1993.

Johnson, M. "Toward a History of Theoderic's Building Program." *Dumbarton Oaks Papers* 42 (1988): 73–96.

Juvenal. *Juvenal and Persius.* Loeb Classical Library. Latin Authors. Rev. ed. Cambridge, MA: Harvard UP, 1957.

Juynboll, G. H. A. *Muslim Tradition: Studies in Chronology, Provenance and Authorship of Early Hadith.* Cambridge: Cambridge UP, 1983.

Kahane, A. "Antiquity and the Ruin: Introduction." *European Review of History* 18, no. 5–6 (2012): 631–644.

Kaldellis, Anthony. *The Christian Parthenon: Classicism and Pilgrimage in Byzantine Athens.* Cambridge: Cambridge UP, 2009.

Kallet, Lisa. *Money and the Corrosion of Power in Thucydides: The Sicilian Expedition and Its Aftermath.* Berkeley: U of California P, 2002.

Kamen, Henry. *Empire: How Spain Became a World Power, 1492–1763.* New York: Harper-Collins, 2004.

Karmon, David E. *The Ruin of the Eternal City: Antiquity and Preservation in Renaissance Rome.* Oxford: Oxford UP, 2011.

Karttunen, F. E. *An Analytical Dictionary of Nahuatl.* Norman: U of Oklahoma P, 1992.

Keith, Alison. "City Lament in Augustan Epic: Antitypes of Rome from Troy to Alba Longa." In Bachvarova, Dutsch, and Suter, *Fall of Cities in the Mediterranean,* 156–182.

Keller, O. *Die antike Tierwelt*. Vol. 1. Hildesheim: Georg Olms, 1967 [1909].

Kennedy, Hugh. "From Polis to Madina: Urban Change in Late Antique and Early Islamic Syria." *Past & Present* 106, no. 1 (1985): 3–27.

Kennell, S. "Hercules' Invisible Basilica." *Latomus* 53, no. 1 (1994)" 159–175.

Killgrove, Kristina, and Robert H. Tykot. "Diet and Collapse: A Stable Isotope Study of Imperial-Era Gabii (1st–3rd centuries AD)." *Journal of Archaeological Science: Reports* 19 (2018): 1041–1049.

Kip, A. Maria van Erp Taalman. "Euripides and Melos." *Mnemosyne* 40, no. 3/4, 4th ser. (1987): 414–419.

Kister, M. J. " ' 'An Yadin' (Qur'ān, IX/29) An Attempt at Interpretation." *Arabica* 11 (1964): 272–78.

Knight, Alan. *Mexico: From the Beginning to the Spanish Conquest*. Cambridge: Cambridge UP, 2002.

Kockelman, P. "Legend of the Suns: Reproducing the Production of a Nahuatl Text." *Texas Linguistic Forum* 37 (1997): 221–231.

Kopp, Hans. "The 'Rule of the Sea': Thucydidean Concept or Periclean Utopia?" In *Thucydides and Political Order*, ed. Christian R. Thauer and Christian Wendt, 129–149. New York: Palgrave Macmillan, 2016.

Kosmin, Paul J. *Time and Its Adversaries in the Seleucid Empire*. Cambridge, MA: Harvard UP, 2018.

Kraus, C. S. " 'No Second Troy': Topoi and Refoundation in Livy, Book V." *Transactions of the American Philological Association* 124 (1994): 267–89.

Kulikowski, M. *Rome's Gothic Wars: From the Third Century to Alaric*. Cambridge: Cambridge UP, 2007.

Kurke, Leslie, and Carol Dougherty, eds. *Cultural Poetics in Archaic Greece: Cult, Performance, Politics*. Oxford: Oxford UP, 1998.

Lafferty, S. "Law and Society in Ostrogothic Italy: Evidence from the Edictum Theodorici." *Journal of Late Antiquity* 3, no. 2 (2010): 337–364.

Lanciani, R. *Pagan and Christian Rome*. New York: Houghton, Mifflin, 1892.

———. *The Ruins and Excavations of Ancient Rome*. New York: Houghton, Mifflin, 1900.

———. *The Destruction of Ancient Rome*. New York: Macmillan, 1903.

Landels, John G. *Engineering in the Ancient World*. Ancient Culture and Society. London: Chatto & Windus, 1978.

Lang, Mabel. "Herodotus and the Ionian Revolt." *Historia: Zeitschrift für Alte Geschichte* 1 (1968): 24–36.

Lapidus, I. M. "Muslim Cities and Islamic Societies." In Lapidus, *Middle Eastern Cities*, 47–79.

———, ed. *Middle Eastern Cities: A Symposium on Ancient, Islamic, and Contemporary Middle Eastern Urbanism*. Berkeley: U of California P, 1969.

Lara, J. *City, Temple, Stage: Eschatological Architecture and Liturgical Theatrics in New Spain*. South Bend, IN: Notre Dame UP, 2004.

La Rocca, Cristina. "Cassiodoro, Teodato e il restauro degli elefanti di bronzo della Via Sacra." *Reti Medievali Rivista* 11, no. 2 (2010): 25–44.

Lassner, J. "The Caliph's Personal Domain: The City Plan of Baghdad Reexamined." *Kunst des Orients* 5 (1968): 24–36.

———.*The Topography of Baghdad in the Early Middle Ages*. Detroit: Wayne State UP, 1970.

Lateiner, D. "A Note on ΔΙΚΑΣ ΔΙΔΟΝΑΙ in Herodotus." *Classical Quarterly* 30, no. 1 (1980): 30–32.

———. *Latin Erotic Elegy: An Anthology and Reader*. London: Routledge, 2002.

Latour, Bruno. *Reassembling the Social*. Oxford: Oxford UP, 2007.

———. *On the Modern Cult of the Factish Gods*. Durham: Duke UP, 2010.

Laurence, R. "Milestones, Communications, and Political Stability." In Ellis and Kidner, *Travel, Communication and Geography in Late Antiquity*, 43–58.

León-Portilla, M. *The Broken Spears: The Aztec Accounts of the Conquest of Mexico.* Boston: Beacon, 2007.

———. *Aztec Thought and Culture: A Study of the Ancient Nahuatl mind.* Norman: U of Oklahoma P, 2012.

Lewis, B. "The Islamic Guilds." *Economic History Review* 8 (1937): 20–37.

———. *The Political Language of Islam.* Chicago: U of Chicago P, 1991.

Lewis, Charlton Thomas, William Freund, and Charles Short. *A Latin Dictionary: Founded on Andrews' Edition of Freund's Latin Dictionary.* Oxford: Clarendon P, 1969.

Lewis, John David. *Solon the Thinker: Political Thought in Archaic Athens.* London: Duckworth, 2006.

Linders, T. "The Location of the *Opisthodomos*: Evidence from the Temple of Athena Parthenos Inventories." *American Journal of Archaeology* 111, no. 4 (2007): 777–782.

Lintott, Andrew. "Electoral Bribery in the Roman Republic." *Journal of Roman Studies* 80, no. 1 (1990): 1–16.

Livy. *History of Rome.* Vol. 14, translated by Alfred C. Schlesinger. Cambridge, MA: Harvard UP, 1961.

———. *Ab Urbe Condita.* Vol. 1, edited by Robert Maxwell Ogilvie. Oxford: Oxford UP, 1974.

———. *Ab Urbe Condita.* Vol. 2, edited by Robert Seymour Conway and Charles Flamstead Walters. Oxford: Oxford UP, 1919.

Lockhart, James. *The Nahuas after the Conquest: A Social and Cultural History of the Indians of Central Mexico, Sixteenth through Eighteenth Centuries.* Stanford, CA: Stanford UP, 1992.

———. *Of Things of the Indies: Essays Old and New in Early Latin American History.* Stanford, CA: Stanford UP, 1999.

Lombardo, P. A., "Vita activa versus vita contemplativa in Petrarch and Salutati." *Italica* 59, no. 2 (1982): 83–92.

Lopez Lujan, L. "Echoes of a Glorious Past: Mexica Antiquarianism." In Schnapp, *Discovery of the Past*, 273–297.

Loraux, Nicole. *The Invention of Athens: The Funeral Oration in the Classical City.* Cambridge, MA: Harvard UP, 1986.

———. *The Mourning Voice: An Essay on Greek Tragedy.* Cornell Studies in Classical Philology. Townsend Lectures Series. Vol. 58. Ithaca, NY: Cornell UP, 2002.

Low, Polly, ed. *The Athenian Empire.* Edinburgh Readings on the Ancient World. Edinburgh: Edinburgh University Press, 2008.

Lucan. *Pharsalia.* Edited by W. E. Heitland. Hildesheim: Georg Olms Verlag, 1971.

Lupher, David A. *Romans in a New World: Classical Models in Sixteenth-Century Spanish America.* History, Languages, and Cultures of the Spanish and Portuguese Worlds. Ann Arbor: U of Michigan P, 2003.

Luraghi, Nino. "Author and Audience in Thucydides' 'Archaeology.' Some Reflections." *Harvard Studies in Classical Philology* 100, no. 1 (2000): 227–239.

———. *The Ancient Messenians: Constructions of Ethnicity and Memory.* Cambridge: Cambridge UP, 2008.

Lycurgus. *Oratio in Leocratem.* Edited by N. C. Conomis. Leipzig: Teubner, 1970.

Lysias. *Lysias: Selected Speeches XII, XVI, XIX, XXII, XXIV, XXV, XXXII, XXXIV.* Edited by Charles Darwin Adams. Norman: U of Oklahoma P, 1970.

———. *A Commentary on Lycias, Speeches 1–11.* Edited by S. C. Todd. Oxford: Oxford UP, 2007.

MacAuliffe, Jane Dammen, ed. *The Cambridge Companion to the Qurān.* Cambridge: Cambridge UP, 2006.

——. *The Tasks and Traditions of Interpretation*. In MacAuliffe, *Tasks and Traditions of Interpretation*, 181–210.

MacDowell, Douglas M. "The Oikos in Athenian Law." *Classical Quarterly* 39, no. 1. new ser. (1989): 10–21.

Macek, Steve. *Urban Nightmares: The Media, the Right, and the Moral Panic over the City*. Minneapolis: U of Minnesota P, 2006.

Machiavelli, Niccolò. *Tutte le opera*. Edited by M. Martelli. Florence: Sansoni, 1971.

MacMullen, Ramsay. *Christianizing the Roman Empire (A.D. 100–400)*. New Haven, CT: Yale UP, 1984.

——. "Cultural and Political Change in the 4th and 5th Centuries." *Historia* 52, no. 4(2003): 465–495.

Maier, Charles S. *Among Empires: American Ascendancy and Its Predecessors*. Cambridge, MA: Harvard UP, 2006.

Mann, Michael, and John A. Hall. *States in History*. London: Blackwell, 1986.

Marcellinus Comes. *The Chronicle of Marcellinus*. Translated by Brian Croke and Theodor Mommsen. Sydney: Australian Association for Byzantine Studies, 1995.

Marcus, L. S. "Renaissance / Early Modern Studies." In Greenblatt and Gunn, *Redrawing the Boundaries*, 41–63.

Martin, John Levi. *Social Structures*. Princeton, NJ: Princeton UP, 2009.

Marx, Leo. *The Machine in the Garden: Technology and the Pastoral Ideal in America*. Oxford: Oxford UP, 1964.

Massignon, L. *Explication du plan de Kûfa (Irak)*. Paris: Imprimerie de l'Institut français D'archéologie orientale. 1935.

Mathisen, R. *Ecclesiastical Factionalism and Religious Controversy in Fifth-Century Gaul*. Washington, DC: Catholic U of America P, 1989.

Mattingly, D., ed. *Economies beyond Agriculture in the Classical World*. Leicester-Nottingham Studies in Ancient Society. Vol. 9. London: Routledge, 2001.

Mazzotta, Giuseppe. *The New Map of the World: The Poetic Philosophy of Giambattista Vico*. Princeton, NJ: Princeton UP, 1999.

McCormick, John P. "Machiavelli against Republicanism: On the Cambridge School's 'Guicciardinian Moments.'" *Political Theory* 31, no. 5 (2003): 615–643.

Meserve, Margaret. *Empires of Islam in Renaissance Historical Thought*. Harvard Historical Studies 158. Cambridge, MA: Harvard UP, 2008.

Mieggs, R. "The Political Implications of the Parthenon." *Greece & Rome*, suppl. 10 (*Parthenos and Parthenon*) (1963): 36–45.

Mikalson, Jon D. *Athenian Popular Religion*. Chapel Hill: U of North Carolina P, 1987.

——. "Religion in Herodotus." In Bakker, de Jong, and van Wees, *Brill's Companion toHerodotus*, 187–198.

Millar, Fergus. "P. Herennius Dexippus: The Greek World and the Third-Century Invasions." *Journal of Roman Studies* 59, no. 1/2 (1969): 12–29.

Minchin, Elizabeth. "Commemoration and Pilgrimage in the Ancient World: Troy and the Stratigraphy of Cultural Memory." *Greece & Rome* 59, no. 1 (2012): 76–89.

Mindle, Grant B. "Machiavelli's Realism." *Review of Politics* 47, no. 2 (1985): 212–230.

Mitchel, Fordyce. "Athens in the Age of Alexander." *Greece & Rome* 12, no. 2, 2nd ser. (1965): 189–204.

Moctezuma, Eduardo Matos. *The Great Temple of the Aztecs*. London: Thames & Hudson, 1988.

Momigliano, Arnoldo. "Sea-Power in Greek Thought." *Classical Review* 58, no. 1 (1944): 1–7.

——. *Alien Wisdom: The Limits of Hellenism*. Cambridge: Cambridge UP, 1975.

——. *The Classical Foundations of Modern Historiography*. Sather Classical Lectures. Vol. 54. Berkeley: U of California P, 1990.

Montesquieu. *Deux opuscules de Montesquieu*. Bordeaux: G. Gounouilhou, 1891.

Moorhead, J. " 'Libertas' and 'Nomen Romanum' in Ostrogothic Italy." *Latomus* t. 46, fasc. 1 (1987): 161–168.

———. *Theoderic in Italy*. Oxford: Clarendon P, 1992.

———. "Totila the Revolutionary." *Historia* 49, no. 3 (2000): 382–386.

Morales, Ambrosio de, and Florián de Ocampo. *Las antigüedades de las ciudades de España: Que van nombradas en la Corónica con las averiguaciones de sus sitios y nombres antiguos*. En la Oficina de Don Benito Cano, 1792.

Morgan, J. C. "The Character of Aeneas in the *Iliad* and in the *Aeneid*." *Kentucky Foreign Language Quarterly* 2, no. 1 (1955): 26–30.

Morley, N. *Metropolis and Hinterland: The City of Rome and the Italian Economy*, 200 BC–AD 200. Cambridge: Cambridge UP, 2002.

Morony, Michael G. *Iraq after the Muslim Conquest*. Princeton, NJ: Darwin P, 1984.

Morton, Timothy. *Dark Ecology: For a Logic of Future Coexistence*. New York: Columbia UP, 2016.

Moyer, Ann E. "Historians and Antiquarians in Sixteenth-Century Florence." *Journal of the History of Ideas* 64, no. 2 (2003): 177–193.

Moyer, I. "Herodotus and an Egyptian Mirage: The Genealogies of the Theban Priests." *Journal of Hellenic Studies* 122 (2002): 70–90.

Mundy, Barbara E. *The Mapping of New Spain: Indigenous Cartography and the Maps of the Relaciones Geográficas*. Chicago: U of Chicago P, 1996.

———. *The Death of Aztec Tenochtitlan, the Life of México City*. Austin: U of Texas Press, 2015.

Munn, Mark. "Thebes and Central Greece." In Tritle, *Greek World in the Fourth Century*, 66–106.

Musto, R. G. *Apocalypse in Rome: Cola di Rienzo and the Politics of the New Age*. Berkeley: U of California P, 2003.

Namatianus, Claudius Rutilius. *Il ritorno*. Turin: Einaudi, 1992.

Neuwirth, Angelika. "Structural, Linguistic and Literary Features." *Cambridge Companion to the Qur'an* (2006): 97–113.

Nicholls, W. J. "The Urban Question Revisited: The Importance of Cities for Social Movements." *International Journal of Urban and Regional Research* 32, no. 4 (2008): 841–859.

Nichols, D. L. "In the Shadow of the Pyramids: The Postclassic Teotihuacan Valley." *Constructing, Deconstructing, and Reconstructing Social Identity* 2 (2013): 65–82.

Norden, Eduard. *Die Römische Literatur / Eduard Norden*. Leipzig: Teubner, 1927.

Ober, Josiah. *Fortress Attica: Defense of the Athenian Land Frontier, 404–322 B.C.* Mnemosyne, Bibliotheca Classica Batava. Supplementum 84. Leiden: Brill, 1985.

———. *Mass and Elite in Democratic Athens: Rhetoric, Ideology, and the Power of the People*. Princeton, NJ: Princeton UP, 1989.

———. "Thucydides' Criticism of Democratic Knowledge." In *Nomodeiktes: Greek Studies in Honor of Martin Ostwald*, ed. Ralph M. Rosen and Joseph Farrell, 81–89. Ann Arbor: U of Michigan P, 1993.

———. *Athenian Legacies*. Princeton, NJ: Princeton UP, 2005.

———. "Wealthy Hellas." *Transactions of the American Philological Association (1974–)* 140, no. 2 (2010): 241–286.

O'Donnell, James J. *Cassiodorus*. Berkeley: U of California P, 1979.

———. *The Ruin of the Roman Empire: A New History*. New York: Ecco, 2008.

———. Review: Peter Heather, *The Fall of the Roman Empire: A New History*; Bryan Ward-Perkins, "The Fall of Rome and the End of Civilization." *Bryn Mawr Classical Review* 2005.07.69.

O'Gorman, Edmundo. *Reflexiones sobre la distribución urbana colonial de la ciudad de México: XVI⁰ Congreso Internacional de Planificación y de la Habitación.* [S.l: s.n., 1938.

———. *The Invention of America: An Inquiry into the Historical Nature of the New World and the Meaning of Its History.* Bloomington: Indiana UP, 1961.

O'Hara, James J. "Callimachean Influence on Vergilian Etymological Wordplay." *Classical Journal* 96, no. 4 (2001): 369–400.

Orlando, Francesco. *Obsolete Objects in the Literary Imagination Ruins, Relics, Rarities, Rubbish, Uninhabited Places, and Hidden Treasures.* New Haven, CT: Yale UP, 2006.

O'Sullivan, T. M. "Death *ante ora parentum* in Virgil's *Aeneid.*" *Transactions of the American Philological Association* 139 (2009): 447–486.

Osuna Cabezas, M., ed. *Góngora Vindicado: Soledad primera, ilustrada y defendida.* Zaragoza: Prensas Universitarias de Zaragoza, 2009.

Ovid. *Amores, Medicamina Faciei Femineae, Ars Amatoria, Remedia Amoris.* Edited by E. J. Kenney. Oxford: Oxford UP, 1994.

———. *Metamorphoses.* Edited by R. J. Tarrant. Oxford: Oxford UP, 2004.

Owensby, Brian Philip. *Empire of Law and Indian Justice in Colonial Mexico.* Stanford, CA: Stanford UP, 2008.

Page, Max. *The City's End: Two Centuries of Fantasies, Fears, and Premonitions of New York's Destruction.* New Haven, CT: Yale UP, 2008.

Pakkanen, J. "The Erechtheion Construction Work Inventory (IG 1³ 474) and the Dorpfeld Temple." *American Journal of Archaeology* 110, no. 2 (2006): 275–281.

Palombi, D. *L'Archeologia a Roma tra Ottocento e Novecento.* Rome: L'Erma di Bretschneider, 2006.

Papazarkadas, N. *Sacred and Public Land in Ancient Athens.* Oxford: Oxford UP, 2011.

Paul, G. M. 1982. "'Urbs Capta': Sketch of an Ancient Literary Motif." *Phoenix* 36: 144–55.

Pauw, Cornelius de. *Recherches philosophiques sur les Américains, ou Mémoires intéressants pour servir à l'histoire de l'éspèce humaine, par mr. de P***.* Cleves: J. G. Barstecher, 1772.

Payen, P. *Les Iles Nomades.* Paris: ENS, 1997.

Peirano, Irene. *The Rhetoric of the Roman Fake: Latin Pseudepigrapha in Context.* Cambridge: Cambridge UP, 2012.

Penrice, John. *A Dictionary and Glossary of the Qur'an.* Mineola, NY: Dover, 2011.

Pimentel, J. "The Iberian Vision: Science and Empire in the Framework of a Universal Monarchy, 1500–1800." *Osiris* 15 (2000): 17–30.

Plant, I. "The Influence of Forensic Oratory on Thucydides' Principles of Method." *Classical Quarterly* 40, no. 1 (1999): 62–73.

Platina, Bartolomeo. *Lives of the Popes.* Vol. 1, edited and translated by Anthony F. D'Elia. Cambridge, MA: Harvard UP, 2008.

Plato. *Opera.* Vols. 3–4. Edited by John Burnet. Oxford: Oxford UP, 1922.

Plutarch. *Plutarch's Lives.* Vol. 4, *Lysander and Sulla,* translated by Bernadotte Perrin. Loeb Classical Library, Cambridge, MA: Harvard UP, 1916.

———. *Vies.* t. 3, 4, 6, 7, 9, and 10. Edited by R. Flacelière and E. Chambry Paris: Les Belles Lettres, 1957.

Pocock, J. G. A. *Barbarism and Religion.* Vol. 3, *The First Decline and Fall.* Cambridge: Cambridge UP, 2005.

———. *Barbarism and Religion.* Vol. 4, *Barbarians, Savages and Empires.* Cambridge: Cambridge UP, 2008.

Polignac, François de. *Cults, Territory, and the Origins of the Greek City-State.* Translated by Janet Lloyd. Chicago: U of Chicago P, 1995.

Potofsky, A. "French Lumières and American Enlightenment during the Atlantic Revolution." *Revue française d'études américaines* 92 (2002): 47–67

Preston, R. "The Structure of Central Place Systems." *Economic Geography* 47, no. 2 (1971): 136–155.

Procopius. *The Wars of Justinian*. Edited by Anthony Kaldellis. Translated by H. R. Dewing. Rev. ed. Indianapolis, IN: Hackett Publishing, 2014.

———. *Elegies, I–IV*. Edited by L. Richardson. Norman: U of Oklahoma P, 2006.

Quint, David. *Origin and Originality in Renaissance Literature: Versions of the Source*. New Haven, CT: Yale UP, 1983.

———. *Epic and Empire: Politics and Generic Form from Virgil to Milton*. Literature in History. Princeton, NJ: Princeton UP, 1993.

Rabel, R. "Agamemnon's Empire in Thucydides." *Classical Journal* 80, no. 1 (1984): 8–10.

Ramage, Edwin S. "Augustus' Treatment of Julius Caesar." *Historia: Zeitschrift für Alte Geschichte* 2 (1985): 223–245.

Raynal, Guillaume-Thomas. *Histoire philosophique et politique des Etablissements et du Commerce des européens dans les deux Indes*. Geneva: Jean-Leonard Pollet, 1781.

Reade, J. E. "The Ziggurrat and Temples of Nimrud." *Iraq* 64, no. 1 (2002): 135–216.

Redfield, James. "Herodotus the Tourist." *Classical Philology* 80, no. 2 (1985): 97–118.

Reynolds, Joshua J. "Proving Power: Signs and Sign-inference in Thucydides' Archaeology." *Transactions of the American Philological Association (1974–)* 139, no. 2 (2009): 325–368.

Ricoeur, Paul. *Memory, History, Forgetting*. Chicago: U of Chicago P, 2004.

Robertson, Noel. "The True Meaning of the 'Wooden Wall.'" *Classical Philology* 82, no. 1 (1987): 1–20.

Roller, Matthew B. "Exemplarity in Roman Culture: The Cases of Horatius Cocles and Cloelia." *Classical Philology* 99, no. 1 (2004): 1–56.

Rosenthal, Franz. *Knowledge Triumphant: The Concept of Knowledge in Medieval Islam*. Vol. 2. Leiden: Brill, 2007.

Rosivach, V. "Autochthony and the Athenians." *Classical Quarterly* 37, no. 2 (1987): 294–306.

Rossi, Andreola. *Contexts of War: Manipulation of Genre in Virgilian Battle Narrative*. Ann Arbor: U of Michigan P, 2004.

Roux, Georges. *Ancient Iraq*. 3rd ed., rev. New York: Penguin, 1993.

Roy, J. "'Polis' and 'Oikos' in Classical Athens." *Greece & Rome* 46, no. 1, 2nd ser. (1999): 1–18.

Ruiz, T. "Expansion et changement: La conquête de Seville et la société Castillane." *Annales* (1977): 548–560.

Rutilius Namatianus, Claudius. *Cl. Rutilius Namatianus*. Edited by J. Vessereau. Paris: A. Fontemoing, 1904.

———. Castorina, ed. *De Reditu*. Classici Greci e Latini con testo a fronte, ser. 2. Florence: Sansoni, 1967.

———. *Il ritorno*. Edited and translated by A. Fo. Turin: Einaudi, 1992.

Sahagún, B. de. *Códice florentino*, vols. 1 and 11, 1979. https://www.wdl.org/en/item/10612/.

Sahlins, Marshall. *Apologies to Thucydides: Understanding History as Culture and Vice Versa*. Chicago: U of Chicago P, 2004.

———. *Historical Metaphors, Mythical Realities*. Ann Arbor: U of Michigan P, 2004.

———. *The Western Illusion of Human Nature: With Reflections on the Long History of Hierarchy, Equality, and the Sublimation of Anarchy in the West, and Comparative Notes on Other Conceptions of the Human Condition*. Chicago: Prickly Paradigm, 2008.

Sahlins, Marshall, and David Graeber. *On Kings*. Chicago: Hau Books, 2017.

Said, S. "Herodotus and Tragedy." In Bakker, de Jong, and van Wees, *Brill's Companion to Herodotus*, 117–147.

Salmon, John. "The Economic Role of the Greek City." *Greece & Rome* 46, no. 2, 2nd ser. (1999): 147–167.

Salutati, Coluccio. *On the World and Religious Life.* Translated by Tina Marshall. Cambridge, MA: Harvard UP, 2014a.

———. *Political Writings.* Translated by Stefano Baldassarri. Cambridge, MA: Harvard UP, 2014b.

Salzman, Michele R., L. Ellis, and F. L. Kidner. *Travel and Communication in the Letters of Symmachus.* London: Routledge, 2004.

Sannazaro, Jacopo. *Latin Poetry.* Translated by Michael C. J. Putnam. Cambridge, MA: Harvard UP, 2009.

Sannazaro, Jacopo, and Luigi Portirelli. *Arcadia di M. Jacopo Sanazzaro.* Milan: Società Tipgrafica de' Classici Italiani, 1806.

———. *Latin Poetry.* Edited and translated by M. Putnam.Cambridge, MA: Harvard UP, 2009.

Sanzio, Raffaello, and Baldassarre Castiglione. *Lettera di Raffaello d'Urbino a papa Leone X,* 1519. (https://it.wikisource.org/wiki/Lettera_di_Raffaello_d%27Urbino a papa_Leone_X), accessed July 2018.

Sarris, Peter. *Empires of Faith: The Fall of Rome to the Rise of Islam, 500–700.* The Oxford History of Medieval Europe. Oxford: Oxford UP, 2011.

Sartre, Maurice. *Histoires Grecques: Snapshots from Antiquity.* Revealing Antiquity 17. Cambridge, MA: Harvard UP, 2009.

Schmitt, Carl. *The Nomos of the Earth in the International Law of the Jus Publicum Europeaum.* New York: Telos Press, 2003.

Schnapp, Alain. *The Discovery of the Past.* New York: Harry N. Abrams, 1997.

———, ed. *World Antiquarianism: Comparative Perspectives.* Los Angeles: Getty Publications, 2014.

Schwenk, C. "Athens." In Tritle, *The Greek World in the Fourth Century,* 8–40.

Scott, J. *Against the Grain: A Deep History of the Earliest States.* New Haven, CT: Yale UP, 2017.

Scott, Michael. *From Democrats to Kings: The Brutal Dawn of a New World from the Downfall of Athens to the Rise of Alexander the Great.* London: Icon Books, 2009.

Scullard, J. *The Elephant in the Greek and Roman World.* Ithaca, NY: Cornell UP, 1974.

Seaford, R. *Money and the Early Greek Mind.* Cambridge: Cambridge UP, 2004.

Segal, Charles P. "Gorgias and the Psychology of the Logos." *Harvard Studies in Classical Philology* 66, no. 1 (1962): 99–155.

Selden, Daniel L. *Hieroglyphic Egyptian: An introduction to the Language and Literature of the Middle Kingdom,* iii–xx. U of California P, 2013.

Sell, B. D., and L. M. Burkhart, eds. *Nahuatl Theater: Nahua Christianity in Performance.* Norman: U of Oklahoma P, 2012.

Sells, M., ed. and trans. *Desert Tracings: Six Classic Arabian Odes by 'Alqama, Shanfara, Labid, 'Antara, Al-A'sha, and Dhu al-Rumma.* Cambridge: Cambridge UP, 1989.

Shahîd, I. *The Martyrs of Najran.* Subsidia Hagiographica 49. Brussels: Societe des Bollandistes, 1971.

———. *Rome and the Arabs: A Prolegomenon to the Study of Byzantium and the Arabs.* Washington, D.C: Dumbarton Oaks, 1984.

Sharon, M. *Black Banners from the East: The Establishment of the Abbasid State: Incubation of a Revolt.* Jerusalem. Leiden: Brill, 1983.

Shaw, M. "New Wars of the City: 'Urbicide'and 'genocide.'" *Cities, War, and Terrorism: Towards an Urban Geopolitics* (2004): 141–53.

Shipley, Graham. *The Greek World after Alexander, 323–30 B.C.* Routledge History of the Ancient World. London: Routledge, 2000.

Siewert, Peter. *Der Eid von Plataiai.* Vestigia. Vol. 16. Munich: Beck, 1972.

Sirago, V. "I Goti nelle Variae di Cassiodoro." In S. Leanza, *Atti della settimanadi studi su Flavio Magno Aurelio Cassiodoro.* Sovra Mannelli: Rubbetino, 1983.

Smith, Adam. *The Wealth of Nations.* New York: Random House, 2000.

Smith, Julia M. H. *Europe after Rome: A New Cultural History, 500–1000.* Oxford: Oxford UP, 2005.

Solmsen, L. "Speeches in Herodotus' Account of the Battle of Plataea," *Classical Philology* 39, no. 4 (1944): 241–253.

Sommerstein, Alan H. *Greek Drama and Dramatists.* London: Routledge, 2002.

Spencer, Diana. "Lucan's Follies: Memory and Ruin in a Civil-War Landsape." *Greece & Rome* 52, no. 1, 2nd ser. (2005): 46–69.

Squillante, Marisa. *Il viaggio, la memoria, il ritorno: Rutilio Namaziano e le trasformazioni del tema odeporico.* Vol. 15. Naples: D'Auria M., 2005.

Staples, Blaise D. "Graeco-Roman Ruins in the New World." *Arion* 11, no. 2, 3rd ser. (2003): 21–42.

Starr, C. "Thucydides on Sea Power." *Mnemosyne* 31 (1978): 343–350.

Steinmetz, G. "Colonial Melancholy and Fordist Nostalgia: The Ruinscape of Namibia and Detroit." In *The Ruins of Modernity,* ed. Julia Hell and Andreas Schönle, 294–320. Durham, NC: Duke UP, 2010.

Stoler, A. L. "Imperial Debris: Reflections on Ruins and Ruination." *Cultural Anthropology* 23.2 (2008): 191–219.

Stone, A. "From Ritual in the Landscape to Capture in the Urban Center: The Recreation of Ritual Environments in Mesoamerica." *Journal of Ritual Studies* (1992): 109–132.

Sturz, Friedrich Wilhelm. *Lexicon Xenophontevm.* Leipzig: Libraria Gleditschia, 1801.

Syme, Ronald. *The Roman Revolution.* Vol. 1. Rev. ed. Oxford: Oxford Paperbacks, 2002.

Tamiolaki, Melina. "A Citizen as a Slave of the State? Oligarchic Perceptions of Democracy in Xenophon." *Greek, Roman, and Byzantine Studies* 53, no.1 (2013): 31–50.

Teaford, Jon C. *Cities of the Heartland: The Rise and Fall of the Industrial Midwest.* Indianapolis: Indiana UP, 1994.

Thom, Martin. *Republics, Nations, and Tribes.* London: Verso, 1995.

Thompson, Homer A. "Athens Faces Adversity." *Hesperia: The Journal of the American School of Classical Studies at Athens* 50, no. 4 (1981): 343–355.

———. "Buildings on the West Side of the Agora." *Hesperia: The Journal of the American School of Classical Studies at Athens* 6, no. 1 (1937): 1–226.

Thucydides. *La Guerre du Peloponnese.* Vols. 1–6. Edited by J. Romilly et al. Paris: Les Belles Lettres, 1953.

Tibullus. *Tibulli Aliorumque Carminum, Libri Tres.* Edited by J. P. Postgate. Oxford: Oxford UP, 1924.

Tilly, C. *Big Structures, Large Processes, Huge Comparisons.* New York: Sage Foundation, 1984.

———. *European Revolutions, 1492–1992.* Oxford: Oxford UP, 1993.

Tissol, Garth. "Ovid and the Exilic Journey of Rutilius Namatianus." *Arethusa* 35, no. 3 (2002): 435–446.

Tod, M. *Greek Historical Inscriptions.* Vols. 1–2. Chicago: Ares, 1985.

Todd, S. C. *A Commentary on Lysias, Speeches 1–11.* Oxford: Oxford UP, 2007.

Todorov, Tzvetan. *The Conquest of America: The Question of the Other.* New York: Harper & Row, 1984.

Tolan, J. "Muslims as Pagan Idolaters in Chronicles of the First Crusade." In Blanks and Frassetto, *Western Views of Islam,* 97–117.

Trigger, B. *A History of Archaeological Thought.* Cambridge: Cambridge UP, 2006.

Tritle, Lawrence A., ed. *The Greek World in the Fourth Century: From the Fall of the Athenian Empire to the Successors of Alexander.* New York: Routledge, 2013 [1997].

Trout, Dennis E. *Paulinus of Nola: Life, Letters, and Poems.* The Transformation of the Classical Heritage 27. Berkeley: U of California P, 1999.

Various Authors. *Patrologiae cursus completus*, Ser. Latina. Edited by J.-P. Migne. Paris: 1844.

Various Authors. *Gothicarum et Langobardicarum rerum scriptores aliquot veteres.* Vols. 1–4. Leyden: Maire, 1618.

Vergil. *Opera.* Edited by R. A. B. Mynors. Oxford: Oxford UP, 1969.

Versteegh, Kees. *Arabic Language.* Edinburgh: Edinburgh University Press, 2014.

Veyne, Paul, ed. *A History of Private Life: From Pagan Rome to Byzantium.* Cambridge, MA: Harvard UP, 1987.

Virilio, Paul. *The Paul Virilio Reader.* European Perspectives. New York: Columbia UP, 2005.

Viscido, L. *Studi sulle Variae di Cassiodoro.* Sovra Manelli: Rubbetino, 1987.

Vlassopoulos, C. *Unthinking the Greek Polis.* Cambridge: Cambridge UP, 2007.

Volney, C. *Les Ruines, ou, Meditation sur les revolutions des empires.* Paris: Dessenne, Volland, Plassande, 1791.

Wallerstein, Immanuel. *The Modern World-System II: Mercantilism and the Consolidation of the European World-Economy, 1600–1750.* New York: Academic P, 1980.

Wansbrough, John E. *The Sectarian Milieu: Content and Composition of Islamic Salvation History.* 1978; Amherst, NY: Prometheus Books, 2006.

———. *The Modern World-System.* Berkeley: U of California P, 2011.

Ward-Perkins, Bryan. *From Classical Antiquity to the Middle Ages: Public Building in Northern and Central Italy, AD 300–850.* Oxford: Oxford UP, 1985.

———. *The Fall of Rome: And the End of Civilization.* Oxford: Oxford UP, 2005.

Ward-Perkins, J. Ward. "Nero's Golden House." *Antiquity* 30, no. 120 (1956): 209–219.

Wardropper, Bruce W. "Góngora and the Serranilla." *MLN* 77, no. 2 (1962): 178–181.

Weber, Max. *The City.* Edited by Don Martindale. Translated by Gertrud Neuwirth. New York: Free Press, 1958.

———. *Economy and Society: An Outline of Interpretive Sociology.* Berkeley: U of California P, 1978.

———. *The Agrarian Sociology of Ancient Civilizations.* London: Verso, 2013 [1924].

Wehr, Hans. *A Dictionary of Modern Written Arabic.* Weisbaden: Otto Harrassowitz Verlag, 1979.

Welch, Tara S. *The Elegiac Cityscape: Propertius and the Meaning of Roman Monuments.* Columbus: Ohio State UP, 2005.

Weller, Charles H. "On the Interpretation of Thucydides II. 15." *Classical Review* 16, no. 3 (1902): 158–160.

West, Stephanie. "Herodotus' Epigraphical Interests." *Classical Quarterly* 35, no. 2, new ser. (1985): 278–305.

Westgate, R. I. Wilfred. "The Text of Valla's Translation of Thucydides." *Transactions and Proceedings of the American Philological Association* 67, no. 1 (1936): 240–251.

Wheatley, Paul. *The Places Where Men Pray Together: Cities in Islamic Lands, Seventh through the Tenth Centuries.* Chicago: U of Chicago P, 2001.

Wheelan, Joseph. *Jefferson's War: America's First War on Terror, 1801–1805.* New York: Carroll & Graf, 2003.

Wheeler, B., and ويلار برانون. "Arab Prophets of the Qur'an and Bible." *Journal of Qur'anic Studies* 8 (2006): 24–57.

Whittaker, C. R. *Land, City, and Trade in the Roman Empire.* Collected Studies Series CS408. Aldershot, UK: Variorum, 1993.

Wickham, Chris. *The Inheritance of Rome: A History of Europe from 400 to 1000*. Penguin History of Europe 2. London: Penguin Group, 2009.

Willamowitz, U. "Die lebenslänglichen Archonten Athens." *Hermes* 33, no.1 (1898): 119–129.

Wilson, John. " 'The Customary Meanings of Words Were Changed'—or Were They? A Note on Thucydides 3.82.4." *Classical Quarterly* 32, no. 1. new ser. (1982): 18–20.

Wittenburg, A. "Les Ruines comme mémoire des crimes du passé." *European Review of History* 18, no. 5–6 (2012): 799–810.

Wolf, Eric R. "The Social Organization of Mecca and the Origins of Islam." *Southwestern Journal of Anthropology* 7, no. 4 (1951): 329–356.

———. *Sons of the Shaking Earth*. Chicago: U of Chicago P, 1962.

Wolff, Etienne. "Quelques aspects du *De reditu suo* de Rutilius Namatianus." *Vita Latina* 173 (2005): 66–74.

Wood, Ian. "Theoderic's Monuments in Ravenna." In *The Ostrogoths from the Migration Period to the Sixth Century: An Ethnographic Perspective*, ed. S. J. Barnish and Federico Marazzi, 249–278. Woodbridge, UK: Boydell & Brewer, 2007.

Woodward, Christopher. *In Ruins: A Journey through History, Art, and Literature*. New York: Vintage, 2003.

Woolf, Gregory. "Movers and Stayers." In *Migration and Mobility in the Early Roman Empire*, ed. Luuk De Ligt and Laurens Ernst Tacoma, 438–461. Leiden: Brill, 2016.

———. *The Life and Death of Ancient Cities*. Oxford: Oxford UP, 2020.

Wormald, Patrick. "The Decline of the Western Empire and the Survival of Its Aristocracy." *Journal of Roman Studies* 66, no. 1 (1976): 217–226.

Worthington, Ian. *Ventures into Greek History*. Oxford: Oxford UP, 1994.

Wyttenbach, Daniel Albert. *Lexicon Plutarcheum et vitas et opera moralia complectens . . . ad editionem Oxoniensem emendatius expressum*. Lipsiae [Leipzig]: T. O. Weigel, 1843.

Xenophon. *Commentarii, Oeconomicus, Convivium, Apologia Socratis*. Edited by E. C. Merchant. Oxford: Oxford UP, 1922.

———. *Four Books of Xenophon's Anabasis*. New York: American Book, 1885.

———. *Historia Graeca*. Oxford: Oxford UP, 1985.

———. *Opuscula*. Oxford: Oxford UP, 1985.

Yaqut, F. Wustenfeld, ed. *Geographiches Worterbuch*. Vol. 1. Leipzig: Brockhaus, 1866.

Zavala, S. "Hernan Cortes ante la justificacion de su conquista." *Revista de Historia de America* 92 (1981): 49–69.

Zeitlin, Froma I. "Playing the Other: Theater, Theatricality, and the Feminine in Greek Drama." *Representations*, no. 11, no. 3 (1985): 63–94.

Žižek, S. *Iraq: The Borrowed Kettle*. London: Verso, 2004.

———. *Violence: Six Sideways Reflections*. New York: Picador, 2008.

Zumbo, A. "Sugli excursus zoologici nelle Variae di Cassiodoro." In *Cassiodoro: Dalla corte di Ravenna al Vivarium di Squillace*, ed. S. Leanza, 191–198. Soveria Mannelli: Rubbetino, 1993.

Zuntz, Günther. *The Political Plays of Euripides*. Manchester: Manchester UP, 1955.

ff mefffffffff fffffffffffffffffffffffffffffffffffffffffffff

Nahuatl language, 90, 101–102, 104, 112

Narbonne, 51

nationalism, 2, 132n33; and ruins in early modern Italy, 93–95, 140n11

Nazis, 118

neighborhoods: in early Islamic urban planning, 71; ruination of, 8, 77, 81, 83–84

Nero, 49

Numantia, 37, 39, 40, 44, 112, 129n2

oath of Plataea, 32–33, 128n46

Ogier de Busbecq, 90

oikos, 26, 35; *hira* and, 12–13; *polis* and, 22, 29–31, 36

oligarchy, 14–15, 28, 30–32. *See also* elites: Athenian

Olynthus, 31, 35

oratory, Athenian, 127n36; courtroom, 31, 128n45; political, 5, 20, 32 29, 127n35

Orosius, 38–39, 50, 94

Ottoman Empire, 94–95; conquest of Constantinople by, 90; Cyriac of Ancona's relations with, 90–91; use of ruins as *casus belli* by, 91

Ovid, 52

Oviedo, Gonzalo Fernando, *Historia general y natural de las Indias*, 107

Pagden, Anthony, 101

pastoral, 27–28, 53, 108–110

patronage, architectural, 57, 133n41; literary, 85

Paulinus of Nola, 52

Peloponnesian War, 6, 15; Athenian penalties at end of, 27–30, 127n33; ruins made by Athens during, 25–26; Thucydides' account of, 23–25

Pericles, 21, 23, 125n24, 126n26

Persepolis: Alexander's destruction of, 34–36, 129n48; ruin of, 6, 10

Persia, 69, 85–87; Alexander and, 33–36, 128n46, 128n47; cultural influence on early Islam of, 73–76, 78–79; imperialism of, 37; Ionian revolt from, 10, 11; Islamic conquest of, 70–72, 87; Persian Wars, 6, 11- 17, 22, 23; Scythia and, 19. *See also* Sassanid Dynasty

Peru, 107, 112

Petrarch, 2, 93–94, 111

Phocion, 32

Phrynichus, 25

pietas: toward one's estate, 53; toward Troy, 44–46, 49, 51, 104

Pisistratids, 13, 15

Pisistratus, 31

Pizarro, Francisco, 112

Plataea: destruction of, 15, 18; failed colonization of, 14; oath of, 32–33

Pliny the Elder, 90

Plutarch: on Alexander, 34–36, 129n48, 129n50; Boeotian, 35; on Pericles, 128n46; on Phocion, 32; on Theban proposal to destroy Athens, 27–28, 127n35

polis. See city-state

Polybius, 6, 40–41

polytheism, 55, 66

preservationism. *See* conservationism

Procopius, 55, 60–61

prophecy: in Islam, 7, 64–67, 79; of the "wooden wall," 14, 20

Ps.-Aristotle, *Sir al-Asrar,* 86

Qadi al-Quda'i, al-, *Dastur*, 82–83, 85

qarya, 70

qasida tradition, 84–85

qass tradition, 70, 86–87

Quetzalcoatl, 98, 102–103, 142n33

Qur'an, the, 62–70, 77, 80, 83, 84, 86, 136n30, 137n46; accusations of plagiarism against, 67; anti-urbanism in, 65–66, 69–70, 87, 134n10; proof and evidence in, 63–65, 67; ruins in, 7, 67–68, 82, 87

Raphael (painter). *See* Santi, Raphael

Ravenna, 56, 57, 60, 119

Raynal, Abbé de (Guillaume Thomas Raynal), *Histoire philosophique des deux Indes*, 110–112

Reconquista, the, 8, 95–99

Renaissance, European, 89, 91; antiquarianism in, 91, 116; ruin-making as barbarism in, 94, 105–106, 111, 139n4. *See also* antiquarianism; barbarism; humanism

requerimiento, 97

Revelation, Book of, 49

revelation, Qur'anic. *See* Qur'an, the: proof and evidence in

revenge (and ruin-making): Persian, for Sardis, 6, 11–12; Greek, for Athens, 32–35, 123n3, 124n6, 128n47

Roman Empire, 44; fall of, 5, 140n11; harmful nature of, 38; Islamic Civilization and, 73, 75–76, 87; "post-Roman," 7, 55; ruin-making by, 37–41, 104–105, 112–113